CW00449412

EAST TO WEST MIGRATI(

Research in Migration and Ethnic Relations Series

Series Editor:
Maykel Verkuyten, ERCOMER
Utrecht University

The Research in Migration and Ethnic Relations series has been at the forefront of research in the field for ten years. The series has built an international reputation for cutting edge theoretical work, for comparative research especially on Europe and for nationally-based studies with broader relevance to international issues. Published in association with the European Research Centre on Migration and Ethnic Relations (ERCOMER), Utrecht University, it draws contributions from the best international scholars in the field, offering an interdisciplinary perspective on some of the key issues of the contemporary world.

Other titles in the series

Transnational Social Spaces: Agents, Networks and Institutions
Edited by Thomas Faist and Eyüp Özveren
ISBN 0 7546 3291 1

Roma and Gypsy-Travellers in Europe: Modernity, Race, Space and Exclusion
Angus Bancroft
ISBN 0 7546 3921 5

International Migration Research: Constructions, Omissions and the Promises of Interdisciplinarity
Edited by Michael Bommes and Ewa Morawska
ISBN 0 7546 4219 4

**EUROPEAN RESEARCH CENTRE
ON MIGRATION & ETHNIC RELATIONS**

East to West Migration
Russian Migrants in Western Europe

HELEN KOPNINA
Haarlem College and Amsterdam Fashion Institute, The Netherlands

Routledge
Taylor & Francis Group

LONDON AND NEW YORK

First published 2005 by Ashgate Publishing

2 Park Square, Milton Park, Abingdon, Oxfordshire OX14 4RN
52 Vanderbilt Avenue, New York, NY 10017

Routledge is an imprint of the Taylor & Francis Group, an informa business

First issued in paperback 2020

British Library Cataloguing in Publication Data
Kopnina, Helen
  East to West migration : Russian migrants in Western
  Europe. - (Research in migration and ethnic relations
  series)
  1.Russians - England - London - Social conditions
  2.Russians - Netherlands - Amsterdam - Social conditions
  3.Russians - Foreign countries - Ethnic identity 4. Russia
  (Federation) - Emigration and immigration 5.Great Britain -
  Emigration and immigration 6.Netherlands - Emigration and
  immigration
  I.Title
  305.8'91710421

Library of Congress Control Number: 2005933680

ISBN 978-0-7546-4170-4 (hbk)
ISBN 978-0-367-60426-4 (pbk)

Contents

List of Tables		*viii*
Acknowledgments		*ix*
Preface		*x*
Introduction		1
	Theoretical Objectives	2
	Note on Comparisons	6
	Methodology	8
	Ethical Considerations and Practical Difficulties	10
	Organization	12
1	Migration	16
	1.1 Contextualizing Migration	17
	1.1.1 Contemporary and Classical Theories of Migration	18
	1.1.2 Motivation	19
	1.1.3 Why do Some People Stay?	21
	1.2 Historical Note	23
	1.2.1 Movement in Russian Cultural Imagination	23
	1.2.2 'Waves' of the Twentieth Century	24
	1.3 'New' Russian Migration	26
	1.3.1 Internal Migration	27
	1.3.2 New Migration to 'Far Abroad'	29
	1.3.3 Russians in Britain and The Netherlands	30
	1.3.4 Different Groups of 'New' Migrants	31
2	London and Amsterdam: The Tale of Two Cities	39
	2.1 The Setting	39
	2.2 Reflections	45
	2.3 The Tale of Two Cities	47
3	Community	77
	3.1 What is 'Community'?	78
	3.2 Establishing Invisibility	83
	3.3 Reasons for Invisibility	84
	3.3.1 The Outsiders' Perspective	84
	3.3.2 Lack of 'Established' Community	86

	3.3.3	Insiders' Perspective	87
	3.3.4	Antagonism	91
	3.4	Paradoxes of Absence	95
4		**Subcommunities and Subcultures**	**99**
	4.1	Diversity of Russian Migrants	100
		4.1.1 Class	102
	4.2	Subcultures	105
	4.3	Types of Subcommunities	109
		4.3.1 Inclusive Subcommunities	110
		4.3.2 Exclusive Subcommunities	114
		4.3.3 How are Subcommunal Boundaries Drawn and Maintained?	120
		4.3.4 Note on Comparison between London and Amsterdam Subcommunities	125
5		**Social Networks and Informal Economic Activity**	**129**
	5.1	Informal Economic Activity	131
		5.1.1 Business, Bribes and Barter	131
		5.1.2 Reciprocity and Gift Exchange	136
	5.2	Social Networks	140
		5.2.1 *Svyazi* and *Kontakty*	140
		5.2.2 Friendship	145
	5.3	Typifying the Migrants: Who Interacts with Whom?	149
		5.3.1 Doomernik's Classification	149
		5.3.2 Capital and Networks	154
		5.3.3 Brief Note on Employment	156
6		**Cultural Discourses**	**158**
	6.1	Culture: Brief Survey of Contemporary Debate	159
	6.2	Discussing Culture	161
		6.2.1 Cultural Differences and Similarities	162
		6.2.2 Stereotypes	171
		6.2.3 Culture as Behaviour	173
		6.2.4 Culture as Religion	176
		6.2.5 Culture as Heritage	178
		6.2.6 Assimilation and Acculturation	181

7   Ethnicity and Identity   187
    7.1 Culture and Ethnicity   187
    7.2 'Russian' Ethnicity and Nationality   188
         7.2.1 Ethnic Community: the Case of Soviet Jews   190
    7.3 Discourses on Ethnicity   192
         7.3.1 Ethnicity through Memory   192
         7.3.2 Ethnicity through Physical Difference   195
         7.3.3 Ethnicity through a Hierarchical Scale   197
    7.4 Ethnic and Cultural Identity   199

Conclusion   205

Bibliography   *208*

Appendix 1   *Legal Migration Statistics*   *221*
Appendix 2   *List of Informants*   *226*
Appendix 3   *Russian Institutions in London and Amsterdam*   *231*

Index   *240*

List of Tables

A1a Number of immigrants in The Netherlands from countries
of the former Soviet Union by citizenship and year, 1990–98   222

A1b Number of immigrants in the United Kingdom from countries
of the former Soviet Union by citizenship and year, 1990–98   223

A2a Number of asylum applications in The Netherlands from
countries of the former Soviet Union by citizenship and year,
1990–99   224

A2b Number of asylum applications in the United Kingdom from
countries of the former Soviet Union by citizenship and year,
1990–99   225

Acknowledgments

As this book is based on the research done for my PhD dissertation, I want to thank my supervisor, Professor Caroline Humphrey, for being both critical and supportive and for making me review the ways of writing and thinking ethnographically. Special thanks to Cambridge University faculty members and students who had the patience to sustain my excitement and my struggles in writing this book. Thanks to Remco Oostendorp, Anita Sharman, Robbert Jan Roet for proofreading and commenting on parts of my book. The last two years of the publishing process felt lighter and more inspiring through the emotional and creative support of this book's photographer and my partner, Engelbert Fellinger. Thanks to the support of my family without whom I would not have found the energy and discipline to finish this book. Last but not least, I thank all my informants without whom this research would not have been possible.

Preface

The objective of this book is twofold: to present an ethnographic account of Russians in London and Amsterdam, and to address some traditional anthropological topics, such as community, culture and ethnicity. I explore the concept of 'community' through examining different aspects of the lives of Russian migrants in London and Amsterdam. My objective is to determine to what extent the Russians may be said to form 'communities.' To this end, I explore the phenomenon of Russian 'invisibility' in London and Amsterdam. This 'invisibility' is caused both by external (relatively small numbers, geographical dispersion, etc.) as well as internal (social and cultural diversity, antagonism, etc.) factors. In this book I concentrate on the latter factors which reveal the way the community debate enters the migrants' discourse.

By examining the body of theoretical work on 'community' as well as analysing migrant interactions and conversations, I discovered that the term 'community' is inadequate for describing the situation of the Russians both in London and in Amsterdam. Throughout the book, I argue that the Russian migrants are highly diverse, both socially and in terms of their views and adaptation strategies. They are also divided by mutual antagonisms, prompting most of them to reject their belonging to a 'community'. I postulate that Russian migrant social structures can best be described through the concept of subcommunities, or groups based on social, ethnic, class, interest and other distinctions.

The concept of subcommunities is largely descriptive of the situation of Russians in London and Amsterdam, but is insufficient as an analytical tool for examining established theories in the fields of anthropology and migration. The discussion on subcommunities is thus further elaborated by chapters on the topics of social relations, informal economy, and cultural and ethnic identity in order to add analytical value and to establish relevance to a subcommunity's approach to the study of migrant groups.

I came to the conclusion that although Russians' views may be described as 'contextual' or 'shifting' (dependent on the migrant's membership of the subcommunities), 'community', 'culture', 'ethnicity', etc. are still seen by most as fundamental and self-evident categories. Throughout my book, I warn against embracing postmodern theories that present the migrants as cultural 'hybrids'. I attempt to present an ethnography that describes Russians' diverse circumstances and views, and simultaneously defends the legitimacy of the notions of community, culture and ethnicity 'deconstructed' by postmodern theorists.

To my children
Eve Madingley, Kai Tristan and the child about to be born

Introduction

The Economist article entitled 'The Coming Hordes: Migration in the European Union', speaks of Eurosceptics, trade unions and some governments that fear that enlargement of the European Union will bring a stream of migrants from Eastern Europe chasing jobs and social security benefits (*The Economist*, 2004: 25). On the other hand, the benefits of such migration are being praised. They can be seen as economic and political, as well as cultural, assets to the host countries. Such movements from east to west, whether feared or desired, are at the forefront of the social and political agendas of most West European countries. However, studies and predictions of large movements of people from east to west tend to be macro-scale and rarely address the grass-roots level situation of the migrants themselves. This can be partially explained by the fact that many new entries are undocumented or illegal migrants, and quantitative study methods are insufficient to reveal the 'how many' and 'why' and 'how' of their presence in the country. This book addresses the issue of east to west migrants from the grass-roots perspective. It is based on case study and micro-analysis which reveals not only general trends in such migration, but also the details of migrants' lives and circumstances.

My research is concerned with the study of the Russian-speakers in The Netherlands and Britain, particularly in Amsterdam and London. I define Russian-speakers as those born in the countries of the former Soviet Union (CIS), for whom Russian is a native language, independent of their ethnicity. I shall henceforth refer to the Russian-speakers as Russians. My research is limited to those Russians who have entered the receiving country for the first time between 1990 and 2004.

The original research took place in London between July 1998 and February 1999, and from March 1999 to October 1999 in Amsterdam. I have revisited the 'fields' each year through 2003, keeping in touch with my informants in both countries. I spent three weeks in June of 1998 and in September of 2003 in Russia (Moscow and Zagorsk), and three weeks in July of 1999 in Belorussia (Minsk and Grodno). Throughout that time, I lived among the families and friends of my 'English' or 'Dutch' informants. By going to Russia and Belorussia, I hoped to find out more about contemporary Russian culture by visiting the families and friends of the migrants.[1] My goals were as follows: to investigate how 'representative' the migrant population was of the Russian population 'at home'; to bring to light motives for migration; to compare social backgrounds of Russians in London and Amsterdam; to investigate differences between 'back home' in contrast to 'migrated' attitudes on specific issues; to investigate actual networks from Western countries to Russian cities; and to research the childhood roots of at least one key informant.

The initial stage of my research (two months in London and Amsterdam) involved the acquisition of information about different groups of Russians and Russian institutions. I investigated the 'community at large', including all the Russians (legal or illegal residents), visiting members of 'settled' families, their friends and business associates, as well as officials working for the Russian institutions.

The second stage of my research involved isolating a number of more or less distinct groups of individuals. Some groups were defined on the basis of the Russians' legal status in the receiving country; others were self-assigned. I isolated groups like 'independent artists', 'commuting businessmen', 'asylum seekers', 'illegals' and the like. Membership of some of these groups sometimes overlapped or shifted. In both London and Amsterdam, the number of such groups ranged from seven to 20, depending on how specific I wanted the group boundaries to be. I selected individuals or units (like families) from each of those groups as my key informants. Thus, I had 11 key subjects in both London and Amsterdam.

While other European capitals have a history of receiving Russian migrants, I chose London and Amsterdam because both cities have a relatively new and proportionally small Russian population. The Russian migrants in Britain and The Netherlands have so far not been extensively studied by social scientists. However, the phenomenon of 'new Russian migration' in Britain and The Netherlands is also known to other West European countries, as I shall further discuss in 'Note on Comparisons'.

Theoretical Objectives

Generally, my research aimed to achieve the following goals: 1) to describe, as accurately as possible, the living circumstances and views of the migrants; 2) to analyse those views in relation to larger cultural contexts; and 3) to examine contemporary theories on such traditional anthropological topics as community, culture, and ethnicity in the light of ethnographic evidence.

More particularly, I questioned the usefulness of the anthropological concept of community in investigating the everyday life of the migrants. I attempted to determine to what extent the Russians may be said to form 'communities' by exploring the phenomenon of Russian 'invisibility' in London and Amsterdam.

The literature I have consulted can be roughly divided into the following categories: literature on migration (including literature on Russians in Britain and The Netherlands; history and scope of Russian migration; theories of migration; and ethnographies of other migrant groups); literature on Russian contemporary history and culture; and literature on a range of theoretical topics, such as community, ethnicity, culture, social networks, and transnationalism.

The topics of ethnicity and transnationalism deserve special attention. John Rex (2003) discussed the nature of ethnicity in the process of migration. arguing that most modern societies may be termed plural and multicultural, with ethnicity comprising an essential part of this multiculturalism. My own article on ethnicity in Singapore (Kopnina, 2004) focuses on the fact that national and ethnic identities in modern day society may simultaneously overlap, negate or reinforce each other. In the case of my respondents, I have noticed that the ethnic Russian category (such as Georgians and Estonians from the respective countries, or Jews from the Russian Federation), sometimes being opposed, at other times fitting into it. I shall discuss this phenomenon in more detail in the chapter on ethnicity.

An excellent volume on *Ethnicity*, edited by Hutchinson and Smith (1996), offers an array of useful articles on the subject, such as the editorial article addressing shared memory and constructions of the common past; or Brass and Nash's articles dealing with ethnic identity formation and surface pointers. Two other edited volumes, Baumann and Sunier's *Post-migration Ethnicity* (1995) and McDonald's *Inside European Identities* (1993), include articles addressing the wide range of issues related to the contemporary challenges of urban minorities, people's perceptions of themselves as members of certain ethnic groups, and external labelling and group assignment mechanisms imposed from the outside.

Finally, the topic of transnationalism deserves special mention. Vertovec defines transnationalism as a set of sustained, border crossing connections (Vertovec, 2003: 2). He specifies a number of previously identified typologies of it, based on binary distinctions such as 'transnationalism from above' and 'transnationalism from below' (Smith and Guarnizo, 1998); 'narrow' and 'broad' (Itzigsohn et al., 1999), etc. Vertovec discusses transnationalism mostly in terms of migration, particularly addressing the question of what is new about transnationalism. Vertovec relies on Portes et al. (1999), arguing that movements of migrants and the networks they built a hundred years ago were not truly transnational in terms of 'real time' social contact. 'Rather, such earlier links were just border-crossing migrant networks that were maintained in piecemeal fashion as best as migrants at that time could manage' (Vertovec, 2003: 3).

Thus, as a description of the real-world changes that affect migrants, transnationalism seems to give an accurate description of large numbers of people who, due to intensifying economic inequalities between countries, move to places of greater opportunities, commute between countries of origin and receiving countries, and maintain links with their friends and relatives abroad. Transnationalism can also be described as an entity contrasted with, or supplemental to, notions of nation or diaspora (Vertovec, 2001). However defined, transnationalism has also inspired theoretical debates on culture. The concept implies that people have not only become more mobile and connected to countries other than their own, but have, as it were, stripped off certain constraints of culture and become 'transcultural'.

Staring (2001), an anthropologist studying illegal Turks in The Netherlands, cites the pioneers of transnationalism who observed that migrants build social fields that link together their countries of origin and destination. The migrants

> take actions, make decisions, feel concerns and develop identities within social networks that connect them to two or more societies simultaneously. Strongly improved communications technologies as well as improved means of transportation, support the development of transnational networks, and shape the opportunities for immigrants to maintain close-knit ties with other network members in other parts of the world. (Staring, 2002: 2)

As Rouse (2002) argues in his study of Mexican migrants in the USA, transnational migrants from communities independent of territorial or purely ethnic restraints. Transnational migrants do not just move from their country of origin and settle in a new place forever. Instead, they alternate locations, spanning networks over different countries, involving not just individuals but groups and institutions (Rouse, 2002). Rex (2003) distinguishes between two types of transnational migrants: those migrating from economically backward countries and sending remittances home, often retaining the myth of return, and those that are part of more extensive migration movements,

> who migrate to a number of countries and who intend to go on living abroad and exploiting whatever opportunities are available within the several countries. For them there is an international community distinct both from the community of

the homeland and that of the nations in whose territories they are temporarily or permanently settled. (Rex, 2003)

As I shall further argue in this book, Russian migrants may be said to form subcommunities quite distinct from the traditional definition of the clearly delineated community, and to engage in international networks.

Additionally, and relevant to the presently discussed case of Russians in two Western countries, new categories of transnational migrants have emerged. These include, among others, unskilled labour migrants, undocumented migrants (Hagen, 1994), highly skilled workers (Vertovec, 2002) – particularly IT workers employed through global 'body shopping' as termed by Xiang, 2001; and trained occupational specialists drawn back from their diasporas to contribute to the development of their homelands (Meyer and Brown, 1999).

Questions centre on the concept of community. The central question is: do Russians in London and/or Amsterdam form communities and, if not, what are the alternatives?

During my fieldwork, I discovered that the concept of 'subcommunities' describes Russian migrants' circumstances more accurately than that of 'community'. Yet, not everything found in my ethnographic data can be accounted for by the 'subcommunities' approach. This warrants the exploration of alternative methods and ideas that elaborate upon this approach. To deepen the theoretical value of the concept of 'subcommunities', I posed questions related to the concepts of 'culture', 'ethnicity', 'identity', 'informal economy' and 'social relations'. How do social networks affect the unity of or divide 'subcommunities'? How is the cultural identity of the Russians related to their membership of a 'subcommunity'?

I further attempted to place these questions in the context of contemporary debates on the condition of globalization and transnationalism. Finally, I asked whether my data adds new insights to the contemporary theories of migration in anthropology.

As I chose to concentrate on the above-mentioned topics, I had to exclude other topics related but not vital to the objectives of my research. I had to exclude sections comparing the legal background and policy landscapes of The Netherlands and Britain. I did not include a media analysis or the study of the attitudes that the Russians and members of the host societies had toward each other. I also did not include a section on crime. There is only a limited mention of some theories of modernity and transnationality based on the works of Appadurai (1991), Gellner (1994), Strathern (1995), Grillo (1998), Castells

(2000), Vertovec (2002) and Rex (2003). Also, regrettably, I could not fit in a comparison with other migrant groups (such as Indians in Britain or Turks in The Netherlands) or with other Russian groups in other West European countries, although some mention of it is made throughout the book.

Note on Comparisons

Special note has to be made about the value of comparing London and Amsterdam. A comparison of these two cities is problematic because of the difference in size and scale (while Amsterdam's population barely exceeds 700,000, that of London is about 11 million; Amsterdam is compact while London sprawls widely, etc.). Having spent an almost equal amount of time in each city, I had to spend a higher amount of energy during my first stage of research in London in an attempt to compensate for larger numbers and distances.

Before starting fieldwork, I expected to find significant differences in Russian migration patterns between these cities. I hoped the discovery of these differences would lead to valuable insights into the differential effects of host culture and legal institutions and policies in the receiving countries on Russian migrants. Surprisingly, I discovered that despite different cultural, political and social features of the receiving countries, similarities between Russian groups and attitudes in London and Amsterdam were significant. Similarities and differences in the migration policy and in the model of immigrant incorporation present in the two countries have indeed been changing throughout the period of my fieldwork. Although the national model of immigrant incorporation (Bauböck, 1994) is still relevant to my case, the scope of my book does not allow me to give extensive detail of such changes.

At present, EU governments are split on the issue of opening up labour markets. Some countries, like Germany and Austria, have secured agreements allowing the restriction of labour in-flows from Central Europe. The Netherlands and, to a lesser degree, Britain, promise to open their labour markets immediately (*The Economist*, 2004: 25; http://europa.eu.int/comm/ publications/). At the same time, efforts at controlling, monitoring and finally reducing migration flow between new EU states are continuing (Circular Letter 'Fortress Europe': http://www.fecl.org/circular/2302.htm). Common approaches to asylum and immigration policies are being formulated by the members of the European Council. Member states share with the Commission the right to initiate proposals until May 2004 in the fields of immigration and asylum (Information and Communication unit of the Directorate-General Justice and Home Affairs of the the European Commission, B-1049 Brussels, December 2002).[2]

Geographically, both London and Amsterdam are situated in Western Europe not too far from Russia.[3] They are both cosmopolitan and multicultural, with attractive commercial, cultural and social opportunities. In this way, they are similar to Paris, Berlin and New York, and sit in contrast to smaller cities with large concentrations of Russians, such as Lyon, Munich or Denver. This makes both cities attractive for young, enterprising migrants. As larger cities, both London and Amsterdam offer those who seek anonymity a place to hide. They also offer employment and housing in an informal market, and entertainment for the leisure class or tourists.

More specifically, Russians in both London and Amsterdam have proportionally low numerical representation. Both cities lack established Russian communities. The Russians, therefore, are geographically dispersed, as well as socially distant from each other. Their cultural institutions are scattered throughout both cities. Social clustering occurs only in churches, at club venues, or in the homes of members of subcommunities.

Legally defined groups present in London and Amsterdam, such as 'asylum seekers', 'temporary contract workers', 'spouses of Western citizens', etc. are very similar. Also, 'subcommunities', the largely self-defined categories based on informal social ties, professional affiliations, interests, etc., are similar in both cities. This includes groups like 'unemployed housewives', 'seasonal artists' and 'intellectuals'.

Perhaps most significantly for this study is the fact that Russians in London and Amsterdam do not significantly differ in their opinions on the topics chosen for my research. Issues such as the lack of a sense of 'community', mutual antagonism between the groups of migrants, use of social networks, and perceptions of culture and ethnicity, had large individual rather than inter-country variation.

There were, however, slight differences within all of the above-listed categories, and these are itemized below.

First, there are differences in the admission policies of the receiving countries. Distinct groups such as homosexuals, admitted as asylum seekers in The Netherlands or language students in prestigious universities in Britain, are examples of such distinct groups.

Second, there is an element of self-selection taking place in Russia as Russian immigrants come from different social pools. For example, New Russians may choose to send their children to Britain to study English. They have little interest, however, in their children studying Dutch. They do not see Dutch as the 'language of the future'.

Social policies, including migration procedures and welfare provisions, differ in Britain and The Netherlands. Although this has had some effect on the adaptive strategies and living conditions of the migrants, I found that neither the mechanisms of subcommunity formation, nor the discourse of the migrants on the topics of community, culture, ethnicity or identity were affected by those differences.

A comparison between London and Amsterdam (or Britain and The Netherlands) did not produce contrasting results. This might be due to the lack of significant Russian presence before the new wave of migrants arrived in Britain and The Netherlands, or the Russians' relatively small numerical mass in both cities. Other possible factors are discussed throughout the chapters of this book. I might have obtained more contrasting results from comparing, for example, London and Berlin, or Amsterdam and Paris. However, I see the results of this comparison as a very interesting discovery precisely because so few differences were found. The fact that my informants' stories and views, both in London and Amsterdam, are consistent with each other makes it possible to speak of Russian invisibility and fragmentation (as in the chapters on community and subcommunities), Russian versus Western values (as in the chapter on social networks) or Russian versus Western identity (as in the chapter on culture). A very different set of questions would have been required if inconsistencies between Russian views in the two cities had been found. To speak very plainly, the fact that Britain and The Netherlands *are* different, but Russians in both cities are more or less 'the same', provides an interesting contribution to our knowledge of Russian migration to Western Europe in general.

Methodology[4]

Since many of my informants were illegal, and their presence was statistically invisible, participant observation seemed a particularly suitable method of eliciting knowledge about them. Dealing with 'invisible communities', I have discovered that there may be some special advantages to observational, unobtrusive data collection in urban life. Among the diversity of cultures in the city, some may be conspicuous, and others hardly noticeable to the outside (and, therefore, not easily identified). Any instrument but the highest possible degree of immersion in these cultures may be too insensitive (Hannerz, 1980: 309).

To enter the field and expand contacts, I used the snowball method, expanding on the 'leads' I already had both in London and Amsterdam. The bulk of my research involved participating in the migrants' common activities as well as conducting structured and unstructured interviews. Themes of the interviews were chosen in accordance with my area of interest, namely, 'community'. I have also collected personal histories and life stories of the informants, involving their lives in the CIS as well as their migration history.

I have accumulated information about the following items:

1 *Institutions*: a list of formal and informal institutions founded by or for Russians. This includes addresses, a short summary of functions, and a short participation report when applicable. These institutions include Russian churches, bookstores, libraries, cafes, restaurants, clubs, discotheques, business and commercial centres, banks, clubs, etc.

2 *Statistics*: pertaining to the numbers and categories of Russians admitted or expelled from Britain and The Netherlands. This includes data on age, sex, marital status, ethnic origin, city of origin, occupation and political status of the new arrivals.

3 *Legal documentation*: information on immigration laws, work permits, political asylum procedures, cultural exchange programmes, etc.

4 *Short biographies*: brief data on informants' age, sex, marital status, ethnic origin, city of origin, occupation and political status.

5 *Interviews*: ten structured interviews with officials and organizers of cultural events; 50 unstructured interviews with the migrants; 15 interviews with Russians from the CIS; and 12 interviews with those connected to Russians by way of work, marriage or friendship.

6 *Western press articles*: paper press, television and radio reports on Russians in Britain and The Netherlands. I have also collected some materials on the CIS, reflecting attitudes towards Russians and the CIS.

7 *Russian press articles*: mostly taken from the Russian publications in London, such as *London Courier*, *Evropeiskii Vestnik* and *London Info*; and unofficial press in The Netherlands. These were articles pertaining to the life of Russians in London and Amsterdam, Russians' attitudes towards Britain and The Netherlands, advertisements and reviews of Russian cultural events.

8 *Electronic mail and Internet collection*: mostly from *Russian London* (about 600 subscribers) in Britain and *Russen in Nederland* (about 100 subscribers) in The Netherlands, both Internet groups advertising cultural

events and matters of personal interest to Russians. I have also used information from *Info-Russia*, a worldwide Internet group for Russian scholars and other professionals working abroad.

9   *Brochures, fliers and other event announcements* relating to Russian cultural life.

Ethical Considerations and Practical Difficulties

Urban context presents certain conceptual as well as practical problems. Urban anthropology requires extraordinary effort in finding and establishing connections with members of the chosen community due to the size and complexity of the city:

> The uncertain or blurred boundaries of many units of study are not only a characteristic problem of urban anthropology but can also be a source of practical difficulties in the field worker's daily life. Network chains run on without a visible end, new faces keep showing up while others drift out of the picture. (Hannerz, 1980: 313)

Urban challenges faced by the migrants include broad social, economic and welfare concerns. Aside from migrants' worries about their legal status, many are busy finding information, employment and housing; organizing insurance, medical care and education for their family members. Adaptation to the new locality is often very pragmatic. It often includes enrolling in language courses, contacting institutions and organizations, establishing business contacts and the like. Migrants can become caught in this urban whirlpool, taking an ethnographer with them on sometimes purely practical and extremely time-consuming excursions that have little to do with the traditionally anthropological subjects of study. In a city as immense as London or as intricate as Amsterdam, lots of time and energy is expended establishing and following the contact. Yet, the challenges of 'multi-sited ethnography' are counterbalanced by the advantages of having such an exciting field to explore. The diversity and unpredictability of urban encounters, and the freedoms presented by the urban environment, provide continuous surprises and challenges.

Initially, many migrants were suspicious of my motives and unwilling to disclose what they viewed as secret information. Sometimes, it was difficult to ask Russians direct questions about their migration history. Despite my assurances that I did not work for any secret service or collect taxes and that my research was purely academic, migrants were afraid that information they gave me could somehow hurt them.

> Fieldwork and intensive face-to-face interviewing with Russian immigrants is not easy. Most fear outsiders and remain guarded throughout preliminary discussions. Experiences in their homeland cause many to be withdrawn and unwilling to give information about their past life ... Most view outsiders as intruders and are unwilling, at first, to divulge details of past and present experiences, living in fear of repercussions. Those who are willing to talk are usually uncomfortable with tape recorded interviews or even by detailed note taking by the interviewer. (Hardwick, 1993: 12)

I discovered that some migrants were embarrassed to talk about their legal status (or the lack thereof) since they were 'fictionally' married or had obtained false documents to strengthen their asylum seeker's case. Others were embarrassed to talk about their work because they were unemployed or worked on the black market or were criminally involved. Some had jobs inferior to their formal professional level. Migrants were not always willing to disclose their 'social networks' in order to protect their friends against further inquiries and not to give away some useful contacts. To ensure their anonymity, respondents' names and conspicuous personal details used in this book were changed.

I discovered that the best way to get at these issues was through indirect inquiry conducted in an informal atmosphere. I made a rule of introducing myself as a researcher, but adapted the introduction of my research objectives to the expectations of the potential informant. For example, confronting religious members of the Jewish community, I told them that I was interested in religious Russian Jews, not mentioning the fact that I was also interested in the Orthodox Church. Sometimes, in order to take the pressure off the unwilling informant, I had to pretend I was interested in something the informant himself could not be helpful in, except for referring me to the more knowledgeable people.

Problems also arose by doing 'anthropology at home' (Jackson, 1987), and 'anthropology by the native ethnographer' (Abu-Lughod, 1991; Raj, 1997; Strathern, 1987). I was simultaneously treated as 'one of them' (because of the common origin and language), and as an outsider (US citizen, 'previous wave', and 'researcher'). This made my position in relation to the chosen community ambiguous.[5] I define myself as a 'cosmopolitan' – a position that shapes my views on life in a way that might be unacceptable to a more 'nationally embedded' or 'locally committed' individual.[6] The fact that I am

Russian and have lived in Western Europe made me a 'member of the familiar species' and often I found myself monopolized by the Russians against 'the Westerners'.[7] Sometimes Russians assumed that I already knew something because they felt that it was 'common knowledge', discounting the fact that I was a teenager when I left Russia.

Despite my 'Russianness', I was rarely seen as a member of any one group, since Russians assumed that as a researcher my objectives were different from theirs. My participation in the activities of divergent groups, my attendance of different churches, etc., indicated my lack of loyalty to any one segment of the population. This outsider status had some advantages, as sometimes people confided in me more easily than they would have if I were involved in one group's affairs more directly. Alternatively, the outsider status also meant that some people, not usually inclined to pour their souls out to strangers, excluded me from more intimate events in their lives.

My age, gender, family situation, ethnicity and education also played a role – positively and negatively – in my ability to enter certain 'circles'. I found it hard to speak to certain groups, like middle-aged professionals (who found me too young) or certain young men (who did not take me seriously). At the same time, I was welcomed by groups like 'Russian wives' and young professionals. Being pregnant gave me unexpected access to older migrants and families. I have tried to minimize my authority as a former Soviet citizen and aspired towards academic objectivity – it is up to my readers to judge whether I have succeeded.

Organization

The seven chapters of this book are positioned to reflect the sequence of my inquiry into the subject of 'community'.

The chapter on migration gives an overview of classical and contemporary migration theories in general, and the history of Russian migration in particular. The 'new wave' of the 1990s is particularly addressed.

'Breathing life' into the previous chapter, the chapter on London and Amsterdam presents a setting for my research. It also provides brief biographies of my key informants. This chapter gives a spatial and temporal framework to the following chapters.

The chapter on community introduces theoretical debates on community and establishes the phenomenon of 'Russian invisibility' in London and Amsterdam. This chapter addresses external factors, such as low critical mass and the lack of physical markers that may account for the invisibility of Russians from the perspective of outsiders. It also focuses on internal divisions that account for the fragmentation of Russian migrants and their lack of interest in or awareness of the 'Russian community'.

The chapter on subcommunities presents an alternative perspective to an 'invisible community'. I argue that although Russians and members of the host societies might not recognize Russian presence en masse in London and Amsterdam, they do nonetheless form and notice smaller units of families, friends or colleagues. These subcommunities are based on diverse factors like social class, profession, or interests.

The chapter on social relations clarifies how subcommunities become operational. It also discusses the evolution of the migrant's experience as he learns to adapt the social and economic methods learned in the CIS to his new environment. Groups of migrants are further classified on the basis of their diverse adaptation strategies.

Chapters on culture and ethnicity raise issues concerning migrants' perceptions of themselves and others. I also tackle larger theoretical issues, such as the postmodern critique of classical theories of culture and ethnicity. I develop the argument that although 'community', 'culture' and 'ethnicity' mean different things to different people, ideas of origin and belonging are still important to people. The chapter on ethnicity culminates in a discussion on migrant identity, and ties the topics of community, culture and ethnicity together. This is accomplished through my argument against contemporary theories that tend to 'deconstruct' these concepts.

I summarize the findings from the previous chapters in the Conclusion. I conclude that although the concepts of community, culture and ethnicity are interpreted differently by migrants, they are still understood and used as reified and significant categories. The use of those concepts also depends on the migrant's membership subcommunities, which influences the migrant's world view and social positioning.

Notes

1   I left Russia for the United States in 1989, and since the issue of my American passport had not been back to Russia. Also, my knowledge of Russian culture was largely limited to Moscow which is not exactly representative of the rest of the country. During my trips to Russia and Belorussia I visited some of the families of my informants, discovering, perhaps most significantly, that their awareness of the 'world on the other side', and particularly accuracy of information on topics ranging from living conditions of their migrant family

members to the system of government in Western countries was much higher than I expected (perhaps based on my own experience as a former Soviet citizen).

2   Some of the policy-development landmark treaties developed during the period of my fieldwork include: the 1990 Dublin Convention making member states responsible for handling asylum applications (re-evaluated by the Commission in 2003, aiming to avoid situations of 'refugees in orbit' by allocating responsibility to a member state for examining an asylum application); the Treaty of Amsterdam in 1999, which established a common European asylum system; a communication on a common policy on illegal migration (COM(2001)672), adopted by the European Council in 2002, formulates a common policy on illegal migration.

3   This may provide an interesting contrast to Russian settlements in Israel, the USA, Canada, and Australia where, I would postulate, migrants have less of an opportunity to commute back and forth because of relative expense and time of travel; while in France and Germany one may expect similar patterns of commuter migrants to emerge.

4   I find it an important aside to point out my own bias in conducting fieldwork, which is my 'positivistic' (for the want of a better term) as opposed to 'postmodern' view of 'reality'. I make a distinction between 'reality' or 'facts' on the one hand, and 'social reality' or 'interpretation' on the other hand. As a researcher, I am interested in both social reality and reality although I realize that the latter is harder to discover. For example, hearing the story of an illegal migrant about the way he entered a receiving country, I also wanted to find out whether this story is 'true'. I believe that if 'truth' is known or at least suspected, the informant's story can be better understood. I believe that the social scientist's strength lies in his ability to synthesize diverse accounts that testify to the existence of a certain fact. It seems that when postmodern social scientists testify to the respondents' ability to 'create' or 'construct' or 'contest' their 'reality', they simultaneously undermine the respondents' common sense in perceiving reality as such. I agree with Scheper-Hughes who does not deny that there are certain 'facts' that need to be reported accurately – objectively – by an anthropologist, but this objectivity disintegrates at the stage of interpretation or even initial arbitrary choice of subject: 'Obviously, some events are "factual". Either 150 or 350 children died of hunger and dehydration on the alto do Cruzeiro in 1965; here the ethnographer has a professional and a moral obligation to get the "facts" as accurately as possible. This is not even debatable. But all facts are necessarily selected and interpreted from the moment we decide to count one thing and ignore another, or attend this ritual but not another, so that anthropological understanding is necessarily partial and always hermeneutic' (Scheper-Hughes, 1992: 23).

     Most respondents cannot afford the luxury of living in artistically constructed worlds of meanings, and their reactions, it seems to me, testify to the existence of the solid mutually intelligible world with which they interact, employing imagination and humour. I tried to be as sensitive as possible to the respondents' opinions and attempted to understand what they were getting at. This was achieved by asking the same question twice, rephrasing the answer and presenting it back to the respondent for inspection, listening to what a respondent tells other people in different situations, by asking other people about him, and above all by rigorous participant observation.

5   Debating the question of whether the interviewing of Soviet immigrants could be done by former immigrants themselves, members of the research team on life in the Soviet Union argued that emigrants' interviews would elicit more valid responses than those who were not intimately acquainted with life in the USSR; others claimed that emigrants' interviews would to some extent impose their own expectations on respondents, or that respondents

would not trust emigrant interviewers with whom they were unacquainted (Miller, 1987: 373).

Through statistical and qualitative analysis of the data gathered by the 'native' researchers, it was decided that their success rate in eliciting truthful and open responses was about the same as for the non-immigrant interviewers.

6   'Cosmopolitans were considered as those committed to professional skills, having little loyalty to the community in which they lived and having reference groups which were not specific to the community' (Jansen, 1969: 65).

7   In Barth's contribution to *Ethnicity* (ed. J. Hutchinson and A.D. Smith, Oxford University Press), he states that the 'identification of another person as a fellow member of an ethnic group implies a sharing of criteria for evaluation and judgment. It thus entails the assumption that the two are fundamentally "playing the same game", and this means that there is between them a potential for diversification and expansion of their social relationship to cover eventually all different scores and domains of activity' (79).

Chapter 1

Migration

Introduction

In this chapter, I address some theoretical topics of migration, summarizing contemporary critique of classical theories. I argue that although the criticisms of classical migration theories are partially valid, contemporary theories often lack the interdisciplinary and humanitarian approach of the classical theories. I refer to the work of the sociologist Halbwachs (1960), whose classical volume *Population and Society* I find particularly relevant to the understanding of modern migration patterns. I argue that few contemporary works on the anthropology of migration show the intellectual vigour necessary for expanding migration theories in general or providing ethnographies that have the potential of becoming 'anthropological classics'. However, there are impressive advances in migration anthropology regarding questions of migrant motivation and social context (Baumann, 1995; Gardner, 1995; Hardwick, 1993; Raj, 1997; Rouse, 2002; Rex, 2003).

Secondly, I address the issues related to the history of Russian migration, including a discussion of its significance for Russian culture. I also include a brief survey of 'waves' of Russian migration to the West in the twentieth century.

Thirdly, I briefly examine the recent history and the social context of migration to Britain and The Netherlands. As mentioned in the Introduction, I shall not attempt a detailed comparison of Russian migration to these two countries. The results of my research show that Russian migration to both Britain and The Netherlands exhibits similar features, such as the proportionally low numerical mass and the lack of historically formed 'established community' in both countries.

The bulk of this chapter focuses on the issue of 'new' migration during the 1990s when not only Russian, but international migration patterns changed from prior forms (although 'new' movements may still include traditional patterns). I refer to the sociological studies of Codagnone (1998) and Snel et al. (2000), pertaining to Russians in Britain and The Netherlands respectively, as well as to Hammer et al.'s (1998) volume on new international migration. The concept of transnational migration, with references to new types of 'community studies', is particularly relevant here (Rouse, 2002; Vertovec, 2002; Rex, 2003). I give particular focus to the phenomenon of illegal and generally unregistered migration. I stress the need for more ethnographic studies of the new migrants in order to elicit detailed knowledge about the groups which, although numerically large, are statistically invisible. I refer to groups of Russian migrants, such as asylum seekers, commuters, contract workers and 'new Russians' who reflect the social diversity of the new wave.

I do not attempt, however, to dwell upon statistical data in the case of the new migrants as such data can be largely misleading. Statistical data on Russian migrants in Britain and The Netherlands will only be mentioned in so far as it indicates certain trends in official (or registered) migration, or hints at the gap between the suspected numbers of migrants and the available numbers. I also do not extensively address migration policy in Britain and The Netherlands.[1] This information is too vast to be included in this chapter. A summary of legal information can be found in Appendix 1 of this book.

1.1   Contextualizing Migration

Migration has been a vast subject in social sciences since the beginning of the twentieth century. Anthropology did not seriously address the subject until the 1970s, when anthropologists showed increasing interest in studying urban communities and 'ethnic groups' in their own 'back yard'. This led to a shift of ethnographic attention to migration (Baumann, 1995; Calgar, 1997; Hannerz, 1996, etc.). The new focus is due to the reformulations of the old conceptions of social processes in general, and of culture in particular (Boissevain, 1975; Abu-Lughod, 1991. These are the topics discussed in the chapters on community and culture. Recent anthropological interest in migration can also be explained by the spread and recognition of the actual phenomenon in Western Europe, as well as increased government funding for projects that instruct migration policy (Akhbar and Shore, 1995).

Yet, there are still too few works in anthropology that attempt a holistic ethnographic account of particular groups of migrants, and still fewer that attempt to tackle and bring insight to general theories of migration. I shall mention, in the following sections, such notable exceptions of anthropological works as Baumann's (1995) study of Asian migrants in Southall, Hardwick's (1993) study of Russian migrants on the Pacific Rim, Raj's (1997) book on Hindu Punjabis in London, and Rouse's (2002) study of Mexican migrants in the USA. It appears that anthropologists have yet to discover ways of addressing the topic of migration using their methodological advantage as 'trained ethnographers' and their theoretical commitment to holistic analysis. My research attempts to exploit both the methodological and analytical potential of anthropology. In this way, I seek to contribute new insights to the study of migration in general, and to Russian migration in Western Europe in particular.

1.1.1 Contemporary and Classical Theories of Migration

Contemporary migration theories, such as those presented in the inter-disciplinary volume *International Migration* edited by Hammer et al. (1997) and by Courgeau (1995), are often dismissive of the classical theories which they present as rigid and one-dimensional. 'Transnationalism', 'hybridity', and 'cosmopolitanism' became popular terms used in anthropology to describe groups of migrants (Appadurai, 1991 and 2002; Cheah and Robbins, 1998; Moutsou, 1998; Carruthers, 2002; Ong, 2002; Rex, 2003). These terms stem both from 'globalization' concepts, and postmodern anthropological critique of classical theories as static and closed in opposition to dynamic and open conceptions. However, despite the fact that the conditions of migration might have 'globalized' (relative freedom of movement, spread of information technology, etc.), the results of my research make me sceptical about certain contemporary theories. Although contemporary critique of the classical theories is relevant, there is little in the way of alternative theories produced in the postmodern period.

Some of the classical theories produced since the beginning of the twentieth century adopted a macro-approach to the study of migration without particular attention to ethnographic details. They tended to operate with rather simplistic economic theories (like Ravenstein, 1889; Lee, 1969). Still, these classical theories retain their appeal and relevance due to their interdisciplinary and humanitarian nature.

An example of such an insightful work is that of the sociologist Halbwachs (1960). Halbwachs conjures up and simultaneously challenges the idea of a migrant community, raising issues highly relevant to my arguments in the chapters on community and subcommunities. Halbwachs speaks of a migrant as a member of a group who 'becomes an immigrant by the [virtue of the fact that] he begins to share the circumstances of other men who form a group, beside whom he works, and in the midst of whom he lives' (Halbwachs, 1960: 113). Migrant groups form 'collective conceptions' which are 'particularly coloured by the mental and moral reaction of the group toward their physical surroundings' (Halbwachs, 1960: 114). This does not mean, however, that a migrant 'mixes' with other migrants. This point is crucial to my argument developed in the chapter on subcommunities about various factors that set groups of Russian migrants apart, preventing them from forming a unified community:

> The immigrants, as a group, have no ambition or concern except to go from one country to another. This exhausts whatever their minds can really have in common. Each one in the group preserves his individual ends and preoccupations, all the more because he is separated from his group of origin, and from this point of view he is not in solidarity with the others. (Halbwachs, 1960: 115)

Halbwachs accentuates that migration is not just an unobstructed move from one country to another. He explains that it is, rather, a difficult passage that requires breaking the hold of one's own country and resisting 'repulsion' from the country of destination. 'If men were, then, only inert dust like the sand of the dunes, they would be distributed here and there at the mercy of chance, they would turn aside from obstacles, they would be scattered into vast open spaces, now attracted by some, now repulsed by others like magnetic particles' (Halbwachs, 1960: 191). Although the migrants of the 1990s are relatively free to move from country to country and do not necessarily feel 'exiled' or cut off from their country of origin, their sense of purpose, as well as their feeling of 'rootedness' in space and time, suggests that they are guided by rational and clear motives. As I shall further discuss, motivation is often the factor that distinguishes migratory waves and that characterizes individual migrants within such waves.

1.1.2 Motivation

Earlier studies often represented migration in macro-terms, as a sort of unified phenomenon in which the masses are guided by more or less clear-cut motivations (Ravenstein, 1889; Jackson, 1969; Lee, 1969; Taylor, 1969). These motivations were often described in terms of 'push and pull' factors, discussing migrant behaviour as a rational and unobstructed balancing of the 'plus and minus' considerations. The actual dynamics and social processes involved in migration were rarely discussed. These theories often concentrated on economic or political motivation in exclusion of other factors (see brief summary and critique of these theories in Hammer et al., 1998 as well as Courgeau, 1995; Davis, 1988; Melotti, 1997).

As I shall discuss further in the section on new migrants, although migration of the 1990s is often viewed as a 'selfish' migration (Glenny and Stone, 1990), my interviews with the migrants revealed a complexity and diversity of motives that could not be described as merely 'economic'. Although 'nothing can compare with the desire inherent in most men to "better" themselves in material respects' (Ravenstein, 1889: 286), I believe that economic motivation alone is never enough. Recent studies of illegal migrants show that 'economic motivation' may also be broken down into related social and cultural motives. These include providing financial support for the 'stayers'; the element of 'adventure' and 'challenge' present in the decision to migrate; or the opportunity to get specific education or jobs (Hammer and Tamas, 1997; Staring, 1999). Halbwachs (1960) notes that migration 'is not primarily or exclusively a question of economic motives', but a path that involves deeper collective processes.

Fischer et al. (1997) criticize the rigidity of classical theories regarding motivation which view the migrant as a rational utility maximizer. Contrary to the assumptions of mostly economic classical theories, they assert that migration is not cost- and risk-free. Rather, they stress that potential migrants are a heterogeneous group of people who do not have access to perfect and cost-less information, and who do not behave in an unconditionally rational manner. In sum, the potential migrant is not an autonomous human being but is embedded in the social context. The authors argue in favour of the dynamic view of the migration decision, emphasizing the significance of 'pioneers' and 'chain migration' in the early waves of migration. Anwar, an anthropologist of migration in Britain, noted that in the case of Pakistani workers, pioneer migrants decisively influenced those who followed 'by their letters, visits and remittances home, demonstrating economic opportunities' (Anwar, 1995: 238).

In contrast, Russians in the CIS, Britain and The Netherlands demonstrated that, in this modern age of open commuting and relatively easy information flows, those whose families already reside abroad may decide *not* to migrate precisely because their expectations become more realistic. In this respect, we may question Fischer et al.'s (1997) criticism of the classical theories. Modern Russian migrants *do* appear to be more informed and freer to choose whether to stay or go than members of the previous waves. Although my data on Russian migrants does show that the migrants are both socially heterogeneous and influenced by diverse motives, as Hammer et al. (1997), few recent migrants are guided by dreams and illusions, the way previous waves might have been. They do not tend to imagine Britain and The Netherlands to be countries of unlimited opportunities where they will effortlessly find employment, housing and the like (Staring, 1999). Rather, many Russians evaluate available information and realize that migration might not be their best alternative. Instead, their options have broadened to include a temporary trip abroad or, perhaps, the choice of staying home altogether.[2]

1.1.3 Why do Some People Stay?

Hammer and Tamas (1997) ask this question about contemporary migrants. Indeed, given the continuous lack of political and social stability, and the deteriorating economic conditions in many countries of the CIS, it is surprising that so many Russians choose against permanent settlement in the receiving country.

> The question is not why so many migrants left East for West, but actually why so many – given large differences in economic well-being between East and West, ethnic tensions and violence – have *not* taken the step towards the wealthier and relatively safe close-by countries of the EU. (Snel et al., 2000: 29)

Returning to the critique of the classical theories which viewed migration as a direct outcome of economic and political turmoil in the country of origin, Codagnone, an anthropologist of European migration, suggests that the decision *not* to move is as complex as the decision to move.

> The predictions about massive emigration from the post-Soviet space were based on the assumption that worsening economic conditions and rising unemployment would be followed by waves of economic migrants ... Then why has, if not massive, at least more considerable out-migration from Russia and the other republics not occurred so far? The fact presents a challenge to the standard assumptions of migration theory and suggests that economic deprivation alone does not determine mobility decisions. (Codagnone, 1998)

During my trips to Russia and Belorussia, I met the families and friends of my 'Dutch' or 'British' informants. They were more aware of migration options than those whose families have not migrated. For these Russians, migration was rarely considered a viable solution to economic or political problems. In fact, those who visited their relatives or friends abroad generally had a more negative attitude to migration. As the father of my Amsterdam informant put it: 'I've seen where and how [my daughter] lives and it's not all as rosy as I expected. I'm glad to be staying here [in Belorussia]' (Grodno, 1999). During the Soviet times, the iron curtain left the West veiled in the aura of mystery; and far away countries promised to bring freedom and riches. Presently, few illusions about the West are left in the CIS. With more realistic information available regarding the conditions in the receiving country (threat of unemployment, social isolation and devaluation, etc.), many Russians prefer to stay at home.

Some CIS citizens are still enamoured by the idea of 'leaving for the better world'. They do not see this, though, as practically feasible, either because of economic or social reasons. My acquaintance in Moscow said: 'I'd love to go [to the West], but I haven't even got the money to pay the fare [for a ticket]. I don't know anybody in any [foreign] country; I don't speak any languages – I don't think I've got a chance' (Moscow, 1998).

Others reported that migration was not even on their minds. As the friend of my Belorussian informant from London aptly put it: 'When you live in a sty you cannot imagine what it's like to live in a castle. I don't want to hear about how rich or happy somebody else is. Envy eats you up more [than the actual situation at home]. It might be better there [in the West] but I'm here and that's as far as I'll get' (Minsk, 1999).

On the other hand, the answer to why people stay may lie in the increasingly restrictive migration policy of the West European countries.

> In the near future, large quantities of emigration are unlikely to occur as the majority of countries in the West are concerned about the flow of emigrants from East European countries and Russia and take defensive measures, including more severe laws of entry and introduction of stringent migration quotas to limit the undesirable migration. (Tishkov, 1996: 41–2)

In the second half of the 1990s, migration policy has tightened throughout Europe. In Britain and The Netherlands, restrictive policies reflect both the political and sociocultural climates of the two countries (see Appendix 1 for more details on migration and citizenship laws in both countries).

We have thus far mentioned some of the classical and contemporary theories of migration relevant to migrant groups in general. We shall now explicitly address the place of Russian migration both in Russian culture and history, and in internal and international waves of the twentieth century.

1.2   Historical Note

1.2.1 Movement in Russian Cultural Imagination

Russia may be said to have a long-standing tradition of migration, in- and outside of its borders. Because of its large territory, and its social and cultural diversity, people within Russia have been on the move for hundreds of years.

Two displacement ideas loom large in Russian popular and literary imagination: that of migration, and that of 'exile' (*ssylka*) from the motherland. Although 'migration' implies voluntary choice, and exile is understood as a requirement to leave accompanied by a sense of loss and isolation, both are deeply fused in Russian imagination. Migration, like exile, is often perceived as forced. Thus, economic or political motives for migration are both justified and resented, leaving Russian expatriates with deep feelings of guilt for 'betraying the motherland' and an almost obsessive sense of longing and nostalgia. This proves true for everyone from farmers to intellectuals – and these remain persistent themes in Russian literature. This unique cultural configuration, fusing migration, forced exile and nostalgia, seems to be a consistent feature of Russian population movements throughout history.

Kotovskaya and Shalygina (1996) speak of *othodniki*, men who temporarily moved into the cities in search of seasonal work in the nineteenth century. Indeed, since the freeing of the surfs, movement from the country to the cities has been a strong and self-perpetuating demographic force. After *perestroika*, back-to-land campaigns became widespread and a few hundred ·thousand city dwellers found the incentive to move back to a land attractive enough to dare to 'return to the roots' (Bridger and Kay, 1996). Despite these internal movements, most Soviet citizens were not allowed to leave their national territory, and had difficulty moving between the republics.

These land-to-city and city-to-land movements, as well as citizen's inability to cross the borders, have deep roots in Russian culture. The idea of movement, freedom and possession (either of land in the country or of opportunities in the city) – the very concept of the road, *doroga* – are all deeply embedded and intertwined in Russians' cultural psyche. Russians have developed a strong cultural imagination for the concept of 'going places' precisely because the surfs, or *kolhozis* (or for that matter, the Soviet citizens) were not able to migrate freely. 'Going places', however, was often associated with a sense of guilt, since Russians were pressed to stay not only by the letter of law, but also by an elaborate system of cultural symbols. Notions like 'home' or 'native land' have become the anchors for the ships of free Russian imagination. Many have tried to shake off the chains that tie them to these anchors, yet remain fearful of what might happen to them once they are at the mercy of the sea. To continue this marine metaphor, it appears that the wind in Russian sails was generated not only by external forces of nature, but by an inner need to escape the imprisonment of the harbour. Those who left were referred to as *predateli*, or traitors, as dissidents leaving for the West were described. *Rodina* (Mother Russia), or *otechestvo* (fatherland) – metaphors evoking family ties and native homes – were opposed to *chuzhbina* (the foreign land), and seen as hostile and dangerous. Willems describes the Russian political refugee this way: 'Alone in a foreign land …; his stay seems only temporary at first; until the shock of indigence and downward social mobility makes him realize its permanence; he becomes a "stateless" person, a man without a country …; culturally, he is torn between isolation on an island of exiles and immersion in a sea of foreigners …' (Willems, 1972: 3).

1.2.2 'Waves' of the Twentieth Century

In the nineteenth century, most Russian migrants left for America, Canada, Germany and France. In Britain the 'most prominent émigré community was made up of Poles displaced by the Russian empire territorial gains, rather than by Russians themselves' (Kelly, 1998: 297). However, members of the Russian political opposition, although not numerous, were quite influential. They were particularly drawn to Britain, publishing a number of Russian journals and newspapers (Kaznina, 1997: 3).[3] At the same time, Russian migration to The Netherlands was negligible and can be said to be 'accidental'. A handful of Russians, planning to go to Germany and France, remained in The Netherlands. These were mostly political or religious refugees.

Twentieth-century 'waves' consisted mostly of intelligentsia and politically or ideologically motivated individuals. These 'waves', which spread massively into America, Canada, France, Germany, Israel and other countries, may be broken into a few phases. Only a few hundred Russians went to Britain and The Netherlands throughout the first three-quarters of the century.

The first wave concerns the period just before and after the Russian Revolution of 1917. This included famous revolutionaries like Lenin, who continued activities abroad for which they had been persecuted in Russia. These were mostly political exiles who wished to return to Russia if circumstances allowed (although some remained abroad till their death). The movement after the Revolution involved those threatened by the new regime: members of aristocratic families, the cultural elite, and political activists trying to influence events in Russia from abroad (descendants of both groups can still be found in Britain). Malia (1994) estimates that emigration of the old upper classes after the Civil War comprised 1.5 million. 'For the most part, these émigrés were not "White Guardists" but intelligentsia whose skills were cruelly lacking for the post [Civil] war reconstruction' (Malia, 1994: 137). London has been a hub for the literary elite, although to a lesser degree than Paris or Berlin (Kaznina, 1997). Besides the elite, other social classes suffered population displacement after 1921. Almost a million in total poured into continental Europe, France, Germany, Poland, Latvia, Yugoslavia, Bulgaria and Czechoslovakia. They included peasants, workers and impoverished aristocrats (Glenny and Stone, 1990; Vishnevsky and Zayonchakovskaya, 1994). 'Every strand of opposition was represented in the new communities, from monarchists and former courtiers through ex-ministers, conservative and liberal, to Socialist Revolutionaries, anarchists and Social Democrats of different hues' (Kelly, 1998: 299).

> The first wave is associated with revolution and Civil War in Russia; it was a tragic exodus of over 2.5 million people. Among them were soldiers and officers, Cossacks and students, musicians, writers, scholars. They were Russia's intellectual and cultural elite. The result was that Russian culture, language, lifestyle were to be found not only in Moscow, Petersburg, Kostroma or Rostov, but also in Paris, Berlin, Prague. (Freinkman-Chrustaleva and Novikov, 1995: 150)

The second wave originated after the Second World War and involved predominantly ethnic Germans as well as a few Russians taken to work in Germany during the war and fearing return to their motherland (the latter group was mostly present in The Netherlands).

> Among them were hundreds of thousands of involuntary emigrants – captives, people driven to other countries, displaced persons, who later settled down in many countries of the world. (Freinkman-Chrustaleva and Novikov, 1995: 150)

Malia (1994: 263) estimates that also during the war between one and two million left Russia. A few hundred found themselves in Britain, escaping Stalinist purges (Shilovsky, in Glenny and Stone, 1990: 293–4). The literary elite, with a few exceptions (like the Northern Society in London), moved into the New World – particularly New York – and partially (mostly Ukrainians) to Canada (Kelly, 1998; Hardwick, 1993).

According to Codagnone (1998), the third wave originated in the 1950s and intermittently ran until the 1980s. It consisted of ethnic Jews, Germans, Poles and Greeks. Some moved from other European countries into London and Amsterdam (notably from Germany in the latter case). 'Emigrants from the third wave were the people who were exiled from the USSR or left it because of persecution for political, cultural, or nationality reasons' (Freinkman-Chrustaleva and Novikov, 1995: 151).[4]

Glenny and Stone (1990) argue that the third wave originated in the 1970s and ran into the mid-1980s. In the 1970s, during the relaxation years between East and West, a new wave of political dissidents, mostly Russian Jews, left for America, Israel and Western Europe (Siegel, 1998; Doomernik, 1997). A few hundred Russian Jews joined the Amsterdam Jewish community in the early to mid-1980s (Snel et al., 2000). Codagnone (1998) attributes this wave to the Western diplomatic pressure that relaxed Soviet controls, enabling some 340,000 individuals to leave Russia. This migration is characterized by those who disagreed with the Soviet system and were highly educated (Snel et al., 2000: 61).

To sum up, the earlier waves of Russian migrants had 'common themes' – either ethnic, religious or political – that kept them together:

> One very striking feature of all three waves – inevitably, of the first more than the others – is the way in which the immigrants have kept together. There is now a kind of émigré international that will look after you in any city in the non-communist world ... (Glenny and Stone, 1990: xvii–xviii)

The fourth wave began in the late 1980s, during *perestroika*, when more Jews and ethnic Germans, as well as Greeks and Armenians, departed for their respective motherlands (Siegel, 1998). While it is still an 'ethnic' migration, economic factors figure strongly in it, thus it is not entirely characterized by a common theme. It can be 'distinguished from simple economic migration by the advantages (pull factors) deriving from the absence of barrier to entry and entitlement to citizenship in the destination countries' (Codagnone, 1998).

1.3   'New' Russian Migration

The new wave of migration, to which my research is devoted, occurred in the 1990s, right after the break-up of the Soviet Union. It can be seen as an extension of the fourth wave, though it is characterized by a much greater social and ethnic diversity and by a wide range of motivations (economic being the predominant ones).[5] The 'new' migrants represent groups such as Armenians from Azerbaijan, Jews from Siberia or Russians from Estonia. Though this book is concerned with the migrant communities in London and Amsterdam, most of the 'new' Russian migration has not been international but instead has occurred within the CIS as formerly Soviet borders suddenly became international (Shlapentokh et al., 1994; Tishkov, 1996).

1.3.1 Internal Migration

In the Soviet and post-Soviet period, internal migration refers to the movement of population to and from the republics, including the Russian Federation. These movements are relevant to my own research for two reasons. Firstly, many of the motivational factors involved in internal migration are similar to those involved in external migration. Political and ethnic unrest, economic turmoil, professional and daily life and insecurity, all contributed to population movements in Russia. The second reason is that the life of an immigrant in the receiving society, be it 'far or near abroad', and the mechanisms of adaptation he uses for adjusting (or not) to the receiving society, are best seen in cross-national analysis. Examining the situation of Russians in the 'near abroad', or their circumstances in Russia after they decide to leave, offers interesting insights into the ways Russians in particular deal with different situations in the receiving countries.

Even in the pre-Soviet time, internal migration existed, manifested differently in different areas. In some cases, such as with Caucasian regions, Russians entered the region as militants or 'pacifiers'. They settled first in the military camps and later, outside of them, to keep the local population in check. Many Russians were trading or working in Central Asia in the nineteenth century, settling mostly in the urbanizing areas. Ukraine and Belorussia have had 'Russian areas' and villages since the time of the spread of the Kiev Empire (Shlapentokh et al., 1994).

The Soviet regime, however, introduced a few significant factors that enabled larger numbers of Russians to move to the newly founded republics. After the founding of the Soviet Union, the republics became part of 'greater Russia' (some later than others, such as the Baltic republics that 'joined' the Union after the Second World War). Russian citizens thought of the republics as an extension of their own motherland. At the same time, the concept of 'motherland' was commonly understood as predominantly (if not dominantly) Russian, and Russians gained special 'ruling majority' rights in the number of republics. These 'rights' were not necessarily legally defined, but were implicit in the social hierarchy structure. Some republics offered better work opportunities for Russians. Others offered a better climate or more comfortable lifestyle.

In every republic, Russians were received with varying degrees of hospitality and received different, although generally favourable, accommodation. Before the fall of the Soviet Union, in 1989, there were about 25 million Russians living outside the Russian Federation. Half of those lived in Ukraine and Belorussia. More than one third resided in the republics of Central Asia and Kazakhstan. The remainder were divided as follows: 6.7 per cent in the Baltic republics, 3.4 per cent in the republics in the Caucasus and about 2 per cent in Moldavia (all figures quoted in Tishkov, 1996). These Russian diasporas consisted of mostly the urban professional strata, and its members enjoyed a relatively high political standing. They took this rank for granted as a result of their natural ethnic entitlement, since they saw themselves as belonging to *starshiy v bratskoy semye* ('the elder of the fraternal family') (Tishkov, 1996: 12–14). After the fall of the Soviet Union these Russians found themselves to be the largest foreign majority in Europe. Suddenly, they realized (or were reminded) that they were not 'at home'. Again, the way the titular population treated them, and the changes in their lifestyle, were different in every republic. This was due to specifications of the ethnopolitical situation, which in turn is influenced by the actions of the governing elite and the attitudes of the titular population (Tishkov, 1996: 55). In Ukraine and Belorussia, inter-ethnic problems are solved in a more democratic and tolerant way than in other republics. This might be partially explained by the fact that Russians, Ukrainians and Belorussians are ethnically similar, and that the Russian minority in the former republics is proportionally large. Except for a few countries in the 'near abroad' where dual citizenship was allowed, Russians were forced to make a choice. They could choose to accept the citizenship of their country of residence, which implied a break with Russia; or, having accepted Russian citizenship, they could become foreigners in their country of residence – an act that practically limited their civil, social and economic rights (Shlapentokh et al., 1994).

In 1992, the Federal Migration Service of Russia was formed to serve as the governmental regulator of migration in Russia. In that same year, the republican long-term programme 'Migration' was developed and approved by the government of the Russian Federation. This programme's main goal is to support refugees and forced migrants from the countries of 'near abroad' (Tishkov, 1996: 42). Up until the present, the programme has been largely unsuccessful in trying to control, regulate or even describe the migrant movement.

Humphrey (1996/7) and Pilkington (1998) report difficulties in the adjustment of ethnic groups who suddenly found themselves to be foreigners in their own country, 'dispossessed' not only of their citizenship, but of their sense of cultural and social belonging as well. Ethnic Russians returning to the Russian Federation from Central Asia suffered difficulties in finding housing and employment, and arranging medical care. They also suffered from social isolation (Pilkington, 1998). Humphrey (1996/97) calls internal migrants 'most radically dispossessed':

> No one knows the true dimensions of migratory processes in Russia and there is no law in place to define these people's rights ... According to the Federal Migration Service there were at the end of 1993 around two million of such 'international' refugees, most of them Russians returning to the homeland from the Baltic, Central Asian, and Caucasian states. (Humphrey, 1996/7: 73)

Although the laws developed to deal with the returned Russian communities were highly ineffective, a forced migrant law was passed in 1993, revised in 1995 and did function throughout the 1990s and is still in existence today (Flynn, 2004).

Further developing my argument about the lack of unified Russian community in London and Amsterdam, I find that the phenomenon of mutual antagonism and mistrust among the Russians – including animosity between the 'old' or 'established' waves and new arrivals – is particularly reflective of the 'cold reception' of the fellow-Russians in the Russian Federation. Internal migrants might be said to have suffered a 'culture shock' due to the social and structural problems of adjustment in Russia, similar to those experienced by migrants 'far abroad'.

1.3.2 New Migration to 'Far Abroad'

As in the case of internal migration, 'new' Russian migrants going to 'far abroad' after the break-up of the Soviet Union, leave for the West for diverse reasons, ranging from socio-political to economic. However, economic reasons are more prominent in both the media and academic publications.

> 'The fourth wave' of emigration is quite different from the previous ones. First of all emigrants of this 'wave' leave the country absolutely freely, without anybody's approbation; most of them leave for abroad with their own possessions, with the documents given to them by their country of origin and consulates of the receiving countries. 'The fourth wave' is often called

> economic ... Indeed, most people leave the motherland not urged by political
> confrontation, not because of fear of repressions, not the search for spiritual
> freedom and possibility of self-expression, as it was characteristic of the
> previous generation migrants. More mundane basic motives account for their
> decision ... (Freinkman-Chrustaleva and Novikov, 1995: 118)

My own fieldwork reveals that, indeed, there are very few 'true political'
refugees fleeing dangerous areas (such as certain Transcaucasian countries),
or the kinds of intellectual and cultural elite seeking freedom of expression as
was the case in the previous waves. As members of the older migration note,
this is a less ideological and more 'practical' migration:

> I would say that the new emigration is ... a political emigration, or to some
> extent – without wanting to offend – it is a selfish emigration, in the sense that
> they are people who no longer want to live in Soviet conditions. But one way
> or another, it is not an ideological or a religious emigration and it is becoming
> less and less so all the time. People become dissatisfied and so they leave. They
> go to Israel, America, wherever you like, not in order to fight Soviet reality but
> in order to escape from it. (Bloom, in Glenny and Stone, 1990: 194–5)

Codagnone (1998) lists a few reasons responsible for the fourth wave of
migration. These reasons are largely supported by my own data from London
and Amsterdam. First of all, the wave of the 1990s was prompted by the
liberalization of migration policies in the CIS. While members of previous
waves were either expelled or fled the Soviet Union, new migrants were
more or less free to leave, either permanently or for travel. Business, cultural
and social exchanges between countries of the CIS and the West began to be
actively encouraged during the Gorbachev era. Also, the break-up of the Soviet
Union caused an intensification of ethnic conflicts and political unrest, creating
a new category of refugees. All these factors, combined with the economic
decline of the countries of the CIS, led to an intensification of migration.
Indeed, Russians I have worked with arrived in London and Amsterdam
voluntarily, seeking better opportunities, and were relatively free to leave or
to commute between their country of origin and Western Europe.

1.3.3 Russians in Britain and The Netherlands

Through interviews with Russians and related sources (such as Russian
publications and Internet sites, or cultural organizers and travel agents), and
through my personal observations, I estimate the number of Russians living

in Amsterdam as approximately 4,000 to 10,000. Estimates for London range from 50,000 to 100,000.

Statistical data of the Russian presence, collected from a variety of organizations including the CBS (Centraal Bureau voor de Statistiek), IND (Immigratie en Naturalisatie Dienst), and EBB (Enquete Beroepsbevolking), to name a few, gives little indication of their real numbers. I have also consulted the Russian consulates in London and The Hague, as well as data published by the Russian Ministry of Foreign Affairs to verify available statistics.

There are slight differences in immigration policies from country to country, reflecting on the number and make-up of certain groups admitted to Britain and The Netherlands. Abridged information on these policies may be found in Appendix 1, as well as in the 'Comparisons' section in the Introduction.

1.3.4 Different Groups of 'New' Migrants

In Britain and The Netherlands, Russians are not the only 'new' migrants. In both countries, 'new' migrants usually possess a different legal status from 'traditional' migrants (who either arrived as refugees, or were invited to work by Western governments). Instead of having permanent legal papers, 'new' migrants often enter receiving countries with temporary, conditional and tourist visas, or falsified documents. This allows them to remain beyond the sphere of formal control. As I shall further discuss in the chapter on social networks and informal economy, instead of having formal jobs or receiving social benefits, many 'new' migrants are self-employed, have 'black jobs' or use their friends and families for informal financial support. Because of the lack of formal work permits, some migrants become entrepreneurs, engage in informal labour or criminal activities, or become dependent on those with legal status (friends, spouses, etc.).

In the study of 'new' Russian migrants in The Netherlands, a group of sociologists, Snel et al. (2000), sums up new migration as possessing four general characteristics:

> new geographic patterns of migration [diverse countries including those of Eastern Europe], new types of migrants, new judicial statuses and new existence strategies of the migrants. However, this does not mean that new migration replaces the 'old' one. It may be said that the new migration patterns exist alongside the old ones. As a result, we may speak about increasing pluralization and fragmentation of migration and migrants. (Snel et al., 2000: 1)

This situation is largely true of Britain (Codagnone, 1998). A large proportion of these 'new' migrants are asylum seekers, refugees, commuters or temporary and seasonal workers – so-called transmigrants and illegals. There is no clear demarcation as to which category a migrant belongs; these categories shift according to migrants' circumstances (as in the case of entering a country on a tourist visa and staying on illegally) or overlap (an asylum seeker may also be a commuter). 'Tourists' may want to 'disappear' from legal attention after their arrival, while illegal migrants might try to legalize their status by means of an arranged marriage, for example (Snel et al., 2000). According to my findings, this situation is equally true of Russians as of other migrant groups.

The legal status of 'new' migrants is subject to change. Through marriage, asylum requests, or medical or psychological 'emergency' cases, illegals try to legalize their status. In London, I recorded a case of a young Estonian man who entered Britain on a tourist visa and suddenly converted to Judaism, declaring to the authorities that as a 'new Jew' he would discriminated against in Estonia. When he was denied asylum, he forwarded another letter to the authorities saying that he wanted to join the Anglican Church. He stated that, since there is (supposedly) no Anglican church in Estonia, his only option was to remain in Britain. He is still waiting for the decision, having spent four years in London illegally. Meanwhile, he is supported by his uncle (who is also illegal but runs his own repair shop registered in his English friend's name) and a number of Russian and English friends.

Thus, asylum seekers, marriage partners and contract workers, as well as commuters and seasonal workers, exemplify large groups of new Russian migrants whose boundaries may shift throughout migration history. As I shall further argue in the chapters on community and subcommunities, neither of these groups is likely to forge a community. Migrants often choose individual survival strategies because of the precariousness of their situation, uncertainty of their legal status, lack of common aims, or the practical need of remaining individually aloof to avoid the authorities' attention. All these factors are responsible for the lack of reliable statistical data on new migrants. After presenting some of the available statistics, I shall briefly discuss some groups in an attempt to sketch their general aims in the receiving countries.

Legal channels of entering both Britain and The Netherlands include asylum procedures,[6] marriage or family reunions, or working contracts. However, according to my research and the growing body of sociological studies of recent migration, the majority of the 'new' migrants are commuters, temporary workers and illegals.

Asylum seekers are a phenomenon created both by the increasing internationalization of the world with its opening of borders, and the receiving countries' migration policies. Unlike regular or traditional types of migrants, an asylum seeker's legal status is fairly uncertain, as the asylum decision and procedures may last for years. Although asylum seekers are supposed to be politically motivated, escaping danger to their lives and livelihoods, most of those seeking refuge in the West are not considered to be eligible for asylum (Eurostat). Hammer and Tamas (1998) warn that distinctions between 'forced' and 'voluntary', or 'political' and 'economic' asylum seekers are too simplistic. Throughout the 1990s, there were only very few areas in the countries of the CIS where a full scale war took place. Yet, overt ethnic discrimination with the use of violence – be it against the Armenians in Azerbaijan, Russians in the former Baltic republics, or Jews in Ukraine – is undeniable. Also, some Russians found themselves in physical danger due to poor economic conditions, as in the areas where no electricity or sufficient food resources were available for the winter (parts of the Russian north and certain areas in the Caucasus). Some asylum seekers – such as thieves fearing retribution or Russian army deserters fearing incarceration – seek to escape the consequences of their own actions. In the process of my fieldwork, I observed a number of bogus applicants, as well as genuine victims, with stories of violence inflicted upon themselves and their families. Other asylum seekers claim that they cannot go back to Russia because of medical or even psychological reasons.

As a result of both delayed bureaucratic procedures and the migrants' immediate desire to acquire jobs and housing, many asylum seekers disappear into the world of illegal existence and informal labour. Especially in The Netherlands, where few rejected asylum seekers are actually escorted out of the country, many of those who are refused official permission to stay remain in the country, avoiding public recognition and averting formal notice. This undocumented phenomenon is described in two instances in The Netherlands:

> The first one has to do with forms of illegal migration and commuter migration which, by their very nature, are difficult to trace and document. The second one has to do with the 'mystery of the processed out asylum seeker'. Do the latter leave The Netherlands or not? There is a particular lack of reliable data on the processed out asylum seekers from the former Yugoslavia and former Soviet Union. (Snel et al., 2000: iv)

Dutch law in regard to the rejected asylum seekers and illegals is rather liberal. I have recorded a story of someone who was denied asylum status and roamed around The Netherlands until he was arrested for theft, identified, and incarcerated for a month. On the day of his release he was given a thousand guilders to 'choose his own airline to fly home with' – an event which he celebrated with his friends, buying drinks 'on the house' until the money ran out.

The situation in London is slightly different. Britain has much stricter admission policies where asylum seekers are concerned. Figures from Eurostat show that while The Netherlands received 16,855 (11.3 per cent of EU15), Britain has only accepted 8861 (6.4 per cent of EU15) asylum seekers from the CIS between 1985 and 1998, of which the largest number arrived after 1991 (Eurostat and IGC).[7] Behind these figures stand the stories of my informants who testify to the uneasy transition from an asylum seeker to an illegal. One of my London informants spent a few weeks in a detention centre adjacent to a prison (without having committed any crime) waiting for the authorities' decision to grant him asylum. However, the decision process took a couple of months which my informant, having been released without the right to claim social benefit or work, spent virtually on the street polishing shoes. When the denial of the asylum status arrived at his friend's address, my informant, afraid of being found at his friend's apartment, 'took permanent residence under a bridge'. During the last month of my fieldwork he joined a team of illegal Russian carpenters and is currently earning 'decent money'. Thus, although illegal entry is more difficult in Britain (because of geographical as well as legal barriers), once a migrant succeeds in entering the country, the process of deportation is as messy and ineffective as in The Netherlands. An informant of Snel et al. speaks of illegal migrants who also stay in Amsterdam for years:

> I estimate that there are a few thousand of Russians and Ukrainians in Amsterdam. A small number of them was legal some time ago, but is now illegal. They appear very legal: they work and speak correct Dutch. There is a much larger group, which has never been legal… They never tried to become legal but they do hold an option of marriage open. They have a sufficient network of Russians and Dutch to enable them to stay here. (S9, in Snel et al., 2000: 70)

Aside from rejected asylum seekers, illegal migrants enter the country on tourist and business visas, sometimes arriving from other European countries. Some of these 'tourists' or 'visitors' simply overstay the official invitations of their families or work contracts. Their temporary return to the CIS becomes problematic, since they are unlikely to be re-admitted to Britain and The Netherlands having once been illegal. 'Illegal immigrants, in a certain sense, are the most important residents of unknown society. Current methods of administration and social sciences cannot adequately observe and register them' (Engbersen, 1999a: 13).

The ethnographic method is probably the only one suitable for eliciting knowledge about this numerically large but statistically non-existent group of people. My encounters with the illegals in London and Amsterdam revealed a great diversity of stories and motives for migration. It also disclosed illegals as a socially heterogeneous group of people.

Other categories of 'new' Russian migrants enter Britain and The Netherlands 'traditionally', through marriage, family reunion or work contract. I shall discuss groups like 'Russian spouses' and 'contract workers' in the chapter on subcommunities. At present, suffice it to say that these groups are not numerically large (numbering a couple of thousand each in London, and a couple of hundred in Amsterdam). They are also geographically dispersed and socially disjoined (except for cases of small groups of 'Russian wives' and professionals, discussed in the chapter on subcommunities).

Another set of 'new' Russian migrants is the *temporary and commuter* migrants. While temporary migrants may reside in the receiving country once (either for work, or visiting families, or staying illegally), commuter migrants usually enter receiving countries on a regular basis (something illegals cannot do unless they find ways of crossing the border unregistered, which is easier to do in The Netherlands, coming from other European countries).

Commuters often do business between countries (selling cars and other goods across borders, common in The Netherlands) or engage in seasonal work (such as summertime musicians and street artists, common in both Britain and The Netherlands). Retaining their families, accommodation, cultural interests and social networks in the CIS, these migrants describe their country of origin as their 'home' while 'working' in the West. Some say they have two homes and work in both countries; others call themselves cosmopolitans without any permanent home. Some speak only Russian, as most of their work involves Russian clients or does not require language ability in the receiving country (selling street paintings, cleaning houses, etc.); others speak many languages to enable them to work in different countries. As further discussed in the chapter on Social Networks, some commuters rely on their compatriots' help with employment, housing and moral support, while others approach the receiving society more directly and independently.

> ... we speak of migrants who – unlike the traditional types of migrants – travel
> back and forth between old and new societies. Transnational migrant lives as
> it were in both worlds and instrumentally uses this circumstance, for example
> for transporting goods. (Snel et al., 2000: 4)

As I shall discuss in the chapter on culture and ethnicity, the ideas of
'transnationality', 'hybridity' and 'cosmopolitanism' have become popular in
postmodern discourse (Grillo, 1998; Cheah and Robbins, 1998; Hannerz, 1996;
Moutsou, 1998; Raj, 1997; etc.). However, as I shall further argue, although
patterns of migration may change, ideas of locality, roots and belonging remain
significant for the migrants. My interviews with commuters in London and
Amsterdam revealed that these migrants found themselves shifting between
two 'worlds' for predominantly economic reasons. Yet, their cultural and
ethnic identities remained rooted in their ideas of place and belonging. As
Richmond notes, 'individual migrants in post-industrial societies are of the
"transilient" type who do not necessarily settle permanently in any one locality
and yet are not "rootless", alienated or marginal men in the sense in which
these terms were understood in the context of traditional or industrial stages
of development' (Richmond, 1969: 280). Indeed:

> Many have limited short-term objectives and plan to return to the previous
> locality, or to move on to another place when these objectives have been
> achieved. The greater the ease with which short-term objectives are achieved
> the more likely it is that the migrant will return or re-migrate ... Migration does
> not necessarily mean the complete relinquishment of all the ties with the former
> country or locality ... Evidence of migrants maintaining relationships with those
> in the former locality are the maintenance of correspondence with relatives
> and friends, remitting money to dependants and creditors, periodic visits to the
> former locality ... and maintenance of a network of social relations in the new
> country, with others from the same locality. (Richmond, 1969: 265)

This can be said to be especially true of the 'new' Russian migrants,
many of whom are actually 'shuttling' between the CIS and the receiving
country[8] with the goal of trade, visiting friends or relatives, part-time work
and the like. Earlier generations of Soviet migrants hardly had this choice.
However, non-Russian commuter migrants do not represent a 'new' pattern of
migration (although they are part of the recent wave of the 1990s). This form
of 'migration' has already been noticed by sociologists in the 1960s: 'Today
it is increasingly apparent that a significant number of migrants spend periods
of their lives outside their country of birth, returning home and perhaps after

a further period setting off again, without the implications of finality usually associated with such moves' (Jackson, 1969: 4). Perhaps as a consequence of such freedom of movement, neither temporary nor commuter Russian migrants in the 1990s seemed to experience the same longing and nostalgia experienced by members of the previous 'waves' for whom the idea of 'exile' marked a clear break with the country of origin.

The last group of 'new' migrants are literally '*new Russians*' or 'rich Russians' who are found both in London and Amsterdam, buying real estate and doing luxurious shopping on the weekends. According to one informant, there are also 'thousands' of rich Russians in The Netherlands. They are described as having 'a lot of money, a house, work and residence permit and often their own business' (Snel et al., 2000: 67). I found it difficult to find and approach this group in both London and Amsterdam. Yet, from my 'higher-positioned' informants, I was able to deduce that although the 'new Russians' use (or launder) their money quite conspicuously in the West, their main businesses are usually based in the CIS.

> … wild Russian capitalism is deeply entrenched in global crime and in global financial networks. As soon as profits are generated, they are sent into the anonymous whirlwind of global finance, from which only a portion is reinvested, once conveniently laundered, into the rewarding but risky, Russian economy. (Castells, 2000a: 192)

Some of these groups of migrants move in and out of the statistical limelight as 'asylum seekers', 'tourists', 'visitors', 'students' or 'contract workers'. In this way, they enter into the shadow of official invisibility as they remain past their visa expiration date or hang in a limbo of unprocessed or rejected asylum seekers.

Notes

1   Such information existed in the first draft of this chapter.
2   In the recently completed project (May, 2001) I have participated in, which was designed by Erasmus University in Rotterdam, a number of illegal Russian migrants were interviewed on the subject of their expectations of The Netherlands and their reaction on arrival. Very few subjects indicated large discrepancies between their original views and the actual reality they encountered once in The Netherlands.
3   Such as 'Svobodnaya Rossiya', 'Nakanune', 'Narodovolets', 'Sovremennik', etc.
4   Anthony Bloom came to Britain in 1949 from France, becoming equivalent to Archibishop of the Moscow Patriarchal Orthodox Church in the United Kingdom. He recalls this time

as 'a time of festivity. It was a remarkable time, when there were Russian organizations, young people, ideology, love of Russia, an ardent, passionate Church life … But it does not exist any more and it cannot be created artificially' (Bloom, in Glenny and Stone, 1990: 195).

5   In 2005, this diversity and motivational range are still present, although the scale of the newest migration remains to be explored. Considering the logistical difficulty of defining 'migrants' and particularly illegal migrants (as opposed to 'temporary workers', 'tourists' and 'visitors' or 'shuttlers', 'returnees', etc.), the numbers of those presently entering Western Europe with an intention to stay are hard to confirm.

6   With some legal differences between British and Dutch entry policies, such as asylum granting to homosexuals in The Netherlands but not in Britain.

7   The recent Immigration and Asylum Bill, amended in Committee in the House of Lords and printed on 28 July 1999, introduces even stricter measures concerning refugees (information found in special report of refugees at http://www.guardianunlimited.co.uk/ refugees). Only in April 2000 – for the first time in four months – has the queue of asylum seekers waiting for a decision fallen below 100,000 (Home Office). Presently, hundreds of extra caseworkers are taken on 'to clear the huge backlog of cases' (*The Guardian*, 26 April 2000: 5). There were some recent changes to the aforementioned policies. In the UK, the Migration Programme terminated its existence in 2001 when federal funding for it was removed. Two laws were introduced in the UK since the Law on Immigration and Asylum: the 2002 Nationality, Immigration and Asylum Act and, since 2004, the Asylum and Immigration Act, both of which have introduced even stricter measures regarding asylum and refugees. In The Netherlands, the consequences of the *Koppelingswet* ('Coupling Law', 1996) – the law linking legal status with qualification for social benefits such as education, medicine and housing, and *Wet Inburgering Nieuwkomers* (WIN, 1996) and *Regeling Inburgering Oudkomers* (2005) – the law of 'enculturating' or integrating the newcomers and 'oldcomers' in the latter case – are felt to be generally restrictive of migrants' lives in The Netherlands. In 2004, new *Regels gezinshereniging en gezinsvorming*, rules specifying family reunions and formation, tightened restrictions for bringing in new family members. *Wet of Identificatieplicht* (2005), or Identification Law, was introduced limiting illegal migrants' ability to 'stay invisible'.

8   While in a foreign country, migrants 'find themselves in minority groups within receiving society' (Jackson, 1969: 5). Shuttling between the two countries does not pin a migrant to a particular minority group.

Chapter 2

London and Amsterdam:
The Tale of Two Cities

Introduction

While the previous chapter introduced Russian migrants as a mass phenomenon, this chapter aims to introduce some of the migrants individually by presenting the stories of some of my key informants. Their names, among others, will be cited throughout the book. Their stories provide a deeper understanding of the personal circumstances and idiosyncrasies which influence their views.

This chapter also aims to set the scenes where my fieldwork took place and present a sketch of 'Russian Amsterdam' and 'Russian London'. As opposed to the following chapters, which develop theoretical arguments, this chapter serves as an ethnographic reference point to the rest of my book. This exercise in social geography aims to familiarize the reader with some people and places, and to make him question what is really known about them and what has yet to be discovered.

This chapter is thus intended as a 'discovery tour' not only of streets and faces, but of my own thoughts as they were influenced by the special people I met during my fieldwork, and the places they inhabited. These discoveries led me to the argument of invisibility of Russians in both cities, of the lack of unified community, the presence of subcommunities, and the curious evolution of social relations and informal economy. These and other observations make Russians in London and Amsterdam an intriguing group of migrants.

2.1   The Setting

Where does one find Russians in London and Amsterdam? Although one may hear Russian spoken on the streets, in neither city is there a street or district that Russians would claim to be a stronghold of their 'community'. Although one will occasionally see matryoshkas and samovars exhibited in the windows of East European souvenir shops, travel agents, or simply in odd places at the markets, neither city has a fixed place where Russians exhibit or sell their cultural artefacts. Russian historical exhibits, ranging from treasures of the czars to Communist banners, visit London and Amsterdam annually, enticing the Western public with the promise of 'familiar exoticism'. A rare Dutch or British child has not cheered at the Russian circus performers, a rare Dutch or British culture lover has never attended a performance of Russian ballet.

The Western public learns about the CIS through the media. They learn about the dark ages when the Great Russian czars visited Britain and The Netherlands; about the Revolution which carried out the mistaken promise of a German political philosopher and overturned not only the Russian ruling class but also influenced politics and ideology in both Britain and The Netherlands (the great idea that corroded its own host country but spread the seeds of socialism which still bloom in Western welfare states). They are taught about the Soviet tyranny and perversion, and about the government of fear and deceit. Yet, this same government turned an agrarian nation into an industrial superpower, and took an active part in one of the bloodiest wars of the twentieth century. They learn about the collapse of this power with very sad and funny stories of fallen bridges, sunken submarines, babushkas selling drugs in the subway passageways, rotten potatoes in forsaken fields, and hungry homeless children on the streets of major CIS capitals. Finally, they learn about corruption and lack of promise, the danger of dealing with the CIS, and hundreds – maybe thousands – of migrants who leave the country like rats escaping a sinking ship. The British and the Dutch hear, read and watch these stories. They watch the Great Northern Bear with her former republics, younger siblings – or were they domesticated prey? – roaring in pain or in the hope of intimidating – what an odd animal, what a pitiful sight!

Let's go back now, to the streets of London and Amsterdam, where the public is so well aware of Russian and Soviet history. Here, museums, concert halls, stores, churches, restaurants and private houses host bits and pieces of that formerly great empire. Where are the Russians? How does one find them? I shall hereby relate two stories of my first informants in London and Amsterdam. These informants, more than anybody, helped me to find others and made me question my own assumptions about the Russians in two different West European capitals.

A year after my fieldwork, in the late winter of 1999, I was walking in Amsterdam with Alena, one of the Russians who knew 'Russian Amsterdam'. Alena had lived in Amsterdam for six years and she seemed to know most of the local Russians. As we set out on our trip from the Symphony Hall toward Leidseplein, the tourist square, the Dutch capital turned into a city of Russians. On the street, a chic-dressed young couple greeted us in Russian, inviting us to come along to a cafe and supplying us with a load of the latest Russian jokes as we passed the more soft-spoken Dutch on our way through the city centre. On Leidseplein we were introduced to a sextet of Russian musicians playing stylized classical music. They turned out to be former St Petersburg Music Academy students. In a cafe, we drank beer with a middle-aged pianist and his ballerina wife who had come to The Netherlands from Israel a couple of years before. As we moved further to another famous Amsterdam square, Rembrandtplein, I was astonished to find out that almost all the artists selling the pictures of Amsterdam by night, bridges and windmills were Russian. Soon, our small travelling group increased in numbers; and as we walked down to Central Station there were 12 of us marching down the bicycle path. We recommended to each other certain Dutch restaurants and performances, and greeted other Russians who seemed to have taken over the cafes on Rokin, the central street of Amsterdam.

We spoke to a shy young man who studied computer programming in Amsterdam. He was about to tell us how he came to reside there when we told him about our own occupation: anthropologists studying Russians in Amsterdam. At that point, the man became more shy, and suggested that we had better talk to his friend, for the latter was a more interesting case. We changed the subject and discussed the Dutch, which initiated another wave of recent immigrant jokes having to do with Dutch national character and their strange country's laws. All the while, the Dutch pedestrians and bikers turned their heads and, involuntarily, their wheels, evaluating this diverse and conspicuously audible group of foreigners. Perhaps they asked themselves: 'Who are those people? Why are they here? Why don't they get off our bicycle path?'

The same winter, I revisited London and met up with an old family friend, Grisha, a middle-aged biologist from Moscow. Although I learned of his whereabouts only after the completion of my fieldwork, I have known Grisha since my childhood. He led me through the now familiar 'Russian London'. Both of us shared a common interest in the Russian presence: Grisha because of nostalgia, and I because of my research. We did not visit street artists or greet musicians. Instead, we took a bus through the streets where Russian bookshops hid their treasures, where Russian restaurants welcomed non-Russian gourmets, where Russian churches secreted the smell of incense even through their closed doors, and where concert halls and museums housed temporary Russian exhibits. Most of all, Grisha and I noticed the streets where our Russian friends lived, as if drawing our own map of London, adapting to this large city, making it more personal.

But neither Amsterdam nor London was 'Russian' for me when I first moved into them. I had to rediscover these cities through my Russian friends and informants.

In the summer of 1995 I had lunch with a Turkish student at an outdoor terrace in Amsterdam. Somehow the conversation drifted towards Russians and my friend said that she had heard that there are lots of Russian girls married to Dutch men. These girls are brought there neither by love nor blind destiny but by a calculated attempt to obtain Dutch citizenship. I took this personally and started to explain to my Turkish friend that, although I was going to be married to a Dutchman, I was already a US citizen. As I spoke, I was tapped on the shoulder by a girl who asked if I was Russian. Our discussion took place in English, and while I was trying to place the girl's accent, she readily declared herself as Russian. Her name was Sveta. Open and chatty, Sveta introduced us to her Dutch boyfriend, a man some 20 years her senior, who placidly stood at the foot of the open terrace, apparently uninterested in us. Allegedly, Sveta met him at a party on her first tourist visit to The Netherlands.

Sveta became my first Russian friend in Amsterdam. At 27, she turned out to be quite a social magnet, especially where the Russians were concerned. With her baby face and completed paediatrician's education, she was idiosyncratic, and yet her friendliness quickly drew people of different ages, ethnicities and occupations into her circle of friends. Sveta married her mentally unstable boyfriend and was drawn into his world of drugs and destitution. She suffered from depression and occasional beatings in their small dilapidated apartment, all the while reassuring her friends of their mutual love and her intention to rid her husband of his drug addiction. Sveta managed to retain her own freedom to leave the house whenever she pleased, go to night clubs and buy drugs using her husband's meagre disability benefit income.

Two years after our meeting on the terrace, I went to visit Sveta in her apartment with the group of Russian friends she introduced me to. Sveta had a concussion after taking a few ecstasy pills in a night club and fainting in the bathroom. She asked for Russian books and music, and gratefully listened to fresh Russian jokes which her friends picked up either from recent travels back home or through the Internet. Sveta became sentimental about her family back in Ekaterinburg, a large city in Siberia. She told us that as soon as she got better she would leave her husband, return home, and work as a doctor – forgetting about the rainy, dreary Netherlands.

In a couple of weeks Sveta recovered. She left her husband (without divorcing him) and started taking intensive Dutch courses, simultaneously applying to a medical school. Presently, she is still formally married although living with her Chilean lover, speaks excellent Dutch and hopes to get her medical diploma by the end of 2001. Sveta and her lover have visited her home town. She returned horrified by the poverty and hardship they found there, and determined to earn money for her family in Russia. Sveta still has a lot of friends, including many Dutch. She hopes to divorce her husband as soon as her residence status is confirmed. In the meantime, she has agreed to pay him 50,000 guilders (the black market price for a fictitious marriage) by the end of her studies.

Having arrived in London for my fieldwork, I did not know any Russians. I found multiple entries for Russian businesses, churches, translation agencies and restaurants in the Yellow Pages and started my investigation by visiting institutions connected to the Russians (see Appendix 3 for the list and brief descriptions of Russian institutions). During my first days of settlement in the east of London, I discovered a small library next door with a notice board at the entrance, posting a large advertisement for Russian lessons. I called the number and an old woman with a heavy English accent told me in Russian that she did not give lessons any more as she was ill. She spoke perfect English and when I asked her how she knew Russian, she replied that her parents were Russian but she herself was born and bred in Britain. I told her about my project and she advised me to contact a retired publisher who 'knew loads of Russian people'.

I called the publisher and he invited me to come for a visit – he lived close to Heathrow Airport. Having met me at the Underground station, this old but energetic man was delighted to 'welcome the new Russian blood'. While walking me to his house, he asked all the questions that I was planning to ask in my own interviews with the Russians.

I was disappointed because it turned out that the publisher was also from the 'old wave', having come to Britain in the late 1940s. Most of the publisher's friends, from what I could deduce, were also 'old wave' and although his stories were captivating, I could not use them for my research. By the time we finally entered his rather run-down apartment with shelves upon shelves of dusty books (all of which he had allegedly published), I was convinced that this fascinating man was a dead end as far as my fieldwork was concerned. Suddenly, from the depths of the publisher's gothic library, emerging like Cinderella from under the spider webs, came my first London informant.

Olga was 26, married to a British man, living away from home (Moscow) for two years. The reason she was renting (actually, just occupying) the old publisher's room was that her husband was in Dubai for work and she wished to stay in London and study. Olga's husband – for reasons never explained

– rented their apartment out. She had no choice, therefore, but to bounce from one friend's apartment to another. The publisher was recommended to Olga by her Russian ex-colleague at the EBRD – the European Bank for Reconstruction and Development – where Olga worked during her first year in London.

A day later, Olga called me and said that she had lived with the publisher for two months, but felt uncomfortable there. She sensed that, although he was both amiable and feeble, the publisher's reputation as a womanizer was substantiated by his present interest in her. If Olga could not pay rent – and she said she could not – she felt obliged to reciprocate the publisher's generosity, but was unwilling to do so. I was looking for a new apartment as well, as my original abode in the run-down area of Bethnal Green was a temporary residence for summer students. Suddenly, Olga felt she had some money to spare and offered to find and share a flat.

Until the end of my fieldwork and the beginning of Olga's official course of study at the University of London, we shared a cheap flat in Golders Green, North London (haunted by a mentally unstable landlady). Olga was seeking out the Russians as much as I was. She was willing to accompany me to all the social events. Being an easy-going companion as well as an attractive young lady, Olga easily drew people to herself and became my perfect fieldwork-assistant.

While 'seeking the Russians out', I also wanted to know about Olga's life in London. She said little about her marriage, except that she met her husband in Moscow while working as a teller for the international bank. They went out a couple of times, fell in love and got married. She moved to London and got a job at the British branch of the same bank. A year later, he left the bank for unexplained reasons. He went to Dubai, but she allegedly wanted either to find work in London or get a 'serious education' at an English university. In the end, she decided to stay and fend for herself. Lonely and unsuccessful, she joined the Baptists – her neighbour at her first flat was one. She also visited the Russian Orthodox church but felt that the Russians there were somehow distant and arrogant. Therefore, she only went there for the 'smell and atmosphere'.

At the end of my fieldwork, Olga was officially enrolled into the East European studies programme at the University of London. She then received disturbing news from home. Expressing concern for her sick grandfather and mother, she suddenly decided to quit university and return to Moscow. Finally, she went to Dubai to join her husband and has since disappeared as a friend and informant.

2.2 Reflections

In some ways, the stories of my first two informants appear rather odd. This was my first lesson in fieldwork: new Russian migrants had strange stories to tell. Although Olga and Sveta had much in common – being the same age, married to Westerners, living abroad for two years and then emerging from the shadows into a more promising and real world – their stories were anything but straightforward. Events in Olga's and Sveta's lives evolved with a speed unknown to most of the members of the resident population at home or in the receiving countries. Decisions and choices were made quickly. As if playing a chess game, one move followed the other, but it was hard to tell who was winning in this rational and yet unpredictable match.

During the later stages of my research, I encountered and heard more bizarre and unusual stories. In London, I found an article about Sir Anthony Buck, a former Tory junior defence minister. He married a Russian widow who came to London as a tourist and tracked him down after seeing an article about his painful divorce in a Russian gossip paper.[1] In Amsterdam, I heard the case of a 'black Russian' (originally Kenyan) who was adopted by his Russian parents in Chechnya and had to ask for political asylum in The Netherlands. Apparently, the Chechens considered him to be a dark Arab and assumed that he was a Muslim, sympathetic to their cause of independence from Russia. They sent him threatening letters ordering him to leave his Russian parents and join the guerrillas in the mountains.

Although these are not 'typical stories', they warned me of the fact that Russians in London and Amsterdam could not be easily distinguished into broad categories of 'asylum seekers' or 'Russian spouses'. Ethnographic method helped me to trace individual stories, such as Olga's and Sveta's, which could possibly tell me more about the Russians in London and Amsterdam than inaccurate statistical estimates. Another thing I learned from Olga and Sveta was that they were not just 'Russians in a foreign country'. Both were quite idiosyncratic and mysterious personalities. There was Sveta, pregnant by her Chilean lover and very busy and tired from her work in the hospital, with her innocent baby face (black hair tucked in a neat pony tail, lively blue eyes, big cheeks, tiny chin and puffy lips). I would sit with her in a coffee shop, watching her thoughtfully rolling a joint and then suddenly falling silent, and staring at the wall, even before she got stoned. I wondered whether she thought of her impoverished Jewish family back home, of her lover playing enchanting South American guitar, or of something completely different and possibly pragmatic, like how to fit everything into her schedule, which office to go to next, or where to get a cheap haircut.

Olga, a blond beauty with wide soft features and a never-failing smile, seemed a more open personality. Olga felt equally comfortable in the Orthodox church, silently lighting a candle and carrying it through the aisles, shrouded in a kerchief; or in a student bar, accidentally forgetting to button up her shirt and watching undergraduate boys from above the rim of her pint of Guinness. She talked, while casting illuminating side glances, especially when young men were present. She laughed during the night so I could hear her in the adjacent room. She would engage in bubbly, optimistic, simple talk which used to rescue me unfailingly from an academic stupor or general mental fatigue. In the beginning, I thought of Olga as a kind of carefree drifter – a good-hearted simpleton and easy companion. Yet, at the end, when she was unhappy with her study and wanting to return to Moscow, when she had disappeared like a Cheshire cat, leaving nothing but her big smile behind – I questioned whether I really knew this person, whether I understood what she wanted in life.

Another striking feature of Olga and Sveta's stories is how much remained unknown. Despite the fact that I developed a personal friendship with both women, I could not reconstruct certain facts, especially concerning their true intentions. For instance, had they married for love, to secure a visa, or something completely different? Maybe they were hesitant to disclose too much because I had openly admitted my interest in the Russians from the start. Maybe I was not allowed into their sacred private spaces because they did not trust me as a person, or because I did not know how to listen.

There were, however, occasional revelations too intimate and too fleeting to be recorded. Once, during the regular happy chatting about her 'cute professor' whose glasses reminded her of her father's, Olga uttered: 'My father was an alcoholic'. This sounded as if her father was dead, and her family disintegrated. She gave the impression that there was nothing for her to go back to. The silence that fell for that unthinkable half-a-minute accentuated the significance of this utterance in Olga's life. Yet, in the next moment, we were back on the cute professor theme, and his glasses reflected nothing but Olga's perfect haircut.

Three years ago Sveta, in one of her cannabis-induced, introverted moods, was talking of her commitment to solving her husband's drug and mental problems. Suddenly, swinging in her chair, she broke into a song in which a woman tells her old and unloved husband that he can cut her to pieces, but she will try to escape him, regain her freedom and return to her lover. On a couple of other occasions, Sveta would recite poetry or prose that contradicted her previous statements. Recently Sveta talked of how she feared her next visit to Russia since 'it's all so depressing out there'. She reflected on how she would rather just send money to her family and invite them to come over, and how she never wanted them to 'end their days in this scary country'. Yet, with her next breath, she recited from the poem of the Russian poet Brodsky, 'I shall not choose a country or a churchyard, I shall return to Vasiliev Island [near St Petersburg] to die'. Were these true revelations? Could I make them 'scientific' and turn them into data and fit them into my book? Thanks to my first informants, I still ponder these questions.

I have learned from these people that, although I was Russian myself, my origin did not always bring me closer to the 'natives' – I felt that it was not the cultural divide that separated me, as the researcher, from them, as 'subjects'. Instead, it was a gulf of interpersonal mystery that will probably always exist between people, even if they come from the same family. This led me to think of the themes I shall later develop in my theoretical arguments about community, culture, ethnicity and identity. I could no longer look at my informants just as Russians living abroad – they were complex personalities, and their stories made me rethink academic and personal theories I have carried with me into the field.

2.3   The Tale of Two Cities

Returning to the tale of two cities and reflecting on the lack of clear comparisons, I keep asking myself: why London? Why Amsterdam? The reasons for the choices made by Sveta and Olga were obvious – their spouses' nationalities. But for other Russians, the choice is not as obvious.

In the case of The Netherlands, the choice is often dictated by chance. Some of the Russians living there admitted to knowing little about this small country prior to moving there ('Which language do they speak there?' 'Is 'Dutch' the same as 'Duits'?). Excluding cases of legal migrants, such as those with Dutch family members or contract workers, many Russians came to The Netherlands from other countries, such as Germany or France (some having been rejected for political asylum, others through doing business between European countries). Others came because they had friends there or had 'heard nice stories' about The Netherlands. The reputation of The Netherlands as a 'cosy friendly country with a good welfare system' (as Sasha, an IT consultant working between The Netherlands and Britain, put it), along with the recognition it has earned (partially) for being tolerant and accepting of foreigners, have attracted Russian migrants. Margarita, a poet from Amsterdam, evoked the 'sweet smell of tulips and world-famous heads of cheese' as a dream she has fostered since her childhood. She sees The Netherlands as a safe haven – a land of comfort. The more prosaic Vika, a rejected asylum seeker and a recipient of welfare benefits from Amsterdam, said bluntly: 'They're generous. You don't have to work, you'll be provided with everything'.

Admissions policies also play a role in attracting Russians to The Netherlands. As one homosexual owner of the former Russian cafe *Oblomov* testified: 'No other country would accept me as an asylum seeker on the basis of my sexual preferences'. The Netherlands used to welcome some of those rejected by the German system of asylum (although presently the admissions policies are becoming significantly stricter, while welfare provisions are becoming increasingly limited). Finally migration has been facilitated by ease of entry. Illegals, tourists – almost anybody from the CIS found it easy to physically enter The Netherlands by bus, train or plane.

Why Amsterdam? 'Big city', 'more opportunities', 'work and connections', 'more fun' – most answers sounded enthusiastic. Most Russians who started off living outside of Amsterdam (having been stationed at asylum seeker's camps or living with their Dutch spouses) admitted to seeing their move to the city as a positive step.

On the other hand, Britain, being 'large and famous' (as Mitya, a biologist working in London put it), seemed the more obvious choice. Many of my London informants testified to 'knowing a lot about Britain'. They also spoke English before coming there (which was not usually the case with Dutch in The Netherlands). Although, like in The Netherlands and everywhere else in Europe, admission policies and welfare provisions are currently subject to change (and in most cases not to the migrant's advantage), Britain used to be known by the Russians as an 'easy country' to enter and adjust to. Zhenya, a computer specialist from London, believes that Britain 'is open to all professionals' and is 'an easy country to settle in, as far as culture and people go'. His wife, Inna, elaborated: 'English culture is fascinating. People can be open if you're friendly with them'. Michael, a retired sociologist receiving a pension in London, reflects that the British 'have an interest in Russia, and have respect for those who are willing to share their knowledge and skills'.

I knew a couple of Russian businessmen and 'new rich' who sent their children to study in Britain. Some of these wealthy Russians even applied for English aristocratic titles. Although not as geographically accessible from the main continent as The Netherlands, Britain did not pose particular problems for Russian 'tourists' to enter, nor for Russian illegals or rejected asylum seekers to 'disappear'.

Why London? This city was chosen for similar reasons to Amsterdam – size, opportunities and interests. However, I have met some Russians who preferred to 'move into the suburbs' or 'live in a smaller city'. They resented the 'noise, dirt, criminality, and high prices' (Mitya). This leads us to the question of what living in London or Amsterdam actually means for the Russians. How do they see and relate to their chosen cities?

Sveta frequents night clubs and cafes, and the theatre:

> I like the buzz of this city. I like famous tourist things and I like things in between, like little bridges and narrow streets where the shop owners know their customers … I like joking on Albert Cuyp [market] … Pigeons on the Dam Square … Still, you know, it's not my city. I don't know where my city is, I must have imagined it back in Ekaterinburg, but it's definitely not here … (Sveta)

Sveta and her husband used to live in the Oud West part of Amsterdam, in one of the early twentieth century brick apartment houses. Sveta described her street as 'folksy but quiet, civilized but trashy as far as garbage days go'. She liked the fact that her street was close to the centre, easily accessible by public transport, and generally a place 'where normal Dutch live'. Some of Sveta's Russian friends lived scattered in the same neighbourhood. Having moved out of her husband's apartment, Sveta lived for a year in different suburbs of Amsterdam, where housing was easier to find. She missed the 'buzz' though, and having started her training and work at the hospital on the outskirts of Amsterdam, Sveta stayed more and more with her lover in the new northern neighbourhood of Amsterdam, Java Island. It is modern, spacious, and relatively cheap – all appealing qualities for the young couple. Now that Sveta is pregnant, she would rather move into the suburbs like many Dutch couples with young children do. Still, she reflects, having grown up in a large city herself, 'children can be happy growing up in Amsterdam as well'.

Olga has a more ambiguous attitude towards London. Having lived in the east, north and centre of the city, she referred to the city as a maze, as a place to get lost. In contrast, her native Moscow, whose population and infrastructure are similar to London, was familiar, friendly, exciting and open. Olga often recalled her evening adventures in Moscow, going from party to party, effortlessly hopping on buses, being given rides by friendly and trustworthy drivers, having *ponchiki* (Russian donuts) at three in the morning, singing and dancing in the parks. I remember her telling me these stories in a loud voice while we were crossing Regent's Park at night. When I asked her why she was talking so loudly, she replied that she 'needed courage in this dark park'. Often Olga told me that she does not understand London. She feels foreign there. On another occasion she complained about London's poor infrastructure, frequent train delays, and traffic jams that are 'worse than in Moscow'. Yet, in conversations with the English, she usually took a more impartial view:

> I don't know whether I like London or not. I like certain parts of it. It depends where you live. This city's too big to just like all of it. (Olga)

London has many faces for the Russians. I contacted Michael, a 69-year-old writer, through the Jewish Care, an organization that helped hundreds of Russian Jews to leave Russia for Britain. Michael, a former anti-Communist activist and a Zionist sympathizer, knew English before he came to London. Knowledge of English, combined with the help of the Jewish Care, enabled Michael and his wife to leave Moscow. They arrived in London in 1992 as refugees because of ethnic and political persecution, and presently live on pensions. Michael already had contact with Britain through his sister who had moved there 20 years earlier. Michael visited his family in 1978, on the basis of the Helsinki agreement, leaving his wife and daughter behind 'as hostages'.

Michael knows a lot about London's history. He quotes from Charles Dickens and Virginia Woolf while walking the streets of the city. His familiarity with the city comes from his literary knowledge and when he encounters something new – like a block of modern flats – he feels it is not only imposing upon the city's original design but 'contradicting the very soul of the city'. Ironically, Michael and Alina live in the extreme north of the city, in zone 4; his block of flats can be reached by a bus which leaves from High Barnet Underground Station every half an hour. The bleak suburbia reminds Michael of his own native city; and since many of the region's residents are (non-Russian) migrants, the 'reference to London is easily lost'. However, Michael and Alina's immediate neighbours are English ('quite an amiable elderly couple with little ambition'). Michael feels sympathetic towards the British:

> I have only kind things to say about this country. The British have this pleasantness about them, a kind of tolerance, one sees smiles on the streets. Alina [my wife] misses snow though. I miss the forests. I don't miss people in the forests as they were rather suspicious and hostile to strangers. (Michael)

Michael wants to organize a course for British people learning Russian in which he would show them the latest Russian movies. In the process, he wants to explain both the idiomatic expressions used in the film and the cultural situations in which the characters' behaviour needs to be explained. He plans to have conversations and tea after each show. Michael feels that just as 'carrying London in my imagination while in Russia' has enriched him, so can the Londoners be enriched by imagining Russian cities.

Imagining London can land one, though, in a city very different from Dickens' and Woolf's tours. Lena represents a more posh, yuppie side of Russian London. I knew Lena from the art school we both attended in Moscow but found her in London almost by accident, having heard of her whereabouts from her mother during my visit to Moscow. Living in a trendy area of Notting Hill, Lena enters her building through a white staircase located between four thin columns.

Lena, an architect who used to work as an interior designer for the summer houses of the New Russians in Moscow, had become a Masters of Arts student at London University in 1996. This allowed her to stay in London on a student visa while living off her Moscow savings. She also received help from her Russian-businessmen parents. Lena applied to a couple of art schools across Western Europe but London's offer seemed the most attractive. Lena, perfectly made up with an impeccably fashionable hair style, is often mistaken for a French or German artist. Lena likes 'living like British aristocracy'. She appreciates the style and taste of London culture which was missing in Moscow. There, apartments were 'stuffed with mass-produced low-quality furniture'. Lena's sense of style is reflected in the interior of her London flat which she shares with a female German banker: perfectly scrubbed wooden floors, minimalist furniture, grotesque but fitting candle holders and an array of modern gadgets ranging from a disco-size stereo system to an air humidifier with aromatic oils.

Lena hosts lavish parties for mostly young successful professionals, very few of whom are Russian (except for her own cousins who work in banks). Cocaine is freely used. Lena frequents the trendiest night clubs, and in her spare time – which is scarce – travels to exotic destinations or goes skiing in the Alps with her Swiss boyfriend.

Lena adores London. London is where life is, where new ideas are understood and innovations (architectural and other) accepted. In London, people know how to enjoy themselves, and one can fully realize one's potential. Lena's knowledge of London's geography is largely limited to places of work and leisure, scattered across the centre and reached by taxi only. Lena's London consists of trendy modern places, plus the airport which she describes as 'the most important place in London, the place you can leave and come back to, dragon's mouth, passageway into freedom'.

The airport is also evoked as an integral part of London by Angela, an ethnic Lithuanian in her late teens, who arrived in London in 1998 with her husband and baby daughter. For Angela, the airport has little to do with freedom. Gatwick is a 'gate that closes behind you'. Once you are admitted to the country as an asylum seeker, the gate to one's mother country shuts and seals London, so one 'feels like a spider in a jar'. The feeling of entrapment follows Angela everywhere in London, and although she comments that the city is 'large enough to encompass her whole country', Angela feels that London's borders are closed. Angela, who 'emigrated to escape', feels claustrophobic and disoriented. Yet, closed spaces have an advantage of becoming familiar. In the months that I knew Angela, she began adapting to London by relating to it practically, like a prisoner who starts decorating his cell and suddenly feels inspired.

I met Angela in the Russian-language Anglican church in Earl's Court. What attracted Angela most about the church was the fact that she could get rent-free Russian videos and audio tapes. Rummaging through 'things one can get for free', or 'get a deal on', Angela admitted to becoming enticed by London. London appears to Angela as a collection of places where things can be obtained (from shopping malls to churches) as well as a place made live by gossip and anecdotes. London is 'bigger than Vilnyus but just as provincial, people know about each other like in a village'. Angela is under the impression that she knows London and its people pretty well, so she does not feel foreign there. At 19, she is interested in discos and clubs which play the 'same music as at home', and although her English is very poor she feels affinity with young people looking for a taxi to take them home after a night out. Angela loves Soho 'because it's international and fun'. She muses about getting her belly button pierced, starring in one of the 'naked movies', and 'getting herself a funky haircut'. She also likes Chinatown because 'they've got cheap food and big portions, plus I adore onions!'. The only bad thing about London is its climate. Angela dreams of living on a sunny island without rain or the sound of traffic.

Angela's idea of 'fitting into London' is by doing things, by knowing people, by constantly moving and discovering new opportunities. The rhythm of the city is reflected in Angela's turbulent personal life. From the start of her stay in London, Angela worked in different jobs, including waitressing, making clothes, house cleaning and baby-sitting, as well as being a 'housewife' for her Lithuanian husband and daughter. Angela managed to fit in British lovers and friends, which 'helped her get familiar with the strange city'. In 1999 her husband left her and she was asked to leave her apartment. Angela found an older British 'sponsor' and a couple of 'lesser comforters', who now fully support her and her daughter. Angela is openly considering 'entering the business', meaning escort services, but feels that at the moment her 'sponsors' give her enough security and she can devote more of herself to her daughter. She still lives in the south of London in Brixton in a rather dilapidated flat but hopes to move in with her elderly sponsor in Chelsea soon. During our last conversation, Angela admitted to 'becoming really accustomed to London' and realizing that despite the closed borders, life in London offers opportunities which she dreamt of before leaving her native country.

'Expanding the borders' is a common practice for Russians living in London. I met Zhenya, 29, his wife Inna, 30, from Yaroslavl, and Zhenya's cousin Mitya, 28, from St Petersburg, through my Canadian friend, a student of Russian and fan of Russian culture. Zhenya and Inna lived with their two-year-old daughter in the High Barnet area of north London in a rented family house. They arrived in London in 1996 because of Zhenya's work as a programmer. Inna, formerly an engineer, became a housewife. Although Zhenya speaks good English, his wife knows very little. In an effort to learn the language, she watched children's programmes, like *Teletubbies*, with her daughter, and talked to English neighbours. Calm and relaxed, Inna admits to being a 'slow and steady learner'. Observing her 'discovery of Britain', starting from the living-room couch and slowly progressing to encompass the whole country during and after my fieldwork, was truly remarkable.

The family rarely visited central London. It was difficult to drive into as well as 'child unfriendly'. They greatly preferred to spend time in the countryside. They travelled to architectural landmarks and monuments not far from London, such as Leeds. Zhenya and Inna's attitude towards Britain was rather positive, thinking of it as a sensible and economically stable country. Inna took up reading English history and sharing her knowledge with her husband at the dinner table in exchange for his stories of office events, undeterred by the persistent international babble of her daughter. Inna also read books on English art and architecture, which were evoked during the family's weekend trips. After three years of life in High Barnet, Inna convinced Zhenya of the beauty of fox hunting, and became a perfectly informed and loyal fan of the royal family.

In 2000 the family moved to New York where Zhenya continued working for the same company. In the latest e-mail, Zhenya wrote that they like the United States and will probably remain there.

Not all Russian migrants are as easily adaptable. Some bring their world with them and remain in it throughout the years of their stay in London. Mitya, who, like Zhenya, is a skilled professional, was invited to work in Britain. He now works as a biologist in the Cancer Research Laboratory near Mill Hill East – one of the northern outskirts of London. Mitya travelled first to Ireland, and then to Britain in 1993 as an exchange student. He got a job in London and stayed on. A highly eccentric character, Mitya stands on the margins of being the life and soul of all parties and a social outcast. He claims to be an ethnic Krivich (denied by his ethnic Russian cousin), one of the 'last true tribes in Russia'. Mitya can talk endlessly about Russian history and religion (particularly Orthodox). He sees Orthodoxy as a growing religion that will some day take over the world. Mitya quotes from Russian historians and theologians at any occasion when he is drunk, which is most of the time when he is not working. Allegedly, he wants to return to Russia to promote the return of monarchy. If that does not work, Mitya wants to devote himself to the 'dismemberment of the corrupt British monarchy, a task that can only be taken on by a Krivich'. Such pronouncements made me wonder about Mitya's scientific credentials, but apparently his colleagues in the Laboratory value him as 'one of the most promising young specialists' but 'very different from the British'.

Mitya rarely comes to London. He sees it as a 'concentration of noise, pollution, over-consumption and other kinds of utter nonsense'. Like Zhenya and Inna, he is rather enamoured of the English countryside, including the 'rolling hills and the ponds with geese' that surround his research centre. On the weekends, he takes a bus into the city and watches the 'countryside yield to industrial development'. Mitya gets off the bus and goes back 'when the sight becomes completely intolerable'. As in the case of Olga and Sveta, Mitya's idiosyncratic character can indeed be described as 'different from the British', but he remains an eccentric in Russian eyes as well. His opinions, readily given to practically all my queries, speak of individual rather than 'Russian' or 'Krivich' imagination. In the chapters on ethnicity and social networks, I shall further develop this thought, as informants like Mitya made me realize how important it was to look not only at the place migrants came from or settled into, but also at who they are and how they find their individual ways of adapting to their new environment. Despite individual eccentricities, informants like Mitya held strong opinions on subjects ranging from 'community' to 'culture'. While I realized that these statements could not be taken as 'representative of Russian opinions' they did represent original voices within collective Russian discourse. Mitya taught me, among other things, that 'being Russian' or 'being Krivich' can have different meanings for different informants, but the importance of ethnic identity for an individual – however it is expressed – cannot be underplayed (the theme discussed in the chapter on ethnicity).

As mentioned in the Introduction, I found little difference between my informants in London and Amsterdam. Since the migration policy of both countries allowed similar groups of people into each city (politically motivated asylum seekers, professionals, students, marriage partners, etc.), it was the individual differences between members of such groups that made Russian views so diverse between, as well as within, London and Amsterdam. Michael, Lena, Angela, Mitya, Inna and Zhenya have all contributed something personal to the city of London. They have created (by the act of imagination) and inhabited their own city. However, they did not necessarily become 'London Russians', either because they still felt like foreigners or because they physically moved. Like most 1990s migrants, my informants rarely saw the receiving country as a final destination (Inna and Zhenya making a home in the US, Lena moving to Zurich after marrying her Swiss boyfriend, Angela suddenly leaving her British sponsor and going back to Lithuania to visit her family for an indefinite period of time – all movements that happened after completion of my fieldwork).

My informants could attach themselves to a place and, to a degree, become part of it. They could also reattach themselves to a different place, either because of work or legal status incentives, nostalgia, or a sense of adventure. But unlike transnational theorists suggest, place and belonging still mattered to the Russians. Despite all their travels, most of them retained their identities and opinions rooted in their past experiences or their individual personalities. Such were the cases of a few informants whom I observed commuting between London and Amsterdam or between other countries.

Sasha is an IT consultant working for Anderson's. He is ethnically Kazakh, born in Moscow. He considers himself a 'rolling stone' but 'stone with the Russian soul'. He is in his early 30s, living in London since 1996. I met Sasha through the 'Russians in London' Internet news-group. Sasha moved to Amsterdam to work for the same company in 1999. He is presently considering transferring back to Moscow unless he gets invited to work in Japan: the latter being a place where he can 'earn real money' and then 'live where he wants'.

In London, Sasha rented a large studio flat in the rich northern suburb of Golders Green. He reflected that his character was somewhat fitting of his surroundings, describing his suburb as 'laid back, with houses ostentatious but withdrawn' – one could only see the top floor of the house behind tall garden plants or fences. Indeed, Sasha seemed to epitomize the stereotypical Golders Green resident, sinking in a comfortable armchair, philosophizing about the future of the world – friendly, homely, talkative, easy to get along with, but also stingy. While boasting about his earnings, he invariably brought Cola bottles to his friends' parties. Sasha liked to celebrate every holiday or occasion in Japanese restaurants and was surprised every time when so few people showed up to join his feast.

At dinner, Sasha liked to muse about the three important things in life: 'balancing work and personal life, travel and knowing other cultures, and fitting in with the people whose mentality is close to yours'. Sasha longs to 'have more free time' as he usually works until 9 p.m. six days a week. He wishes to have more time to travel, not just for work but 'to see the world and to get to know its peoples'. He feels he is an 'anthropologist at heart'. Another of Sasha's favourite after-work themes includes the spiritual poverty of the West, especially the US. Sasha sees the British as not quite European, since 'they are getting more and more commercial. At the moment they are between the Americans and the Europeans'. Europeans, on the other hand, 'do not work as much – but they've got culture'.

Since moving to Amsterdam, Sasha's habits have remained the same. He has even managed to obtain the armchair that makes his Dutch flat (consciously chosen to be located across the street from two Japanese restaurants) look like the one in Golders Green (and, as he admits, like his Moscow flat as well). Yet, Sasha sees the 'world of difference' between the continental (and quintessentially European) country of flowers and his former place of residence. In London, Sasha showed little interest in architecture, but he is very enthusiastic about the beauty of Amsterdam's buildings, the precision of Amsterdam's canals, the cosiness of Dutch cafes and restaurants, and the accessibility of Dutch culture. Sasha is particularly excited about the fact that one can get an annual museum/railway discount card and visit most fine arts museums free. Also, Dutch girls are much friendlier and more open than British girls. Sasha says he likes The Netherlands better than Britain because the 'Dutch are closer to the Russians'.

Recently, Sasha has been thinking about going back to Moscow. He sees himself as a free foreign worker who can go back any time he likes, granted that economic conditions in Russia improve a bit or the political situation becomes more stable. He misses the better social and personal life, air-conditioning in the Russian metro, and sincere friendship. In the meantime, he looks for a 'nice Russian or maybe European girl'.

   Sasha admits that although he likes to live in certain places more than in others, his value system and his personal habits remain the same. Some migrants, however, felt that the place where they lived had changed them, or answered an inner need for change that prompted their move from the mother-country.

   Another case of a London/Amsterdam crossover is that of Margarita, a 40-something poet from St Petersburg. After the publication of my article about the Russian 'community' in London in the *East-West Journal*, I received a phone call from Count Tolstoy, the offspring of the Russian aristocracy, and the organizer of society balls for those Russians who can afford them (both members of the old elite and recent wealthy arrivals). The Count told me (in broken Russian, having been born in the UK) that his primary interest is bringing the Russian communities in Western Europe together. Through the Russian Orthodox Church, the Count knew a number of Russians in Amsterdam (mostly members of the 'old waves') whom he visited regularly. One of his Amsterdam friends was Margarita, who arrived in The Netherlands in 1990 'on a visa of a creative artist'. She became established as a 'new Amsterdam poet' by giving recitals at the Dutch poetry society. Tolstoy advised me to contact her.

   Margarita was naturalized as a Dutch citizen within seven years of her arrival and is now enjoying what she calls 'being Dutch'. I met Margarita in a cafe in the folksy district of Jordan, close to her apartment. Jordan is known for being the trendiest non-tourist part of Amsterdam. Margarita talks only superficially about her poetry, striking me as a very down-to-earth business woman, self-assured, and thoroughly enjoying life. She has no family, and she spoke of Amsterdam as a place where singles can enjoy social and cultural life to their full potential. A couple of times our conversation was interrupted by people waving at Margarita. Others came over to our table to inquire about the latest art exhibit she went to, or to recommend a new theatre production, or to invite her to the 'music evening'.

   Margarita likes to travel in other European countries, but every time experiences relief at coming home. Amsterdam is a true home as it is 'always welcoming. My work's waiting for me; my friends are waiting. When I come back my own street greets me like a rolled out carpet'. I asked whether artistic life in St Petersburg, her home city, was different from here. Like with most other questions about her Russian past, Margarita dismissed it with 'Ah, very different'. Does she miss Russia? Not really, although nostalgia does occasionally come through in her poetry. Margarita said that she 'didn't need Russia abroad' except for a few old friends and the [Orthodox] church. She never sought Russian friends in Amsterdam, nor visited the Russian cafe or

Russian parties of which she was vaguely aware. Apparently, Russia was something that had to do with her past, and which gave inspiration. It also served as a point of reference against which the present could be viewed and valued. 'A person,' Margarita told me, 'does not live between past and present. One remembers the past but lives in the present, and this is where I live now and I love it here.' Thus, I have learned that even poets, whose sensitive souls are supposed to be prone to nostalgia, can absorb every sight and sound of a new place, grow familiar and fond of something which is so different from home and draw inspiration for their art and personal life as they become part of this place.

Amsterdam, like poetry, can be experienced differently by less 'assimilated' migrants. While Margarita's case testifies to the possibility of the happy fusion between the self and the new location, other informants either felt rejected by Amsterdam or rejected it themselves. Like Margarita, Slava writes his own poetry and likes reading that of others. His poetry, though, is used to counterbalance anything foreign he encounters in The Netherlands. Slava, a car salesman, loves to recite Gumilev and Akhmatova, early twentieth-century Russian poets, when talking of Russia. 'In Gumilev's poetry there's a lot of genuine pain and through it comes joy', reflects Slava. Interrupted by a business call from his Russian partner in Germany, his face exhibited more mercantile and pain-free joy: 'New party of Fords!'

Knowing about my research, Slava sent me two poems by Josef Brodsky. According to Slava, these testify to the dreariness of both of my research sites:

> London town's fine, especially in the rain,
> Which is not to be stopped by cloth caps or crowns …
> On a grey day, when even a shadow has no strength
> to catch up with your back, and the money is getting tight,
> in a city where, dark as brick may get,
> The milk will always stand sedately white …
>   (from 'The Thames at Chelsea' by Brodsky, 1980: 90)[2]

> … In this country laid flat for the sake of rivers,
> beer smells of Germany and seagulls are
> in the air like a page's soiled corners.
> Morning enters the premises with a coroner's
> punctuality, puts its ear
> to the ribs of a cold radiator, detects sub-zero:
> the afterlife has to start somewhere …
>   (from 'The Dutch Mistress' by Brodsky, 1992: 30)[3]

Like Sasha in London, Slava likes to muse about cold and distant capitalist countries in opposition to genuine and warm Russia. I shall quote both Sasha and Slava on these points in the chapters on ethnicity and social networks, as their views are reflective of many (although far from all) Russian migrants.

As noted in the chapter on Migration, dependent upon migrant's legal status, age and duration of stay in the receiving country, some of the 'new' migrants still experience their absence from Russia as an 'exile'. Slava, like Sveta, Olga, Angela and Sasha, although socially or professionally 'integrated', cannot experience London or Amsterdam without a twinge of nostalgia. I learned about the pull of a place and the importance of belonging from Slava, while he was jiggling innumerable car keys in his pocket and attentively watching the 'low battery' warning signal on his mobile phone.

I was introduced to Slava through Sveta who studied Dutch in the same class as Slava's girlfriend. Slava, an ethnic Russian aged 30, looked like a proverbial Russian bear, with an unruly straw coloured mane, large, awkward and heavy-footed and equipped with a somewhat unbecoming pair of thick glass spectacles. Slava's half-civilized centaur's appearance reflected his educational history: he used to study history at the University of St Petersburg but soon turned to business. From that moment on, as Slava's girlfriend recalled, he became 'disinterested in the West European history but fascinated by its wealth'. Living in Amsterdam intermittently since 1992, Slava was indeed famous for his devotion to what he termed the 'capitalist cause' which he earnestly served by driving second-hand cars from Germany for sale in Russia. Slava learned Dutch within three years and allegedly had 'contacts' with the border police.

Slava saw The Netherlands as a land of opportunity, as good as any other West European country. Unlike Germany, however, where most of his business originated, The Netherlands was 'safe, comfortable, and friendly'. Slava did not like competition from Russians in Germany or in Belgium. He insisted on his business being clean, while most of his competitors were said to be involved in 'dirty affairs' (selling stolen cars). Slava often contrasted the infamous Antwerp Russian Mafia with legitimate dealings in Amsterdam. He saw The Netherlands as generally 'clean' and admired its liberal laws towards drugs and prostitution. Slava frequented expensive restaurants in Amsterdam, preferring Dutch to foreign food. As soon as he could afford it, Slava moved to the suburbs into a large modern house to 'feel comfortable and yet be close to the place where it's all happening'.

Still, Slava was nostalgic and referred to St Petersburg as 'his city' where his real friends are. Most of Slava's Amsterdam friends were Russians involved in the same business. After his girlfriend left him to go to Canada with an older Russian-Canadian businessman, Slava became increasingly bitter, saying that local Russian women are 'learning to be prostitutes from the Dutch'. In the past year Slava drank heavily and supposedly lost a lot of his assets, having to sell his house in the suburbs. In 1999 he was said to have returned to Russia, although later I heard rumours that he continued his car business in Germany.

A more optimistic case is that of another 30-something St Petersburger, Dima, who could be seen almost every summer evening between 1995 and 1999, selling his paintings in the touristy Rembrandtplein. Dressed like a nineteenth-century French artist, Dima attracts passerbys' attention by casting a welcoming smile, inviting them to 'just take a look' at his pictures with an exaggerated gesture of servility. According to his neighbours, also Russian artists, Dima sells 25 pictures per day (25 guilders each) – more than anybody at the square. 'This shows real Amsterdam', explains Dima to a customer in his good English. 'Not just some monuments, but how Amsterdam lives, feels, moves.'

Most of Dima's paintings are of Amsterdam and The Netherlands, without the windmills and tulip fields. Dima explains:

> I paint what I see. I move back to Russia and I paint Russia. Here I have no nostalgia, but I try to create nostalgic images of the country that is not my own – and it sells. I come here for money. I enjoy Amsterdam, but I have to make 25 pictures per day, so I work like a robot. (Dima)

Dima gives out a page with his abridged biography to his customers. There he gives a deeper description of his watercolour creations:

> Most of his work is dominated by realistic landscapes but some of his paintings can be described as fantastic or mysterious dreams and evasions were we to hear the lament of a Russian soul. His work combines the enigmatic world of Slavic sentimentality with the achievements of the West-European culture. (Dima)

Dima began travelling and painting abroad in the late 1980s. He came to Amsterdam for the first time in 1990. Dima had an exhibition of his work in Amsterdam in 1993 and 1995. 'I come here to work, then I go back to my family in St Petersburg', Dima says, simultaneously keeping a sharp eye and a ready smile for potential buyers. 'Although sometimes I stay in The Netherlands for the greater part of the year, I never think of it as my home.'

However, Dima is not planning to return to his real home and permanent residence with his family for good. In Amsterdam he has his apartment, his friends and his favourite bars. Although, according to the artist, people in Dutch bars do not know how to have a good time and really 'pour their soul out to their neighbours', Dima finds the Dutch friendly and open, not to mention generous. He claims that at least 40 per cent of his clients are Dutch. Considering that the pictures are tourist-oriented, as all artists on the square claim, 40 is a significant percentage. In Russia, Dima says, he had almost no domestic clients, except for petty racketeers that tried to get him to pay an extra rouble for 'protection'. New Russians, Dima remarks, are not interested in art. Old Russians are more interested in potatoes. 'As long as Russia is what it is, Russians have no money to buy my pictures, and Russia is as it is as long as it is – here's my philosophy', Dima reflects half-jokingly.

Dima feels that Amsterdam is a truly artistic city and that it fits him like a glove. Unlike Margarita, Dima sees Russia and The Netherlands as compatible places with different flavours. Unlike Slava, he sees his experience of living abroad as continuous. According to Dima, Amsterdam and St Petersburg share a common appreciation for visual arts and beauty in general. Not just the same canals and hunchbacked bridges, Dima says, but also a 'feel of the wet city, the city of water and old houses'. Reflecting on Slava's description of 'sad joy', Dima concludes his comparison: 'Only in Amsterdam everybody is celebrating this beauty, while in St Petersburg people just sigh of good old times. I am happier here too, and people see it and they buy from me'. Like Margarita, Dima's 'artistic soul' does not suffer nostalgia but uses this new place to create art. Unlike Margarita, Dima – because of his family back home and the lack of legal status abroad – will never turn Amsterdam from a place of seasonal work into a new home.

Other migrants can also relate to the new place by endowing it with familiar features, by mixing the past with the present. Although I have noticed that mostly older migrants tend to view new places through the prism of familiarity, there are also young people I met who carried their short past in the CIS into the new country. They continued to live this way for many years, as if migration never took place. One of my best friends in Amsterdam, Nastya has lived with her Turkish husband and two children in Amsterdam since 1998. I met her through Sveta. Nastya is 24, and presently studying business computer science at the Free University in Amsterdam. She sums up her migration and personal history this way:

> I met Hussein, my husband, in 1995 when I was vacationing with my family in Turkey. We fell in love and I started visiting him in The Netherlands. I got used to his son from the first wife; he began calling me mummy. Hussein owns

a Turkish restaurant. I help him, working there as a waitress. I found some good friends, like Sveta, and we went out together, to the discos and other places. Still, I found it difficult in The Netherlands. Even though I was starting to learn the language, I kept coming back home where I've graduated from the textile institute. I missed my family and we had some problems with Hussein, so I left. In a few months Hussein came for a visit and the old flame lit up again. I got pregnant and after many doubts decided to go back to The Netherlands and get married to Hussein. We never actually got married because of some bureaucratic nonsense with my documents, but we had an official ceremony and now live together with two kids. (Nastya)

Aside from taking care of her two children and following a full-time course of study, Nastya helps her husband in his restaurant on the weekends. Their children are babysat by the Turkish relatives. Although she has little time to go out or even rest, Nastya is lively and enthusiastic.

Of all the Russians I have met in Amsterdam, Nastya seems the 'most (Belo)Russian' – most of her stories are rooted in Belorussia, and her perceptions are shaped by the values and ideas she learned at home. Nastya gives her friends advice based on her Belorussian dormitory experience or her grandmother's village wisdom. Whenever her Dutch or Russian friends have a headache or other ailment, Nastya comes up with a herbal or house recipe, sometimes accompanied by a spell. Even when describing typical Amsterdam situations, like a joking exchange on the market, Nastya speaks of the interacting parties as if they were Grodno's town folk, *devki i parni* (gals and guys). Nastya's Amsterdam seems to acquire a melodic Belorussian lull as it gets transformed into the world she is familiar with. Although there are no birches in Amsterdam, Nastya refers to light bark trees as birches; canals become rivers and springs, parks turn into meadows. She loves wooden shutters (which she calls *stavni*, Russian window shutters) on the windows of the old Dutch houses, wide entrances to staircases (*kryl'tso*), flowerpots installed outside window panes, and other architectural elements that remind her of Belorussian buildings. Nastya seems comfortable in this virtual town, sincerely referring to it as 'home'. Frequent visits to Belorussia, as well as her family's monthly stays in Amsterdam, allow Nastya to keep the link with her real home alive, but even her mother and sister are beginning to view Amsterdam as an extension of their own town.

Irina, a 26-year-old economics student at Amsterdam Economic Institute (HES) makes a clear separation between 'home' and 'here'. Irina, originally from Minsk, has a dual Russian and German citizenship.

We went to Germany first. I was 10 then, but my father and my big love stayed in Minsk. I kept visiting home, for many years I didn't even feel like I'd left. My mother married a Dutchman and started her own business, opened an art gallery in Dordrecht. I went to school here. Learning Dutch wasn't a problem. I study economics at HES and work four times a week in a night shop. (Irina)

Unlike Nastya, Irina's Amsterdam was nothing like home. In comparison to Minsk it was cold and insincere. Irina plans to remain in The Netherlands and knows Amsterdam very well, orienting herself without a map in any part of the city. She speaks perfect Dutch. Still, she feels little warmth for Amsterdam. I met Irina in a Russian cafe *Oblomov* which she visited practically every week. Preceding the meeting, Irina's reputation as a gossiper and a noisy drunk preceded her. Her gossip concerned her numerous Russian friends who, despite Irina's youth, included middle-aged and pensioner migrants. Unlike Sveta who also attracted various Russians, Irina consciously tried to create her own 'circle' – the bigger the better. She desired to live in this circle and to monitor and supervise the activities of its members. She attended every Russian party she had been invited to (or invited herself). She organized Russian gatherings in her own student flat, discussing guests' past history and present conduct right after they left. Irina's knowledge of individual Russians' lives, their secrets and even future plans was simply astonishing. Dressed conservatively in business suits and having a plain but friendly face, Irina's most popular nickname was 'KGB Irina'.

If there was any sense of 'community' in Amsterdam, Irina embodied it. In Amsterdam, where aside from the Russian cafe and the Orthodox church there were no specialized Russian institutions, informally organized gatherings were the only occasions at which Russians could be found en masse. Remarkably, Irina's Amsterdam consisted of invisible lines that connected people, mostly Russians, through their social relationships. Irina traced each line with the precision of a geologist mapping mineral sources. From Rokin to Sumatraplein, from Gerard Doustraat to Utrechtsestraat, Irina knew who lived where, who was connected to whom, how frequently, and why.

Irina lived with various Russian men for periods ranging between a week and a couple of months. Financially independent and always retaining her own student flat as a back-up, Irina would move into her new boyfriend's apartment and typically attempt to teach him about 'true family values'. In some curious way, Irina seemed a bit of a Dutch feminist: independent, outspoken, unwilling to think of settling down and having children, and oriented towards advancement of her own career. Yet, Irina was often seen as 'an example of Russianness' by her compatriot partners, dozens of whom passed through her 'school' during and after my fieldwork. They cited her style of domestication, including obligatory home cooking, evenings with friends with vodka and guitar, the acquisition of new furniture, and invariable passionate fights which sometimes involved physical violence.

Irina has managed to turn her 'exile' and her nostalgia into a practical tool of adaptation: not only does she long for Russia, she has, quite literally, created a miniature model of her mother-country in the middle of Amsterdam. Irina has not only adapted to the place – she has adapted the place to herself. Irina remains one of the central actors in the social life of Russian Amsterdam and one of my most important, although not always benevolent, informants.

Dina, by contrast, carries the nickname of 'Saint'. I met Dina, a 34-year-old Georgian, through Sveta. Dina and her husband lost their jobs (both were engineers) in Tbilisi in 1991 and spent five years in Moscow in painfully unsuccessful attempts to find employment (partially because of the Russians' discrimination against non-Muscovites in general and Georgians in particular). They were dreaming of having enough financial security to start their own family as well as to help their impoverished parents, and were almost driven to despair. Having considered their options, Dina decided to come to Amsterdam to earn money for a year, staying with her aunt (a Dutch citizen of 20 years). She was told by her Dutch lawyer that she could stay for a number of extra months. Having completed a course of Dutch and entered a special training programme, Dina was hoping to find a job that could provide her with a much needed income. She planned to go back as soon as her official visitor's visa expired. However, it turned out that the lawyer had made a mistake, and Dina found herself illegal after a couple of months.

> I have a new lawyer who says that if I want to have any chance of staying legally here, I should go back and ask for permission to return from my country. Everybody tells me I don't have much of a chance to get back once I leave. My lawyer says I won't even be in the computer, that it's safe for me to go back; that there are no laws here on the basis of which they can decide to refuse admission, except for in cases of criminals. I just don't know. It would have been all right if I had something to come back to, but at the moment all I have got is two camps of friends – some have taken my husband's side, some have taken mine; my family is really hostile to my husband; I have no job, no money to bring with me. All I anticipate to find back home are constant reminders of my husband's betrayal and my own failure. I feel like I've lost two years here, not having accomplished much, having only managed to ruin everything I've left behind. (Dina)

She could not continue her training programme, and could only earn money doing 'black jobs' (cleaning, baby-sitting). Meanwhile Dina's father, the only provider for her family in Georgia, had died, leaving her income as the only financial support for her mother and extended family. If Dina returned to Georgia, she was told by her new lawyer, she would never be able to re-enter The Netherlands again.

Although suffering from migraines and often depressed about her situation, Dina manages to spend some time enjoying the cultural life in Amsterdam. If she can afford it, she attends classical concerts, theatre performances and galleries. An insomniac, she admits to walking the Amsterdam streets at night, after work, 'watching the stars dreaming on the surfaces of canals' or observing silhouettes of the Dutch houses and their residents through the windows. Dina calls Amsterdam a 'fairytale' city, full of mysterious lights and church bells, enchanted, misty and mysterious. Dina is interested in the history of Amsterdam – its history of trade and expansion, the taming of the waters, the domestication of nature, practical friendship with neighbours, and acceptance of strangers. She views her own plight, and her lawyer's terrible mistake, as one of the unfortunate manifestations of her fate. Her own presence in the enchanted city is completely accidental; and although Dina views herself as 'poor, childless, loveless' she feels that Amsterdam offers her compassion, the way that books in old Georgia used to offer intellectuals escape from grim reality. Still, Dina's heart is still in Tbilisi.

> I think The Netherlands is a good country. I feel calmer here. I'd never feel at home here; I guess I'm just too old to grow new roots. My history, my soul – all's left in Tbilisi. My family had a turbulent history: Stalin's purges have eliminated the aristocratic side of my family, have taken familial wealth away. Still, I felt that I was enriched living there, with good friends, and books, and things which are just part of me, having been born there. (Dina)

Sveta introduced me to a very different person in the same month as she introduced me to Dina. Vika, 25, arrived in Amsterdam in 1996 from Yaroslavl. Since then, she has mostly lived with Yugoslavian men. She has never worked or learned Dutch. Before the *Koppelingswet* came into existence in 1998, Vika was able to collect unemployment and other social benefits. After the law was passed, she lived off one of her Serbian boyfriend's money.

Vika's current boyfriend is involved in the infamous Yugoslavian 'burglary ring' and spends most of his time in jail, while Vika tries to sell stolen merchandise (computers, mobile phones and other electronic equipment) to her numerous Dutch and Russian acquaintances. At one time, Vika was trying to recruit Russian girls to work for Yugoslavian burglars. Yugoslavians find 'suitable' rich households in need of cleaners (advertised through newspapers) and send Russian girls to 'clean' and effectively take inventory of the valuables. After a few days of work, the 'cleaners' disappear and the burglars come.

Vika spends most of her money on cannabis and tries to 'repair' her flat in the run-down neighbourhood of Jordan. Vika's flat lacks basic plumbing, heating, electricity (for which Vika never pays, staying mostly at her boyfriend's flat) and wallpaper. Yet, Vika sees her apartment as a 'symbol of Amsterdam – kind of trashy but potentially beautiful'. Amsterdam, Vika reflects, also needs a lot of work but is still 'much neater than Yaroslavl'. Generalizing that everything in life needs work, including her own living standards, Vika admits to 'being lazy and spoilt'. Yet, she also sees herself as an 'independent no bullshit spirit' like most Amsterdamers. Vika speaks of the Dutch as having a lot of money and knowing how to take care of it. Sometimes Vika speaks of her own involvement in the criminal world as a revolutionary act of social justice, taking a bit of money from those who can make more and giving it to those who cannot earn any.

Vika dreams of becoming rich some day – either by means of 'getting involved in serious business' (burglary) or 'becoming an artist' for which she feels she has a talent. She wants to be able to send money to her mother and alcoholic stepfather. She also wants her teenage sister to leave Yaroslavl and come to live with her in Amsterdam.

Vika can rarely afford good food. Since she does not cook at home, she sometimes goes without eating till her boyfriend finds out and buys her pizza. Also, Vika's friends and admirers include coffee shop and fast food cafe sellers who often allow her a free treat. Vika looks younger than her age, very fragile and pale with large brown eyes. Despite her fragility, she has a reputation for violent outbursts and uncontrolled behaviour. She used to frequent bikers' cafes in Amsterdam but was asked not to return to either branch after repeated fights in which she allegedly kicked, scratched, bit and almost stabbed the cafe's rather muscular customers. Vika is also not welcome in the Russian cafe *Oblomov (*and later *Kalinka)* because of her unruly conduct. Although Vika's first Yugoslavian boyfriend in Amsterdam allegedly beat and abused her, Vika loves to speak of 'girl-power' and her own strength. Midway between Pippi Longstocking and a hopeless drug addict, Vika attracts and loses men easily. She misses Russia but says it is 'all manure' there and she will never go back.

Through Vika, I met Vadim. Vadim, 21, arrived in Amsterdam from Moscow in 1992 with his mother (married to a Dutchman). A school drop-out,

Vadim founded his own heavy metal band, consisting of two Russian illegal musicians and a Dutch singer. Vadim has an angelic feminine face framed by long wavy hair. He is tall, extremely thin and delicate. Aside from music, his other hobbies include the use of various hard drugs and the organization of (mostly Russian teenage) drug parties. Although speaking perfect Dutch, he feels 'distinctly Russian'. Vadim went back to Moscow a couple of times hoping to form his own band, but could not sustain himself without his mother's support and had to return.

Vadim likes the 'dark holes' of Amsterdam: bikers' cafes with Harley Davidson parts plastered to the wall and tough looking tattooed drunkards supporting their heavy chins with black gloved fists; coffee shops where ageing hippies spend countless hours staring into pastel painted walls and pondering the world's hidden purposes; bridges and parks – congregation sites for the homeless junkies at night; empty stations, or squatter houses on the outskirts of the city. Vadim and his group gave concerts in garages and basements with a mixed audience of stoned teenagers and equally blurry eyed rodents. A budding businessman, Vadim 'hired' some of his friends to paint the basement in which he was illegally rehearsing music. They turned the grim dump into a psychedelic castle of neon graffiti and hanging pieces of cloth which on closer inspection turned out to be small Soviet flags and portraits of Lenin.

Vadim aspired to make his music into an internationally acclaimed combination of Russian and Western heavy rock. Describing The Netherlands as the 'dead fish of music', Vadim felt that Amsterdam gave him little inspiration. Aside from the 'dark holes', there was little to fill what he called an 'emptiness of the heart'. The latest news from Vadim has been bad – he went to Moscow to 'visit his grandmother' for the summer and was caught in a night club selling ecstasy pills (after being warned and ignoring the threats of 'legitimate' sellers). He has been sent to jail. His mother is currently trying to rescue him but the task may require many thousands of dollars.

My informants showed me different sides of London and Amsterdam – sometimes enchanting, sometimes prosaic, sometimes grim, and sometimes full of hope. Michael's literary wanderings across London, or Vika's shoplifting tours of Amsterdam were concealed from outsiders' eyes. Yet each added their own mark to the invisible map of Russian London or Amsterdam. These and many others were the stories that inspired me throughout my research and revealed not only the ways in which Russians lived, but also the ways they differed in their perceptions of places and of themselves. My informants, who carried their pasts – memories, education, moral values, accumulated experience – into different cities, related to the present in ways that could not simply be described as 'Russian' or 'migrant'. Rather, their perceptions made me question my own assumptions based on generalized notions of migratory experience or of Russian experience abroad.

During my fieldwork, I asked myself a number of questions about my informants, such as: how do they survive practically and psychologically in the new environment? Why do they feel Russian (or not)? How do they see themselves and their compatriots in relation to the outside world? In the process of the interviews, however, I discovered that there was no 'Russian consensus' on either of the above-mentioned topics, and no 'real representative' Russian opinions. Migrant perceptions and opinions were as diverse as their personal histories. Although the migrants could still be grouped together on the basis of their legal status, age, city of origin or any other chosen feature, they were first of all individuals, each of whose stories had a different twist.

Through conversations with my informants, I started to understand which ideas were important to them. It appeared that despite their individual diversity, there were certain persistent themes that enabled me to write about 'Russians in London and Amsterdam'. My informants answered the questions I posed above, and their voices will be heard throughout the following chapters, addressing the topics of community, subcommunities, culture, ethnicity, social networks and informal economy. Informants' stories testified to who they were, where they came from, what they hoped to achieve, and how they viewed themselves in relation to their past and present surroundings.

While their place of origin mattered to all my informants, their attitudes towards both the native and the new places differed. Some informants, like Nastya, learned to combine the two worlds by extending the past into the present. She blended elements that made the mother country special with those of a strange land. Others, like Sergei, Inna and Margarita, embraced the 'new', learning about and enjoying new places and people, moving away from the past. Yet others, like Slava, Angela and Sasha, remained nostalgic for the past and critical of their surroundings. At the same time, they learned to live in a new place by adapting in practical ways such as 'earning money', learning the language and finding 'native friends'. All the while, they remained aware of being caught between two worlds but managing to effectively live in one while maintaining emotional links with the other.

It occurred to me that my informants had charted an invisible map of time and space, creating, as it were, an invisible community bound by ideas of 'self' and 'others'. This was a community that was not conscious of itself, but existed as long as individual Russians positioned themselves on this invisible map which stretched throughout the 1990s, spanning the CIS, London and

Amsterdam. This 'community', that will be discussed in the following chapter, is invisible both to the Russians and to the outsider. Although the actual group of people (Russian migrants) clearly exists, 'community' – socially constructed and individually maintained – remains ambiguous.

Notes

1 'From Russia with Love, Sir Anthony weds widow who rang his doorbell', *Daily Telegraph*, 13 June 1994.
2 J. Brodsky (1980), *A Part of Speech*, The Noonday Press, New York.
3 J. Brodsky (1992), *To Urania*, The Noonday Press, New York.

Appendix: Impressions of Russian life by Engelbert Fellinger, Amsterdam, 2004

www.engelbert.org

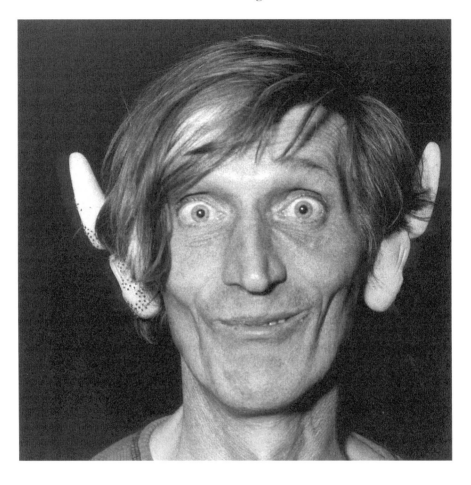

Chapter 3

Community

Introduction

The lack of statistical data on the Russians is striking in the light of the fact that the number of Russians could, by unofficial estimates, add up to hundreds of thousands in Britain and tens of thousands in The Netherlands. Amsterdam and London host the largest number of these migrants. But can we assert that there is a Russian 'community' in London and/or Amsterdam? Why is there so little known about it through Dutch and English academic journals or through the media?

This chapter aims to address some of the issues raised in chapters one and two, namely the existence of the group of migrants whose 'invisibility' is confirmed both by the members of the receiving society and by the Russians themselves. This chapter begins with theoretical questions concerning the concept of community and presents ethnographic data confirming that the concept of community is ill-suited for describing the Russians in London and Amsterdam.

In Rouse's (2002) discussion of transnational migrants (in his study, Mexican migrants in the United States), he challenges the established definition of 'community' as 'discriminable population with a single, bounded space – a territory or place'. Rouse argues that the image of territorially bounded community 'has become increasingly unable to contain the postmodern complexities that it confronts' (Rouse, 2002: 158). The concepts of 'international' or 'transnational communities' imply that not only territorial but also ethnic bounds of community have now disintegrated. Instead, new boundaries of subjective self-identifications are currently being drawn (Vertovec, 2002; Guibernau and Rex, 2003). As I shall further argue, however, global citizenship (Ong, 2002; Rex, 2003) and cosmopolitanism (Carruthers, 2002) do not always account for the strong feelings of almost filial affinity and fixed belonging that migrants themselves experience.

Russians were mostly sceptical about their 'community', making comments such as 'Maybe elsewhere, but not here' and 'They must be talking about Indians (Turks)'. Implicitly, Russians suggest that they understand what a 'real community' should be like while denying its existence at present and in the place they live. They suggest that 'communities' exist elsewhere or at other times. If many Russians felt that a 'Russian community' in their city existed, they did not feel part of it. Russians gave examples of what they thought communities were, such as the Jewish 'community' that congregates around synagogues and cultural issues; or the Russian communities in Germany or France.

While it is problematic to apply the term 'community' to all Russians in London and Amsterdam, both the Russians and the members of the host society do refer to Russian groups that are based on institutional affiliation or interest (church attendants, cafe habitués, newspaper readers, etc.) as 'communities'. Also, Russian migrants may still be referred to collectively as a 'community' in the very limited sense of describing a collection of people with certain common traits, such as their country of origin or present city of residence.

Further in this chapter, I examine the reasons why such a narrowly defined community is invisible. I suggest possible reasons for Russian invisibility, including the lack of established community and the lack of significant critical mass of Russians in London and Amsterdam. Another factor is that most of the 'migrants' are not officially registered as such and thus statistically non-existent. I also address less obvious and more case-specific explanations for invisibility having to do with the Soviet or post-Soviet experiences of the migrants, such as Soviet communitarianism and socialist hierarchization. It appears that most reasons for Russians' animosity towards each other can be understood through examining the historical, social and ethnic background of the migrants. Maybe, the population of Russians at present (and as opposed to the earlier waves who represented particular social classes) is so heterogeneous that we cannot speak of an original community in the first place? Does social fragmentation prevent Russians from forming a unified community or becoming visible as its members? These questions will be addressed later in this chapter, and further developed in the chapter on subcommunities. They also serve as a central theme throughout my book.

3.1   What is 'Community'?

'Community' can be perceived in several ways: as an abstraction, employed for practical purposes by the researcher; as a geographically or socially defined entity; as a symbolic means of expressing group identity; or as a feeling of affinity with a group that shares common characteristics. 'Community' could even be seen as a useless and potentially confusing concept altogether. Thus, the 'measure of migration is ... complicated in a given population by the inadequacy of conceptualization of "community" or society' (Jackson, 1969: 5).

'Community' is a difficult topic in anthropology as definitions and examples of 'communities' are plenty but a consensus on a common term is far from possible to reach. From Benedict Anderson's 'imagined communities' to Anthony Cohen's 'symbolic communities', social scientists suggest different ways of conceptualizing 'community' without the limitations of the old dogmas like 'geographic proximity' or 'common heritage' (Carrithers and Humphrey, 1991). Criticism of a 'community' as a closed, self-contained and static system (similar to the criticism of 'culture', 'ethnicity' and 'identity'), has been widely spread in the 1990s (Al-Rasheed, 1995; Boissevain, 1994; Baumann and Sunier, 1995; Glazer and Moynihan, 1996; Modood, 1997; Smith, 1996).

Yet, while academics were de-essentializing and de-reifying 'community', the concept seemed to prosper in the minds of people who thought they belonged to a 'community' and to those who defined them as such. It has been argued that instead of diffusing in the postmodern world of shifting identities and continuously renegotiated boundaries, the term 'community' (as well as 'culture' and 'ethnicity') remained and even solidified in popular as well as institutional discourse (Chapman, 1994; Baumann, 1995; Eriksen, 1993; Verkuyten et al., 1999). The use of the term 'community' ranges from practical (as in the case of a group collecting joint benefits), to ideological (as in the case of asserting the group's solidarity and ideological unity against other groups). Reflecting contemporary processes of nation-state formations and countering simplistic theories of globalization, 'communities' and 'cultures' are persisting instead of disintegrating. As I shall further discuss in the chapter on culture, the interplay of global and local politics and economics also reflects on academic discourse, complicating the previously used terminology (Akhbar and Shore, 1995; Gardner, 1995; Miller, 1995; Strathern, 1995). Often, after a period of postmodern criticism and deconstruction of the supposedly outdated anthropological terms, they are re-introduced into academic discourse (Childs, 1993; Ekholm-Friedman and Friedman, 1995). There is presently a movement to re-introduce 'community' into academic discourse after years of deconstructing it. I side with the view that despite the problems inherent in the term 'community', it is nonetheless a useful term when it is defined in context.

One may ask what the term 'community' is used in opposition or contrast to. One might look at 'community' as opposed to 'society'. In our case, there are at least two 'societies' of reference: the Russian society in Russia and in the receiving location. If we were to view a migrant 'community' as an extension of the Russian society, 'community' stands not in contrast to, but as an integral part of society. However, a Russian 'community' may be seen as external to the receiving society. As such, Russian 'community' needs to be no more than a collection of people different from their hosts to be called a 'community'. We may also say that 'society' is homologous (homogeneous?) with 'community' in a sense that society is composed of communities (although we cannot speak of the 'British "community"' or 'Dutch "community"' 'at home'). This point will be particularly important to my further developed argument about subcommunities.

For an anthropologist, the most interesting aspect of the 'community' is the social actors' definition of it. In criticizing Kalb's (1998)[1] 'romantic' and 'sceptical' notions of community, Blockland finds it more useful to ask:

> How do people in everyday lives think and act 'community', and what are the characteristics of the social relationships that, according to them, make up their communities, or have nothing to do with communities whatsoever? (Blockland, 1999: 140)

The question 'is there a community?' can best be answered by the Russians themselves, as well as the Dutch and the British in their respective countries. Throughout the following sections, I shall present evidence to the fact that neither the Russians themselves, nor the members of the receiving society, see them as a 'community', while they do use the term to describe groups within a larger group.

> From the conversations with the key informants it has been stressed time and again that there is nothing like a 'community', in a sociological sense, of Russians in The Netherlands. The country of origin is not a sufficient organising principle ... The same is true for the more specific groups, such as, for example, Jews, who, as it has been noted, take part in the activities of the Jewish 'community' in The Netherlands – especially in Amsterdam – but not the Jewish communities organised along the country of origin principle. (Snel et al., 2000: 61)

A similar observation was made by Natalya Shuvaeva, a major Russian newspaper editor, and by Alexander Fostiropoulos, an Orthodox priest in London. Although both of them testified to personally knowing 'hundreds of Russians' by virtue of their profession, and approximating that there are 'tens to hundreds of thousands' of Russians in London, neither of them could describe these migrants as a unified community. Natalya Shuvaeva, however, refers to her newspaper's readership as a podium for a kind of 'community'.[2] Alexander Fostiropoulos also referred to his congregation as a kind of community, but one which is based on religious principles and includes many non-Russians:

> I wouldn't speak of the Russians here as a community. Community in this case can be used only as a collective term. Church membership doesn't make Russians into a community, as the church embraces all Orthodoxies, such as Greeks, Serbians, and British. Our goal at the Church is not to bind Russian-speakers together but to bring forth a greater awareness of Orthodox unity for all nations. Even if sometimes the church fosters a sense of community, this is not its major goal. At the end of the twentieth century the church became less of a religious institution, it seems, a condition that we attempt to rectify. We allow people to be themselves and interact with others, but we don't foster a sense of ethnic identity. One doesn't need to be an Orthodox Christian to be Russian. We can therefore speak only of a community of believers, and different factors make believers into a community. As soon as you try to draw a line around the people, they slip out one by one. It's easy to force the issue of community... But I would speak of the Russians in London and Russians who come to church, not of Russian community. (A. Fostiropoulos)[3]

Father Alexander referred to the 'old community of believers', noting that the previous waves of migrants did perceive the church as a 'community centre'. Thus, the newspaper editor and the Orthodox priest speak of 'communities' which are not encompassing of all the Russians but only those that join in certain activities (reading a Russian newspaper, participating in worship) or belong to certain institutions. Another example of such 'communities' comes from Sasha Kolot, the former owner of the only Russian cafe in Amsterdam, who referred to his cafe's habitués as a 'community'. The director of BCI, the organizer of cultural events in London, also spoke of a 'community' of Russians that assembles during events and cultural festivals.

Participation in events and communal activities is an important topic of Raj's book on Hindu Punjabis in London. She views a 'community' as a dynamic and contextually defined entity. When Hindu Punjabis participate in religious or cultural events in London, they view themselves as belonging to a 'community'.

> ...the Hindu Punjabi temple involves an understanding of a spatially bounded place temporarily coherent with a specific organization and structure. As such, it is a community. It is a community which is spatially defined and comes together at certain moments. (Raj, 1997: 109)

The feelings of 'belonging' or 'being excluded' are often associated with church attendance. Raj asks whether this 'community' membership extends beyond the physical compounds of a temple. Raj notices that the Hindu Punjabi form 'smaller social groups, cliques or "circles of friends" whose existence challenges a view of the temple community as a "unified" group' (Raj, 1997: 109). (I shall further address this point in the chapters on subcommunities and ethnicity.) Despite internal stratification

> ... individuals may see themselves as nominally part of a Hindu 'community' when they are not physically present 'in' the temple. Exploring ethnic and community identity begins with the realization that there is no Hindu Punjabi 'community', in a sense of a whole, but only moments when community occurs, when people gather as a whole, because of a certain criterion of identification. (Raj, 1997: 110)

One must be careful, however, in deciding whether or not a 'community', as Raj herself notes, is contextually bound. Also, what might look like a 'community' to the outsider might not be felt as such to the one assigned to it. Raj employs Anderson's term 'imagined community' to assert Punjabi's membership in a temporary community via temple worship and other practices, emphasizing that temple-attendants spend most of their lives outside the temple in different social fields. Punjabi temple attendance also has a strong social component. This 'leads us to understand the temple, not as a site where "community" meets ..., but a place where friends can be found' (Raj, 1997: 110). This point is especially relevant to the Russian situation. For the Russians, the social component of church attendance, as will be discussed in the chapter on social networks, seems to be of paramount importance to most members of the congregation.

As in the case of Hindu Punjabis, Russians may sometimes be referred to as a 'community' by virtue of their membership of certain institutions or participation in certain events. This 'community' is neither unitary nor stable. Its definition depends on the institution or event which claims to assemble such a community.[4]

As a group of people originating from the CIS and residing in the same city (sometimes reading the same newspaper or going to the same Russian church, cafe or club), Russians in London and Amsterdam present an odd case of factual existence without external recognition or internal awareness. Russian 'community' may be granted its existence conditional on the flexibility of the Russians' and the outsiders' definition of the term. 'Community', thus, appears to still be important for the people who feel they belong to it or observe it, but the actual meaning of 'community' may be contested.

3.2   Establishing Invisibility

I have arrived at the realization of the invisibility of the Russians in Britain and The Netherlands through my conversations with the British and the Dutch, as well as through my media analysis. In most cases, only partial awareness of the Russian presence was admitted. Very few sources claimed to have information on the numbers of Russians present or the characteristics of the supposed Russian 'community'. Russian invisibility was admitted both by the Russians and by members of the host society.

My Dutch informant, interested in 'everything Russian' and one of the founders of an Internet site for Russians in The Netherlands (Rusland.net), was surprised when I told him that there is 'more than a handful' of Russians in Amsterdam. A British co-owner of a Russian cafe in London told me that he knew about the existence of other Russian cafes and restaurants but had no idea who owned them or who their clientele was (most of the owners and clients were in fact, Russian). A Russian organizer of the Russian theme nights and discos in one of London's night clubs said that although he thought there were 'hundreds of thousands' of Russians in London, 'most of them were old and didn't like disco' (Garik). He thought that his clients were the children of the older émigrés (from previous 'waves') and was surprised when I told him that on the basis of my interviews most of his disco-goers were independent new arrivals.

While some of my informants expressed amazement at seeing 'so many Russians' at a party of 20 people and were even more surprised to hear that other guests knew more Russians, others asserted that there are hundreds of thousands of Russians living in London or Amsterdam alone. Some of the Russians that supposed that there were thousands of their compatriots in London or Amsterdam personally knew only a few of them; while others, knowing tens of Russians, assumed these were the only Russians present.

The most common acknowledgment of communal unity is the self-definition as a 'Russian' and an acknowledgement that other 'Russians' are present in London or in Amsterdam. Generalizations like 'we have a hard time adjusting to local culture', or 'the Dutch or the English don't understand us', suggest that these Russians see themselves as part of a distinct group seen in contrast to the other group (this will be further discussed in the chapters on culture and ethnicity). Yet, when asked directly whether they feel part of a community, their answers are ambiguous. Inna, a housewife from London, reflected:

> On the one hand, I'm Russian, I guess I'm part of the Russian community. On the other hand, I don't really have much contact with these people. I don't know who they are. I have my family and my interests, and that's my world; I don't know about theirs'. (Inna)

'I feel like an island in the sea', Sveta, my key informant in Amsterdam, told me. 'Others are also just floating, alone or with their families and friends.' This idea of separate 'islands' supports my further-developed argument about subcommunities. Another informant refers to himself and his family as an 'outpost', or on another occasion as a 'hard working guy for the Russians and hard working Russian for the Dutch'. These statements suggest that although Russians sometimes describe themselves collectively as a 'community', it is usually done along very general principles (such as the country of origin) and in opposition to the host society. Aside from this broad assignment (which does show, nonetheless, the importance of the concept of 'community' for the Russians), few concrete bonding features or conspicuous markers were identified, leaving the idea of a mega-community rather vague and elusive.

The elusive 'now you see it, now you don't' quality of Raj's community is particularly relevant to the Russian case. This elusiveness or invisibility of 'community' as a whole is confirmed both by the Russians and by the outsiders. The question then becomes, how can we explain such elusiveness or invisibility?

3.3   Reasons for Invisibility

3.3.1 The Outsiders' Perspective

The primary reason for Russian invisibility may lie in the simple fact that Russians are still relatively few in London and Amsterdam. There are much fewer Russians in Britain and The Netherlands than other, 'traditional' groups of migrants. The result is that Russians are less conspicuous to the members of the host society and to each other. Low critical mass may affect the cultural unity of the group – the more fragmented the groups of migrants, the less chance they have of sharing common cultural features or participating in the joined maintenance of what Bourdieu (1977) calls 'cultural capital'. As will be discussed in the chapter on social relations, it may be that cultural capital, which has been accumulated collectively but stored individually, is not shared by the group on arrival. Perhaps cultural capital also needs a critical mass to become openly expressed in a receiving society; since it appears that the smaller the number of carriers, the more internalized their culture is. Geographical dispersion and cultural fragmentation, both of which will be discussed further in this chapter, compounded with the migrants' low numbers, are responsible for their invisibility in London and Amsterdam.

Another likely explanation for the Russian 'invisibility' is a matter of superficial similarity with the resident population. As will be further discussed in the chapter on ethnicity, migration studies in Britain and The Netherlands often mention 'race' as an important aspect of relations between the receiving society and the migrants (Baumann, 1995; Bryant, 1997; Castles et al., 1984). Russians, however, are not conspicuously different in terms of colour or dress. Indeed, when I asked my British acquaintance whether he met any Russians in London, he replied that he 'wouldn't know them from the British if he met them on the street'. He also admitted to automatically 'spotting an Indian, even if they are as British [nationality-wise] as I am'. In The Netherlands

> Foreigners are welcomed and made to feel at home to the extent that they have pale skins and come from countries with a Judeo-Christian background. With all others, the Dutch try to be friendly but their efforts at being multi-cultural seem forced. (Portnoy, 2000: 27)

Culturally, however, the Russians may present an odd case for the receiving society (the topic explored in the chapter on ethnicity). In discussing Russian migrants in the Pacific Rim, Hardwick notes the following patterns of settlement and interaction with the receiving society, which might account for intentional 'invisibility':

> Russians also carry the stigma of belonging to a strange and relatively unknown variant of mainstream Christianity. Eastern orthodox dogma and ritual often seem uncomfortably 'pagan' to more fundamentalist Christians ... Experiences in their homeland left many with scars that have not healed, even in the more open environment of the United States and Canada. Their need to remain unobtrusive and geographically isolated has sometimes created 'invisible' ethnic landscapes of anonymity, where only trained eyes can tell they are in a Russian neighbourhood. (Hardwick, 1993: 4–5)

Unless a Russian talks loudly on the street or seeks to attract attention in public places as some 'new Russians' do in expensive shops in London and Amsterdam, he can easily be mistaken for a local or any other European tourist. Russian cultural idiosyncrasy is not initially apparent in dress or behaviour.

Thus, I have isolated a number of possible explanations for Russian invisibility in Britain and The Netherlands: low critical mass in comparison to other migrant groups; an inconspicuous entryway that discourages statistical monitoring; and the lack of any obvious problems associated with their presence. (One exception would be growing concerns with Russian crime, which will be discussed later.) Other significant factors are the novelty of the Russian presence in Britain and The Netherlands, and the lack of established communities. Members of the host societies are not used to the 'Russians coming' (de Lange, 1997) as there is no acknowledged history of hosting this group of migrants.

3.3.2 Lack of 'Established' Community

It appears from my interviews that the lack of established community in London and Amsterdam does have an influence on the invisibility of new arrivals. They have, as Sergei, a theatre director from London notes, 'nothing to join'. A retired school teacher from Belorussia living in The Netherlands for nine years claimed that the 'only Russians in Amsterdam are those found in the old [established] Russian "community"' (Stepa). But, when asked to provide examples of such 'old émigrés', he replied that he only knew a handful of Russians who arrived the same year as him. An Amsterdam Russian Foreign Church attendant suggested that there used to be a community in Amsterdam at the beginning of the twentieth century. This supposedly consisted of the literary elite who attended the church, but 'now they are all dead and their children, along with the newcomers, aren't interested' (Pavel).

The lack of established community is also noted by the Russians in London. Zhenya, a computer specialist working in London, reflected that he expected to meet some 'old and well-rooted Russians' in Britain who 'use samovars to make tea and play balalaikas on Sundays'. He was disappointed to find that the 'only Russians around are as "green" [newly arrived and lacking in tradition] as we are'. Mitya, Zhenya's eccentric cousin, bemoans the lack of 'aristocratic Russian spirit' which, according to him, could have 'dignified Russian presence abroad'. Mitya calls society balls and other events organized by members of the old elite 'parades of fake monarchy'. Michael, a retired sociologist, is even harsher:

> These are thieves who launder their money. They mark their status by going to special gatherings and paying over £200 for the ball (such as *War and Peace*), supposedly for charities. This is a European habit of a servant: to wear a tuxedo of his master. (Michael)

Snel et al. have noted that 'established' community plays little role in tying new Russian migrants together:

> A remarkable difference with the Yugoslavian 'established' community [in The Netherlands] is a very low level of self-organization, at least on a national or ethnic basis, of the formal Soviet citizens. Some informants, however, point out to the importance of informal relations, which are viewed as originating from the old Soviet practices during the communist regime; if there are ties between the more 'established' ex-Soviet citizens, these are characteristically based on friendship or family connections. (Snel et al., 2000: 61)

Russian migration specialists assert that the previous waves of Russian migration exhibited binding characteristics not present among the new Russian migrants. Contemporary scholar of Russian emigration, L.I. Eremenko,[5] quoted by Freinkman-Chrustaleva and Novikov in a book about Russian migrants in Germany, identifies specific features of Russian emigration as part of a special socio-cultural phenomenon:

> 1) lasting adherence of all waves [of Russian migration to the West] to preservation and development of national culture – traditions, customs, belief, and language; 2) openness towards the culture of the host countries, uninhibited interaction with them; 3) loyalty to the roots remaining in their motherland …; 4) interaction between residents of different geographical areas, enabling them not to lose spiritual and cultural values; 5) feeling an organic part of the national culture developing in Russia … We need to add to this rather accurate generalised characterization that many of those processes manifest themselves quite differently among members of the fourth wave. (Freinkman-Chrustaleva and Novikov, 1995: 54)

By contrast, other European capitals have conspicuous established communities. According to the writer Nabokov, French and German Russian diasporas in the first half of the twentieth century formed tight 'colonies':

> In Berlin and Paris, the two capitals of immigration, Russians have formed
> compact colonies ... In these colonies Russians stuck closely to each other. I
> mean, of course, Russian intelligentsia of democratic persuasion ... (Nabokov,
> quoted in Kaznina, 1997: 14)

True. For centuries there has been a Russian influence felt through
trade, royal and official visits, and culture exchange in both Britain and The
Netherlands (Kaznina, 1997; Naarden, 1992). But this influence has often
been restricted to certain cultural or economic areas, without actually spilling,
live, onto the streets of London or Amsterdam. Earlier Russian migrants, who
arrived after the Russian Revolution or the Second World War (after having
been forced to work in Germany by the Nazis) were few in numbers. As
discussed in the chapter on migration, only a few thousand Russians arrived
Britain, and a few hundred in The Netherlands in the twentieth century before
the fall of the Soviet Union. Most have largely integrated into English or Dutch
society. 'Established' Russians did not found lasting ethnic institutions, other
than the Orthodox Church,[6] as was the case with the earlier Russian migrants
in the US, Canada, France or Germany.

I have postulated that the post-Soviet Russians have arrived in a relatively
new ground with no deposit of cultural soil to grow their roots into. The
cultural capital of the 'established' Russians was not enough to provide
cultural nourishment and extensive social support for the new arrivals. In
other countries, where the strong established Russian 'community' supposedly
exists, new arrivals do find themselves part of conspicuous communities. In
London and Amsterdam, Russians have to look hard to find a community to
fit into.

3.3.3 Insiders' Perspective

One reason Russians are invisible to outsiders, as well as to each other, is
that most of them are not 'registered' migrants but temporary, commuting,
'tourist', or illegal. As discussed in the Introduction, most are not interested
in making themselves visible to the authorities. It is not in the Russians'
interest to present themselves as a 'community' because they want to remain
inconspicuous. Furthermore, these 'unregistered' migrants often pursue
individual rather than collective objectives and often come into contact with
each other through competition (for black jobs, sublet housing, etc.) rather than
cooperation (lobbying for their collective rights, etc.). Migrants often choose
individual rather than collective survival strategies for a variety of reasons.

Some live in precarious situations, or are uncertain of their legal status or their future. Alternatively, they might lack common aims, or have a practical need to remain individually aloof to avoid the authorities' attention.[7]

Russians might fail to see themselves as a 'community' if they are largely unaware of, or indifferent to, the presence of their fellow citizens – especially when those come from a social, ethnic or professional milieu different from their own.

> We may speak of a great degree of differentiation of migrants from … the former Soviet Union. We are talking about people who in their everyday life here in The Netherlands, despite the fact that they come from the same country, do not come into contact with each other. (Snel et al., 2000: 71)

From the inside, the Russians express diverse opinions about their own 'community'. The word for a 'community', *obshina*, has similar connotations to the English term. The grammatical stem is shared by words like *obshiy*, 'common'; *obshnost*, 'commonness'; *obshestvo*, 'society'; *obshestvenniy*, 'public'; *obshenie*, 'social intercourse'; etc. Yet, the strict meaning of *obshina* has a more limited connotation than in English. It implies a commune, a group, a tribe, a ghetto, a social enclave. *Obshina* is usually used to describe concrete social groups and cannot be generalized as a '"community" of mankind', for example. *Obshina* is often used to describe a group of outsiders that hold common beliefs or possess common values; people rarely refer to themselves as belonging to *obshina.* Consequently, Russians in Amsterdam never use the term *obshina* literally but imply it in relation to their affiliations. Church-goers, for example, refer to themselves as *prihozhane*, 'congregation', or *veruyushie*, 'believers'. In Amsterdam, *Oblomov* cafe habitués sometimes referred to themselves as Oblomovtsy.[8]

Russians showed only partial awareness of the Russian institutions and very selective participation in Russian events (see Appendix 3 for a detailed list of Russian institutions in London and Amsterdam). Only a few socially active individuals managed to attend many diverse parties and events. Younger informants tended to blame their lack of interest on the presence of other cultural attractions offered by London or Amsterdam city agendas. A teenage hard rock musician from Amsterdam asks: 'Why would I go to a *Sputnik* concert if there's always new and hot stuff at the [Dutch] clubs? If I wanted a Russian disco or music I could get it in Russia – that's not what I'm here for' (Vadim). Older informants give broader reasons, like busy work schedules, or fatigue. As a retired doctor from London testifies: 'I feel like I left my active life back home. Here I'm just floating. I'm too tired to bother about all these events, singing, talking. I just don't have the energy' (Vasya). Many immigrants find themselves detached, worried about practical issues such as obtaining legal documentation and finding work. It could be that Russian cultural events are not attractive or popular enough to forge a sense of 'community', as Sergei, a theatre director from London suggests.

I remember my first visit to the St Luke's Anglican church in London where masses were held in Russian. The Russian priest and his family's band were singing inspiring carols in Russian. Everybody clapped and cheered. Yet, although the congregation numbered less than 30, there was a sense of fragmentation. Russians were scattered throughout the building, in small groups or alone. After the sermon, tea and cookies were served which brought the Russians into closer physical proximity. Still, most groups – consisting of families and friends – stayed intact. I later found out that most people knew the names or even stories of other members of the congregation, but few open contacts were made. I had to be rather forceful to introduce myself and to enter small group discussions, sensing surprise and suspicion in response to my intrusion.

Alienation from one's fellow-citizens may have positive connotations, as a poet from Amsterdam reflected. Potentially, this isolation implies independence and self-sufficiency: 'I don't want to belong to a herd where others instruct my conduct or check my life' (Margarita). It is interesting to note that some of the more negative definitions of *obshina* imply a herd, a narrow-minded and closed group with archaic morals that suppresses individuals. Margarita explains why Russians are reluctant to see themselves as a whole group: 'We had enough of it in Russia. The good thing about being here is that nobody can tell you who you are … [From the outside] they do say who you are, but you can still lead your own life'. Grisha, a biologist from London, confirms: 'Here, I don't need to be part of the group; here I'm just a specialist'.

The reason some Russians felt they did not belong to a 'community' was that they did not have enough things in common (*nedostatochno obshego*) to share with the 'community' members. 'I have my interests; they are work interests. Others have their own work interests', explains a Russian computer scientist from Amsterdam. 'Outside work, I like to go bowling, I like playing chess. I don't know of many Russians who share my hobbies, so I play with whoever enjoys it' (Kirill). A housewife from London adds: 'I don't think other Russians are interested in my life, it's rather boring. I exchange recipes and talk about soap operas with my friends, but actually I'd rather read a book or take some professional course – others don't seem to be as interested in improving themselves' (Marina). A presently unemployed doctor living in Amsterdam feels that contact with the 'Russians' holds him 'back from the future': 'We can talk endlessly about old Russian films, old Russian music, old Russian dachas. I feel empty after these reminiscences because there's nothing new. I'd rather talk about the future' (Lev).

These statements lead us to the following section about a widespread mutual antagonism among the Russians – a phenomenon not unknown by other migrant groups. As the following section suggests, antagonism can take particularly 'Russian' overtones since its roots may lie in Soviet and post-Soviet social history.

3.3.4 Antagonism

Animosity between groups of Russians, or individuals, is a mysterious phenomenon since we have established that the Russians are geographically dispersed and usually content not to have too close contact with each other. Antagonism seems to be both the cause and the effect of the weakness of communal consciousness among the Russians.

Generally, there is a multitude of factors responsible for creating conflict not only between Russians, but within any migrant group:

> Conflicts within a group can stem from a number of sources. Some are closely related to economic and social stratification and the inequitable distribution of wealth, prestige and power. Others reflect traditional rivalries between regions or localities in the former country or opposing political ideologies that relate more to conditions in the sending rather than the receiving country ... Such conflicts frequently coincide with generational differences and are aggravated by them. They necessarily involve some consideration of the processes of social mobility and adjustment experienced by migrants and the ways in which these influence the degree of identification with the new country. (Richmond, 1969: 264)

Even though we have mentioned the lack of established communities, antagonism arises even among the few members of 'older' and 'newer' waves who come into contact with each other. Esman argues that 'even within the same ethnic group mutual support and solidarity may be strained by tensions and conflicts between earlier and later arrivals' (Esman, 1996: 317). I have observed that the 'old' generation, mostly political dissidents or cultural exiles, expresses discontent with the 'new' generation. They feel that this new group lacks political commitment, spirituality, and 'what's worse – stain Russian names' in the receiving country (Glazer and Moynihan, 1996: 135).

Antagonism between the Russians also existed in the supposedly more unified pre-1990s communities. The post-revolutionary 'wave', superficially united in their anti-Soviet views, consisted of

> individuals displaced by a deluge [who] always kept a weather eye on the country to which many at first anticipated returning in a matter of months, the size of the population movement, and the very diverse forces that it involved, [which] meant that internal differences and disputes soon became nearly as important as polemics with the common enemy, the new, Communist Russia ... Inevitably, the cultural life of the Russian emigration was subject to much the same fragmentation and contention as its political existence: here again attitudes to the Soviet Union were crucial. (Kelly, 1998: 299)

Among the recent arrivals, I heard the statement 'I want to have nothing to do with these Russians' from people of different occupation groups and social strata as well as different ethnic denominations (Russian, Jewish, Georgian, etc.). The explanations for this antagonism, however, are varied. Some migrants complained of how dishonest, unreliable and greedy their 'Russian' neighbours and friends were. Others explained their desire to stay aloof from their 'own' group by their wish to 'mix' with citizens of their 'new' country, issuing statements like: 'Since we live in this country, we might as well be friends with its people'. Some others said that they 'did not wish to belong to a ghetto', or brushed my question off with 'We are not on a group tour'. Finally, some said that they do not avoid other Russians intentionally, 'it just happens'.

Some Russians, even those from common ethnic or social backgrounds, found their compatriots' behaviour embarrassing, backwards or irritating. In the interview with Hubert Smeets, a former Russia correspondent in The Netherlands, he mentioned that his Russian wife did not share his enthusiasm for visiting Russia and entertaining Russian friends. He explained that she is tired of the culture of complaints.

> In the beginning my husband often invited Russians to our parties. Some of them had lived in The Netherlands for five years but didn't speak a word of Dutch. But they did complain about everything; food was bad, education was bad. Then I'd say: So, you have to go back. This would almost turn into an argument. (Frantova, 6 August 1999)[9]

Natalya Shuvaeva, a Russian newspaper editor in London, reflected:

Russians like to complain a lot, and the most popular subjects of criticism are the health and education systems. They say that the primary education here is so awful, they wish their children could still study in Russia. Private education is desirable, especially for new Russians. Russians also complain about the useless GPs, their lack of attention. Still, when it comes to serious surgeries, Russians try to bring their family members here to have an operation. (Natalya Shuvaeva, talk in Oxford, June 1999)

But while this 'culture of complaints' breeds familiarity and boredom among the Russians, other cultural experiences teach Russians to treat each other as strangers. Recalling Hardwick's (1993) discussion of 'cultural baggage' earlier in this chapter, part of this 'baggage' is the Soviet inheritance of fear. Among the older émigrés, one reason for keeping aloof from each other is mistrust.

For a long time we held aloof from the Russian colony in London. Those who have not lived under the Soviet regime must find it hard to imagine the psychology of persons who left that paradise during the first decade of the new order. I don't know how it may be today but, at that time, nobody who had previously belonged to the old Russia could be sure of his life and well-being, right down to the last minute of his existence. A careless word spoken in the street might give rise to a denunciation, arrest and imprisonment ... Even when we had spent some time in London, under the protection of English laws, in complete confidence that we were beyond the reach of the Soviet system, we could not shake off our instinctive reactions of fear. (Shilovsky, in Glenny and Stone, 1990: 289)

My elderly informant in Amsterdam reported that although he left Russia during *perestroika* and realizes that the 'spectre of Communism' has diffused, he is still haunted by the idea that the friendlier his compatriot, the more suspicious he is.

The mutual antagonism among the Russians could also be seen in terms of old ethnic and class rivalries suddenly brought to the fore by the relative geographical proximity of the migratory groups (having come from different countries of the CIS and settling in the same city). Their only common desire might have been 'to go from one country to another. This exhausts whatever their minds can really have in common' (Halbwachs, 1960: 115).

As opposed to the geographically proximate communities (such as Turks in The Netherlands (Staring, 1999) or Indians in Britain (Baumann, 1995), when whole neighbourhoods are occupied by residential houses, shops and cultural institutions of one migrant group), Russians in London and Amsterdam avoid such clustering. By contrast, Darieva (1998) and Doomernik (1997) report that Russians *do cluster* and found geographically proximate cultural institutions in Berlin.[10] The same phenomenon is found in Canada (Hardwick, 1993), Israel (Siegel, 1998), and other countries with large Russian populations. This brings us back to the question of critical mass and makes us suspect that for some ironic reason 'the fewer the Russians the less they like each other'. As mentioned in the Introduction and as will be further discussed in the section on comparison in the Conclusion, it is regrettable that the scope of my research did not allow me to make more in-depth comparisons between Russians and other migrant groups, or between Russians in different countries.

Finally, leading into the discussion developed in the chapter on ethnicity, it needs to be noted that Russians actually do come from different ethnic, cultural and linguistic backgrounds. Soviet-style hierarchy of ethnic groups (with ethnic Russians presiding over the top of it), and other forms of state-condoned antagonism between social groups, may account for the fact that Russian-speakers coming from different countries of the CIS, or different ethnic backgrounds, do not want to be seen as part of a group of generalized Russians.[11] The feelings of inferiority or superiority, which will be discussed further in the chapter on ethnicity, were indeed present among ethnically diverse groups of Russian-speakers present in London and Amsterdam. Angela, an ethnic Lithuanian from Lithuania and an asylum seeker in London, referred to the ethnic Russians living in her country and seeking asylum in Britain as 'fakers': 'They are blaming Lithuanians for their misfortunes in order to get an asylum here'. Michael, a Jewish sociologist, now living on a pension in London, felt that the ethnic Russians in Russia did not consider him to be 'one of them' and he did not see any reason why Russians in London should suddenly shed their anti-semitic tendencies. Vadim, an ethnic Russian teenage rock musician from Amsterdam referred to Georgians and Armenians living in Amsterdam as 'non-Russian'. Vadim did not see any reason why outsiders would group them together with ethnic Russians.[12] Thus, 'community' appears to be ethnically divided if acknowledged at all.

Soviet communitarianism (Communism?) might also cause a pendulum effect of rejecting the state-imposed 'spirit of ethnic equality'. Since the sense of the Soviet 'community' was artificially fostered in Russians for many years, their freedom from imposed identification with their fellow countrymen may have led to the rejection of a 'community' spirit altogether. The Soviet propaganda touting the brotherhood of all Soviet peoples irrespective of social class, ethnicity, religion or personal beliefs could have created resentment and cynicism in those striving towards individual freedom and achievement. These issues will be further explored in the chapters on subcommunities and ethnicity.

But how is this antagonism expressed? One expression of social distancing could be gossip, the subject which de Vries investigates in her article on Turkish girls in The Netherlands. Inter-group gossip restricts the individual's freedom. Girls' objections to gossip 'may result in an internal self-differentiation from their gossiping compatriots, but this never implies any desire to cease to be Turkish or to embrace "Dutchification" (*vernederlandsing*)' (de Vries, 1995: 51). Russians of different backgrounds seem to engage in gossip about their close friends as well as more distant acquaintances. Gossip usually involves discussion of personal morals or material inequalities with disapproving undertones. Unlike the case of the Turkish girls, Russian gossip seems to be manifestly negative and may serve to increase social distance between the Russians. To precede the 'boundary maintenance' section in the chapter on subcommunities, we need to note that social exclusion, and even open confrontations and expressions of hostility, are not uncommon among the Russians.

Thus, we are confronted with the lack of 'communal consciousness' and widespread indifference or even antagonism towards fellow citizens among the Russians. Except for small circles of friends or families who form close groups, there appears to be little that holds the Russians together.

3.4   Paradoxes of Absence

Among other factors, the lack of the self-defined 'community' may account for the Russian invisibility in Britain and The Netherlands. Diversity of new arrivals, their backgrounds and present circumstances, as well as the unique antagonism among the Russians may explain the social fragmentation that prohibits the migrants from 'seeing the whole picture'. However, many questions still remain unanswered. For example: if the Russians themselves recognized their 'community', would it become more visible to the outsiders, and vice versa? For whom are Russians in London or Amsterdam a 'community'? And, why does it matter whether there is a community at all?

Clearly, the use of the term 'community' is problematic. Envisioning it as 'shifting, contested, fragmented, imagined, floating and constructed' does not help us conjure up a 'community'. Anthropology, along with philosophy, has long been puzzled by epistemology and the question of how reality is conceived. Some of the postmodern anthropologists suggest that reality is constructed and may only be understood through language, thus existing only in the minds of people. To me, 'social facts' are referential to 'reality' which exists outside human minds and independent of human interpretation of it. 'Community' is an example of such a 'social fact' and refers to a material artefact, namely a group of people perceived as bounded and sharing certain common characteristics. That said, it seems to me that the question of whether 'community' 'exists' is rather irrelevant. The only way to escape the vicious circle of mentioning a 'community', only to deny its very existence later, is through acknowledgment of its use as a 'social fact'. My informants emphasized – implicitly or explicitly – that the idea of a 'community' matters to them insofar as it may be used to identify oneself with or in contrast to their surroundings. Identifying with, or rejecting, the 'community' altogether may suggest how a migrant feels about himself or his place in the receiving society – how he constructs a mythology of the past and envisions the future. Despite all the difficulties, I find the term 'community' useful as a way of conceptualizing a group of people, a distinct minority. Yet the Russian 'community' should not be assumed to carry all the characteristics that a 'community' (both in academic and popular discourse) is said to have. Such similarities might include geographical proximity or cultural or social ties. The only thing that the migrant Russians in the 1990s may have in common is their country of origin and common language. 'Community' appears to be as good a term to discuss such a group as any other, if our ethnographic task is to describe and analyse a migrant group.

On the basis of my data, it might be concluded that there is no self-defined 'community' in either London or Amsterdam. 'Community' may be said to be present by a very limited definition (as the term designating 'Russian presence' in the receiving countries) but its members are invisible to each other and to outsiders. Many migrants, fragmented into small groups, question either the presence of a Russian community altogether or deny their belonging to it. However, most of them share a sense that there is 'something' that stands in the place of 'community'. In the following chapter, I shall discuss subcommunities, which may serve as an alternative to a 'community'.

Notes

1   Kalb, D. (1998), 'The Limits of the New Social Orthodoxy', *Focaal*, 31/32, pp. 237–48.

2   After Shuvaeva's talk at Oxford in June 1999, the following exchange occurred during the question and answer session:

Q5: It looks like there's no real 'community' whatsoever: no one church, or cafe like with the Poles –

N.S.: Most Russians don't want to assimilate or form 'villages', they rather stay aloof from each other. But *LC* does serve as a kind of focal point through announcements of large common events, like the opening of a church for Easter … Readers' letters also form a kind of podium for a community …

Q5: So they are like floating communities, scattered throughout London.

N.S.: There are certain areas where Russians live, like Highgate, Finchley, Docklands (where Russian life evolves around a certain pub), W2 area and Bayswater; Queensway … but indeed, it's hard to pin them down to one area.

3   A. Fostiropoulos makes more interesting observations about the 'community' and anthropology: 'I understand community as both geographically proximate and bound by something in common. Polish immigrants used to settle close together on their arrival in the areas of South-West London and Wimbledon, but now they've also moved apart. Sharing only common language and history isn't enough …'

    I don't think it's generally possible to use anthropological methods to understand the church – church can be seen through theological method and understood through committed religious experience. A good ethnography of the Orthodox Church is Julie Williams' 'To be the Church' (*Communion*, December 1998). Her article speaks not only of the ways the church operates but opens up other agendas about members of the Orthodox church in Scotland. Anthropology can help disentangle casual distinctions, such as national identity forged through religion.

4   By contrast, the Indians in London and Turks in Amsterdam are often seen as stable 'communities' by the media and through common discourse. If this research could expand its scope to include other migrant groups we might be able to gain more insight into the process of creating a migrant community. Comparison between Russian diasporas in different European countries or elsewhere as well as between the Russian and other diasporas may provide a useful clue as to which factors are responsible for creating a Russian communal identity (this subject will be further addressed in the chapter on ethnicity).

5   L.I. Eremenko (1993), *Russian Emigration as a Socio-Cultural Phenomenon*, Candidate of Sciences Thesis, Moscow.

6   At the beginning of the twentieth century, many aristocratic cultural institutions like literary societies, social and political clubs, and printing offices were established in London (Kaznina, 1997). Most of them were rather short-lived, except for a few very select clubs organizing society events like the annual *War and Peace* ball and attended by the children and grandchildren of the pre-and post-Revolutionary aristocratic elite (see the chapter on migration).

7   As might be the case with some other minority groups, calling themselves a 'community' might have practical advantages to the group (Baumann, 1995). Members of a minority 'community' may claim collective benefits from the receiving institutions, no matter how internally divided they are. Yet, the Russians do not appear to be interested in collective lobbying of their own interests. This may be because of the fact that these interests are mostly individual, since most of my informants are relatively self-sufficient, be it through employment, political status or marriage. Only very few would profit from attracting attention to themselves through collective claims.

8   At present, the new Russian cafe *Kalinka,* founded by a group of Armenians, is collecting a
     more ethnically homogenous crowd, prompting non-Armenians to nickname it 'Erevanka'
     and feel excluded from this 'not quite Russian' cafe.
9   From the Dutch newspaper *Trouw*, 'Die Russen klaagden altijd over alles', August 1999,
     p. 2.
10   However, there is contradictory evidence on community formation in Germany, where
     ethnic Russians are said to exhibit more avoidance behaviour than Russian Jews or
     Ukranians: 'There is little affinity found among the [ethnic] Russians. According to experts'
     opinion, Russians are either not seeking or barely seeking communion with each other,
     also stronger communal tendencies and formation of institutions are observed among the
     Jews and Ukrainians' (Fedorov, 1998: 83).
11   As Caroline Humphrey's research in Buryatia and Mongolia suggests, there is a strong
     element of socialist hierarchization present among the peoples of the former Soviet
     republics or autonomous regions, when one ethnic group feels that another group is inferior
     to them. 'Buryats feel that Mongolians are "backward", "crude", "traditional", etc., while
     Mongolians feel that Buryats are stuck-up, too Russianized, etc., the Inner Mongolians too
     subordinate to the Chinese, etc. The hierarchy of independent country, republic, ASSR,
     "autonomous" region, etc. have surprising salience for them – a real question of status and
     rights. People don't want to be associated with others whom they have been taught to think
     of as "inferior"...' (Humphrey, comments on the earlier draft of this chapter, 2000).
12   Also see footnote 7.

Chapter 4

Subcommunities and Subcultures

Introduction

In the previous chapter on community, we have explored the phenomenon of Russian invisibility and the difficulty of using the term 'community' to describe various groups of Russian migrants in London and Amsterdam. Numerically small and geographically dispersed, Russians compose a socially heterogeneous group, where animosities and mistrust between the migrants enhance social distance. In both London and Amsterdam the feeling of common descent and realization that 'We are all Soviets after all', reported in countries where numbers of Russians are greater, such as the former Soviet republics (Tishkov, 1996; Shlapentokh et al., 1994; Panarin, 1999), United States (Miller, 1987), France (Jackson, 1993), Germany (Darieva, 1998; Doomernik 1997), Israel (Siegel, 1998), or Canada (Hardwick, 1993; Shuvaeva, 1999), is challenged by disparities undermining cultural unity.

Nonetheless, as I shall further discuss in the chapter on social relations, strong affiliations between the Russians do exist, ranging from pragmatic to recreational. While no unified community is recognized, the presence of interest groups or social circles is undeniable. As this chapter intends to reveal, subcommunities function similarly to 'communities' as defined in the previous chapter.

This chapter aims to expand upon the exploration of 'community' by exploring the nature of subcommunities. I will examine how they are formed and how they function within the host society. I shall investigate why Russians in London and Amsterdam are best described in terms of subcommunities, and how this approach can aid our understanding of other migrant – or indeed any – urban groups.

Subcommunities may not be specific to migrants but might be a general urban phenomenon. Yet, migrant subcommunities, particularly Russian subcommunities in London and Amsterdam, exhibit a number of specific and unique features. These features, I argue, are inherited from the CIS and are subject to change as the migratory context alters the experience of class, social networks, culture and ethnicity.[1]

As opposed to the numerically larger community, subcommunities may consist of a few individuals. Subcommunities may be based upon common background, family ties, professional affiliation, practical need, friendship, or interests and hobbies. Members of subcommunities are linked by social networks characterized by trust and the fulfilment of mutual expectations. Some subcommunities are formed on the basis of the Russians' legal status in the country, such as 'political asylum seeker', 'spouse of a Western national', 'self-employed seasonal artist', 'temporal contract employee', 'illegal resident', etc. Membership in such subcommunities depends both on self-selection mechanisms and policies of the receiving countries. In this chapter I focus on the former.

I shall start this chapter with a discussion of the diversity of Russian migrants, particularly addressing the issue of class. Cultural and ethnic diversity will be further discussed in the chapters on culture and ethnicity. I shall argue that subcommunities contain subcultures, and expand upon this theme with an example of occupational subculture.

I shall then turn to different types of subcommunities, namely those with inclusive and exclusive membership. I shall further elaborate this classification by distinguishing between large and small, intentional and assigned, open and closed, stable and shifting types of subcommunities. I shall address boundary maintenance mechanisms, with particular mention of the role of liminal and dual members in maintenance and negotiation of subcommunal boundaries. Finally, I shall make a comparative note about subcommunities in London and Amsterdam.

4.1   Diversity of Russian Migrants

We have already addressed the issue of migrant diversity in the chapters on migration and community, and we shall return to this subject in the chapter on social relations. Migrant diversity is both problematic (because of conceptual difficulties of distinguishing 'migration types'), and revealing in regard to the situation of individual migrants (Codagnone, 1998). Distinctions drawn from the outside are usually made on the basis of the migrants' legal status. In The Netherlands, Snel et al. (2000) list about seven categories of Russian migrants, which are very similar to their classification in Britain.

> Although [Russian] 'community' is enormously diverse, with all manner of types of people present as befits those originating from the largest country on earth, they can be divided into various broad categories. Some are in Britain for a finite time – on secondment for companies, engaged in academic research,

or on professional exchange schemes. The families of those people usually accompany them. Others – generally younger, and with or without dependants – are students. They are permitted to stay in the UK for as long as their course lasts, but it is expected that they return home at the end of the course ... A large group of Russian nationals in UK are those married or about to be married to UK citizens. It is overwhelmingly the case that Russian women marry British men ... Lastly, another large group of Russians in the UK are asylum seekers. (O'Connor, 1997: 6)

Aside from their legal status, the Russians can be placed in these categories:

1   temporal: age at arrival, duration of time spent in the receiving country;
2   personal: gender, ethnicity, occupation, and class;
3   transformative: subjective level of integration, such as present occupation.

All of these factors matter for internal distinctions, since Russian migrants themselves rarely group together on the basis of legal status alone.

The temporal category is quite important, as I have observed that the migrants who had lived in the receiving country longer than five years tended to cluster together or to 'mix' with members of the host society, not easily accepting newcomers. This is especially true of the older (above 50) migrants who were generally more conservative in their social choices. Those who arrived in the receiving countries under the age of 15, went to schools and learned the language quickly, tended to 'assimilate' more easily. This group was inclined to abandon their Russian friends as the 'cultural gap' grew proportionally with time of stay in the receiving country.

Generational divide has important implications for forging a 'community':

These practices make Hinduism visible – and act as an affirmation of 'communal' identity ... For the parental generation, it is in these overt and conscious patterns of practice that can be found the essence of what it is to be Hindu. For the younger generation, however, 'Hinduness' is something that needs to be learned and has some specific manifestations. (Raj, 1997: 124)

A similar observation is made by the Orthodox priest in London:

While for some Russians the experience of Russian people formed by the events in their culture is by itself motivation enough to forge a community,

> for others it's a reason to avoid it. Other immigrants in Britain, such as the
> Indians, come through different circumstances. But even Pakistani community
> is difficult to speak about as although the old generation wants a sense of the
> old-fashioned community, the new generation is too rebellious to sustain it.
> (A. Fostiropoulos)

Personal and transformative categories, including ethnicity and occupation in the CIS and in the receiving country, will be discussed in more detail in chapters on culture and ethnicity and social networks. Gender plays a role in the creation of groups like 'Russian wives', or 'single male businessmen', discussed further in this chapter.

4.1.1 Class

Of all these categories, only the question of class presents a certain conceptual problem. Cole asks whether any single criterion can be applied to assign a person to class and discusses the difficulty of dealing with subjective criterion:

> If a random collection of persons are asked merely to what class they belong,
> some of them will probably give no answer at all, and will not know what
> answer to give. If, on the other hand, they are given a list of named classes to
> choose from, most of them will probably be prepared to fit themselves into
> one of the given categories; but it may make a considerable difference how a
> list is drawn up, not merely according to the number of classes that are named,
> but also according to the names that are used. (Cole, 1995: 1)

Belonging to a class is also seen as related to racism (particularly among the 'working class') (Balibar, 2003: 325). The idea of class is important to Russians as a way of distinguishing different social groups in the CIS. The mutual antagonism that many Russian migrants experience towards each other, mentioned in the chapter on community, partially stems from class divisions. 'What those who deny the existence of classes … are really denying is not class but class antagonism as a pervasive phenomenon of … society.' Social boundaries, created in the CIS, and sometimes altered in migration, are nonetheless pervasive phenomena. Although Russian class boundaries are not clearly defined, Russians speak of class as a self-evident and stable category.

Vernacular expressions describing class in Russian range from 'circle': *krug* ('He's not from my circle') to 'level': *uroven* ('He is not at my level').

When asked to extrapolate on these notions, Russians gave examples of such categories as 'intelligentsia', *technar* (technically trained but intellectually limited professional); *hanzha* (materially-oriented snobs and fake aristocracy), 'peasant' (referring not only to agricultural workers but to simple hard working people), or *bydlo* (bums, stupid and ignorant people).

Notably, little explicit mention is made of class in either the Western or Marxist understanding of the term. The hierarchy of Russian 'class' appears value-laden and subjective, rather than being based on inheritance or constructed through wealth or occupation. This is not surprising since

> The two broad types of industrial society ... – capitalist and Soviet – present a number of similar features in their occupational structure and in the general shape of their social stratification, but they also differ widely in their political regimes and their social doctrines and policies, in the manner in which the upper social strata are constituted, and in the historical changes of social structure which they have undergone. (Bottomore, 1991: 33)

In Britain, where discourse on class is still clearly pronounced, Russians felt more self-conscious about their 'class'. The migrants were placed, as it were, outside of the established class categories and branded as 'outsiders'. The chapters on culture and ethnicity explore Russian reactions to external labelling. In the case of being placed 'outside class', Russians evoked differences between their own and Western categorization. Grisha, a temporal contract biologist working in London, reflected:

> [In Russia], the class system is different from the British one. Here class is inherited, you cannot jump from low to high. In Russia, you can get educated or get a job, and it changes your standing ... Here I guess I'm seen as a temporarily employed foreign academic, a class in and of itself. It's a class my friends here fall into. (Grisha)

Here, Grisha uses 'class' as a 'category' – assigned from the outside and fixed. Michael, a retired sociologist from London, gives examples of British vs Russian class:

> While a bookkeeper may earn the same as a cleaner, their social opportunities are incomparable, the level of their social niches is incompatible. In Russia there is different social stratification and different measures of prestige. Class is still important in England, and it's largely based on profession. At some society ball, a simple cleaner is hardly noticed as a human being. They have a

hereditary based class system too, like castes. One may enter from the outside, as high as upper middle, because of money or profession, but one can never get higher or get really accepted. (Michael)

In The Netherlands, class distinctions are less pronounced, and a 'we are all middle class' perspective is publicly shared. Russians in Amsterdam felt somewhat closer to the host society as they too could see themselves as 'middle class', since the Russian class boundaries are more vaguely defined. Generally though, whether being perceived as 'outsiders' or as 'members of the middle class', internal distinctions remained solid. Margarita, a poet from Amsterdam, reflects:

The Dutch can view me as they like, as I'm still a kind of new phenomenon for them, but [the Russians] are quick to assign me a box with the label ... Being a poet in Russia implies both being a member of the leisure class, and being rebellious and unorthodox – both [categories] not generally liked by the Russians. (Margarita)

Perhaps to escape her 'box', Margarita prefers the company of her Dutch friends and views herself as belonging to a 'group of creative thinkers'.

Like Margarita, some migrants experienced a change in their 'class status' positively. The fall of the Soviet Union spurred a drop in the ideologically-based prestige of the 'workers and peasants' there. However, some of my informants felt that in Britain and The Netherlands, the so-called welfare states, positive attitudes toward the 'simpler' occupations were encouraged. A witty middle-aged Belorussian plumber from London reports:

In the Soviet days, plumbers were supposed to be the avant-garde of social change, like all proletariat. We were the exemplary class (*sic*) of citizens. After [the fall of Communism] we were just plumbers, people doing dirty work ... Necessary work, nonetheless – often I would get a bottle of vodka as an extra reward for my services – but still a plumber is a plumber, you address him with '*ty*' (informal 'you' in Russian) ... Now, here I'm Mr Plumber. Here I'm 'excuse me sir, could you check my pipe'. Suddenly, I feel respected again. (Gera)

Sanya, a young construction worker from Uzbekistan, living in Amsterdam, agrees:

Although officially my skill as a construction worker was laudable [in Uzbekistan], the government paid me little money, and my wife's friends [architects] looked down at me, I wasn't from their *krug* ... it was clear from jokes at the dinner table, as if I wouldn't understand those jokes being dumb ... Now here I don't hear any such jokes. I thought that after my Dutch improved I'd hear them, but no, nothing funny. Construction work is serious and what I do is equally important as what you [an anthropologist] do ... Even if you don't think so – and I still suspect some Dutch don't – you cannot say it out loud. It will be like saying 'You're black' to a black person – here it's a taboo. (Sanya)

In London, a recently retired Russian doctor noticed that his colleagues treated nurses and staff with more respect than in the CIS:

It's not just what they'd call sexual discrimination here – pinching some nurse's behind, it's the whole attitude towards assistants, students, cleaners, technicians ... The idea that we are all valuable members of this hospital, we're all specialists. (Vasya)

Migration changes the context in which class in the CIS had been assigned. Some migrants feel liberated from the categories of the old, particularly if they disliked the stigma of their 'class assignment' in the CIS. Others had felt 'established' in the CIS but suddenly became 'outsiders' or 'new phenomenon' in the West. These migrants bemoan their loss of status. Ultimately, migrants begin to create their own categories, reflective of or in spite of the existing ones in the host society. While Grisha internalizes external labelling and views himself in London as a 'temporary contract worker' and places his friends into the same category, Margarita speaks of herself as a member of the creative elite. Gera enjoys being 'Mr Plumber' as opposed to a 'person doing dirty work'. Some migrants carve a niche for themselves outside of familiar categories of class, while others remain bound by labels assigned to them either in the CIS or in the receiving country. These assignments, whether voluntary or imposed, are the basis of subcommunity formation, as individuals either choose or are led to join certain social groupings.

4.2   Subcultures

Given the diversity of the Russian migrants, it is not surprising that subcommunities are also diverse. This diversity is manifested in subcultures contained within subcommunities. Thornton (1997) defines subcultures as social groups organized around shared interests and practices.

> Subcultures often distinguish themselves against others – workers, achievers, 'squires' or the 'mainstream'. They also differentiate among themselves and in so doing create hierarchies of participation, knowledge and taste. (Thornton, 1997: 1)

Like 'community', 'subculture' influences a group member to accept certain norms and customs associated with the group. Membership in a group endows an individual with its own qualities, causing its member to internalize some of the group's most salient characteristics.

> They will become, in their own, their peers' and outsiders' eyes, certain sorts of people: homosexuals, jazz men or whatever. This identity has importance either because it is one that they value – because it is the result of lengthy training and carries high status – or because it is one that is highly pervasive and difficult to get away from. (Salaman, 1974: 15)

One dynamic that might define a subculture is occupation. Perhaps this is due to the Soviet habit of working in a *kollektiv* which transcends pure work experience. Russians attribute great importance to working with other people. To them, fitting into the work environment also implies fitting into a new culture in general.

> To what extent do persons of a given occupation 'live together' and develop a culture which has its subjective aspects in personality? Do persons find an area for the satisfaction of their wishes in the association which they have with their colleagues, competitors, and fellow servants? (Hughes, 1958: 25)

Salaman attempts to answer these questions through introducing the notion of *occupational community*. Salaman defines this as consisting of 'people who are members of the same occupation or who work together [and] have some sort of common life together and are, to some extent, separate from the rest of society' (Salaman, 1974: 19). Werbner states that the work experience 'is so fundamental to men's world view and sense of identity, and the time spent at work … so extensive, that work together becomes a powerful basis for trust and friendship' (Werbner, 1995: 214).

Salaman distinguishes between two types of community: local and cosmopolitan. The distinction is made in regard to the individual's orientation toward the 'immediate, local world of either his town or his work place' on the one hand, and toward the 'wider world of either the "national or international scene" or his occupation as a whole' on the other hand (Salaman, 1974: 39).

This suggests that a migrant whose work might have been more 'locally' oriented might find it more difficult to adjust or share the values of either 'local' or 'cosmopolitan' workers in the host society. Also, certain occupational groups, whose members share similar educational and professional training with members of the host society, could be expected to 'fit in' more readily than other groups where cross-cultural or cross-national differences in training would impair their ability to 'feel at home' in the receiving 'professional community'.

Indeed, many subcommunities in London and Amsterdam centre on 'international' professions or firms. Grisha, a biologist working in London, suggested that the existence of such transnational subcommunities is a universal phenomenon:

> There are certain differences in the way biology is taught in Russia and here. Even studying for purely experimental biology we had to get a great deal of theoretical and even historical information in ... as opposed to a more applied 'hands-on' approach here ... Still, I was surprised how similar English and Russian academic biology was. Except for a number of technical skills I had to learn here, I felt qualified to lead the team from the start ... I've travelled extensively, met other biologists through conferences, consulted them over Internet – and discovered that biology was pretty similar in all industrial countries ... Even professional jokes we share with our team mates are similar to the ones made in Germany. (Grisha)

Grisha mentions both 'technical skills' and 'shared jokes' that can be attributed to the biologist's subculture. Galya, an employee at an international bank in London, notices that her work experience made British society as a whole more comprehensible. It provided a bridge from the professional subculture to the host culture:

> My job description and duties here are similar to those at [the Russian branch of this international bank] ... Initially, having come to this country, I couldn't make sense of things, couldn't understand why people said the things they did, what they found important in life, how they spent their free time ... My job has brought me closer with the British, it became my dictionary for everyday life in Britain. (Galya)

Professional knowledge can also extend to include lifestyle and hobbies, as in the case of Alik, a Ukrainian music technician. Alik admits to 'doing music outside work' and 'not understanding people who don't live by music'.

Now working at one of the most popular Dutch night clubs, he told me of his experience:

> At first, I couldn't find anything I was interested in – just some cleaning jobs, then gardening ... I was looked down at by my employers ... In the meanwhile, I saved enough money to buy some equipment and start 'mixing' [music] at home ... One day I meet this girl and write this piece of music for her, she gets all excited and tells me to go to that club and show my stuff. So I go, and they ask whether I can do this and that, and I tell them that they have an old machine, that if they really want to rock the house they need another type, and they all listen to me. They ask me what music I like to listen to, so I give them a list – this girl told me what their style was – so they listen and before I knew it I was employed and they changed their machine ... (Alik)

Taking 'professional community' as a unit of study implies the methodological requirement to select a few professional groups and examine their 'professional subcultures'. Unfortunately, my fieldwork had time limitations. Still, my impressions from interviews I have done with professionally integrated migrants leads me to think that in some cases, a professional 'subculture' was more important to a migrant than a common national or ethnic identification. Vasya, a recently retired doctor from Moscow, feels he shares more in common with an English doctor than with a farmer from his own country.

> When I meet a Russian farmer, I don't know what to talk to him about. I don't know anything about cows and pesticides. When I meet an English doctor, not even knowing English, I can already communicate with him. Lots of our terminology has Latin origin, also we share the same skills which can be demonstrated without the use of language ... And yes, I'd prefer the doctor's company. (Vasya)

In the interview with Vasya's English colleague, she told me that she had more themes in common with the 'strange doctor from Russia' than with her own neighbours.

Although neither professional migrants nor their colleagues explicitly speak of professional subculture, it is clear that they feel they share something unique. This bond creates a social environment in which particular types of practice, conduct, terminology, jokes and even style (in both discourse and clothes) are used. Fellow workers are seen as more accepting than the host society at large, able to transcend xenophobic prejudices and see a migrant as 'one of them'. Two London-based computer programmers drew an analogy between 'computer language' and 'common language'.

> Whichever country you work in, your knowledge [of computer languages] is a language understood by both employers and colleagues, no matter whether you speak their actual language ... Even our children, having gone to middle school here [in London], not knowing the word of English, found 'something to talk about' with their classmates: computer games, Internet, even elementary programming. (Zhenya)

On the other hand, Russians who came to the West with particularly 'Russian' skills found it initially difficult to relate to both the professional and the host culture. A London musician, Konstantin, used to play balalaika on the streets of his native Kiev. Although his musical skill was appreciated on the streets of London, he reflected that he 'felt like a dancing bear'. In other words, he believed that people did not come for the music but for the novelty and exoticism of his instrument. If anything, Konstanin felt that his professional skill made him socially isolated.

The above examples demonstrate how professionals, integrated into the host society by virtue of their occupation, may be said to share an international, although professionally specific subculture. Individuals like Konstantin, however, are likely to join groups that contain subcultures similar to their own. For Konstantin, other Russian musicians, or Russian friends, would compensate for the lack of social support at work. This leads us to distinguish between the types of subcommunities, based on their ethnic membership.

4.3   Types of Subcommunities

I distinguish two major types of Russian subcommunities: those with exclusive (only Russians) or inclusive (mixed with outsiders) membership. Subcommunities with both inclusive and exclusive ethnic membership assert their distinction and maintain their boundaries by fostering internal subcultures and by excluding non-members from their social circle (*Krug*). The mechanisms that hold these subcommunities together may combine friendship and practical need. Most subcommunity members congregate around a set of common issues or objectives.

Some of these subcommunities are more 'stable' than others. Some retain their membership for years, while others shift from one group to another. Thus,

I also identify 'stable' or 'shifting' subcommunities. Boundaries of stable communities are less penetrable, while shifting subcommunities are more open. Generally, older and more professionally established migrants tend to form stable subcommunities, while younger and illegal migrants form more shifting ones. The chapter on social relations explores the social dynamic of different groups of migrants in more detail.

It is also useful to make a distinction between 'intentional' and 'assigned' subcommunities. In the former case an individual chooses his social surrounding, while in the latter and far less common case he is chosen or made to fit unwillingly. 'Assigned' membership is usually bound with outsiders' judgements, as in the case of assigning a foreigner status to all the Russians or labelling all ethnically diverse migrants from the former Soviet Union as 'Russians'. An example of this is the Association of Russian Artists in Great Britain (ARAGB). Founded in 1998 in London, this organization included a group of Russians from different backgrounds. Peter Belyi, coordinator of ARAGB, acknowledged that these artists were brought together according to a broad concept of their 'Russianness'. The only reasons for uniting were some practical objectives the Association aimed to fulfil, such as exhibiting and selling their work, finding sponsors to help the artists establish their own gallery, as well as initiating a series of educational activities about Russian art. An individual may also find himself 'assigned' to a family and a group of friends acquired through fictitious marriage; and children may find themselves introduced into a parent's chosen circle of friends.[2]

We may further distinguish between large and small subcommunities. Large ones can usually be broken down into smaller subcommunities, as will be further exemplified by youth and intelligentsia subcommunities. Small communities may consist of two or more family units or individuals.

4.3.1 Inclusive Subcommunities

Although personal and migration histories of Russian inclusive subcommunity members are diverse, there are a number of features that characterize them in contrast to exclusive subcommunity members. I asked my informants to describe their social life both in Russia and in the receiving country. 'Friendship' and 'common interests' figure prominently in inclusive subcommunity members' priority lists. Members of inclusive subcommunities report changes in their social life caused by migration. They often evaluate it positively, as they manage to find new friends to share their interests with. Generally, inclusive subcommunity members are optimistic about the receiving country and society and more accepting of its values. As will be further discussed in the chapters on culture and ethnicity, although all Russians tend to reify their ethnicity and culture, their content and significance greatly varies. In the case of inclusive members, ethnic identity is not as important to them as, for example, a professional one.

In order to describe inclusive subcommunities we need to ask how they are formed: when did the subcommunity's members meet for the first time? What served as the basis for their relationship? And, how was this relationship maintained over time? Below I offer a few examples of small inclusive subcommunities.

Youth subcommunities cannot be easily defined or categorized. In the past, most of the literature on youth cultures concentrated on narrowly defined categories delineated by clear behavioural, style, or other social markers (Brake, 1985). Presently, it is widely accepted that youth, like other social actors, have multiple memberships in different groups and affiliate themselves with various individuals or institutions at different levels. Youth switch between various subcommunities and participate in different subcultures (Thornton, 1995). This is generally true of Russian youth in London and Amsterdam who often affiliate themselves with one or more subcultures present in the receiving country. At one level, we may speak of one large subcommunity of Russian youth; but we could also distinguish individual, smaller, inclusive subcommunities based on chosen subcultures.

The story of three friends, ages 16–18, serves as an example. The three arrived in The Netherlands in 1994, having come to visit one of the youths' families. Since then, they have stayed illegally, jointly renting an apartment in Amsterdam. The group dispersed a year ago. Two of the Russian youths joined an all-Dutch music band, while their Russian friend joined a soccer club. Although the three Russian youths still share an apartment and occasionally 'hang out' together, most of their social life evolves around their non-Russian music or sports groups.

As discussed earlier in this chapter, some occupational groups serve as an example of stable inclusive subcommunities. Workers report a greater sense of belonging to their work group rather than to their compatriots outside of work. Members of professional subcommunities reported close social ties with their colleagues and asserted the importance of professional values in their everyday life. In London, a group of IBM computer specialists, consisting of two Russians and five British, spend weekends and plan vacations together. Both of the Russians, Zhenya and Mark, arrived on working contract visas in 1997. They plan to return to Russia when their employment contract runs out in 2001. Meanwhile, they plan to retain close contact with their colleagues:

> Honestly, I don't have time or desire to socialize outside this circle, I came to Britain to work. In Russia I also used to go on holidays with my colleagues and my family, why change old habits? I learn a lot from my British colleagues, they learn from me. We even correct each other's English [laughs]. (Zhenya)

Zhenya does not distinguish between his Russian and British colleagues, except for the fact that they can 'learn from each other'. This positive attitude towards members of the host society is common not only within professional subcommunities, but also in those based on a common interest or hobby.

Two Russian musicians, Andrei and Dusya, assert that their friendship with a Dutch family is based on their love of jazz. They habitually meet at a jazz club in Amsterdam. Andrei worked at a construction site with other aspiring Dutch musicians; but the true friendship started after the discovery of the 'common ground'.

> We discovered that they [Dutch family] also visited New Orleans and like ourselves fell in love with the place. We all live in Holland but New Orleans is like our imaginary island, we all live there ... I guess sometimes you need some neutral common ground, not just Russia and Holland. [Dusya]

Andrei and Dusya organize their social and cultural life around jazz evenings, or gather at their other Dutch friends' apartments for private parties. They say that they feel 'at home' in Amsterdam as their interests or types of friends are not much different from those in Russia.

Many Russians, like Andrei and Dusya, find their social niche outside work. Of the five Russian artists working for the private gallery in London (along with three British and two Europeans), three said that they form friendships with non-Russians outside of their studios and their circles of friend. One of the artists, Zhora, explains:

> When I came here in 1994, I knew this one Russian guy; he invited me to work with them [for the gallery]. It's a nice working group, but I prefer to work on my own, my studio is my work place. Sometimes I go out with Lyosha or others, but usually I have my own friends to have drinks with. Most of them I met through my [British] girl-friend. I don't like to talk about what I do in the studio, so we talk about other things. I also don't like being in the all-Russian circles because, like some artists who talk only of their own art,

they only talk of Russia. I need more fresh air, I'm not just an artist or just a Russian. I learn about the country I now live in from the British and it gives me inspiration. (Zhora)

The choice of a subcommunity may depend on individual character. Another artist, Egor, who arrived in London in 1998 after a long period of country-hopping, is easy-going and sociable. He learned a few languages and finds any social environment acceptable 'as long as people are open and friendly'. Egor belongs to a number of subcommunities, including his own neighbours:

I'm friends with everybody who's friendly. I don't think artists are friendly. They are too individualist for that. If the British, whatever they do in life, are friendly to me, I'm friendly to them. I have wonderful neighbours where I live – three sets of neighbours, in fact. They all live a floor below me, but we tend to a common garden. They don't mind my music, they don't mind that I turned my apartment into a studio and that my turpentine leaks on their heads. I have a Russian roommate who is a street artist, so we invite our neighbours over to drink vodka. (Egor)

Egor also spends time with 'guys from the fitness club' with whom he goes to watch sports events. Sometimes he mixes a few groups of friends to watch home movies or to visit his exhibitions. Egor admits that these 'mixes' do not work too well, especially when the 'more than two' group of Russians is present – 'they tend to cluster together'. Egor also notices that his neighbours and 'guys from the fitness club' socialize together 'out of politeness' and disperse afterwards 'for the lack of common topics to pursue'. This may indicate two things: subcommunities are not limited to migrant groups; and subcultures contained within subcommunities prevent their members from 'mixing'.

Members of inclusive subcommunities might also find each other through institutions such as clubs, discos and restaurants. Veronika, who arrived in England in 1997, is a habitué of the Russian restaurant *Borsh I Slezy* in London, where she and her British husband met another 'mixed' couple:

We met this couple here in a restaurant, when they asked us about Russian food. Jim has a Russian wife; I have a British husband. We come here [to a restaurant] almost every week. We also visit each other at home. Sometimes we just watch TV together. Sometimes we go out for movies. We like food here; we know some people. It's nice to know other mixed couples ... having common concerns. (Veronika)

Veronika knows a few other mixed couples whose shared concerns include 'finding common language', adjusting gender roles, complying to divergent cultural expectations, reaching professional and social objectives in a different country, and bringing up bicultural children. Veronika herself met her husband while he was working in Moscow. She claims that it is only through her commitment to him that she learned to accept her new country of residence. She feels that her new social circle is as satisfying as the one she had in Russia. Veronika also knows a couple of Russian wives who feel that they do not share much in common with their husbands and prefer to socialize with each other, thus forming exclusive subcommunities.[3]

4.3.2 Exclusive Subcommunities

Exclusive subcommunities often recreate hierarchies and preferences distinguishing social groups in Russia. Except for the case of the habitués of *Oblomov* café in Amsterdam, or the congregations in churches in both London and Amsterdam, not many Russian subcommunities cross social class, economic and political status, and generational boundaries. It is rare to find a person who considers himself to be an intellectual in a group of disco lovers. Likewise, it is rare to find a teenager 'hanging out' with older Russians. Internally, exclusive subcommunities are bound by social networks and folklore exchange which often involves direct contact with Russia, and cultural initiation of the second generation.

The key distinguishing characteristic of an exclusive subcommunity is its all-Russian membership. Veronika's example of 'Russian wives' represents a large exclusive subcommunity. This group might then be broken down into smaller subcommunities, as not all Russian wives in London know or communicate with each other. Veronika personally knows of one group consisting of five to seven women (two are not 'as involved', according to Veronika) who live relatively close to each other in the region of South Kensington. All seven are married to British husbands and, for different reasons, are dissatisfied with their marriages. Reasons for dissatisfaction range from the frank admissions of 'I used him only to get to this country, otherwise he's nobody to me', to 'First we were in love; I came here for him; then we had problems, now we cannot work them out'. Some of the common problems these seven women face are social isolation (two women stated that they socialize with each other for the want of better company), lack of personal support and understanding, lack of romantic interest, and in five cases, lack of jobs. Three of these unemployed women desire to work and seek to improve their knowledge of English: one of them started taking English courses at London University, the other one watches English soap operas. Three women have children and feel that their relationship with the children suffers as a result of their dysfunctional marriage. Financial insecurity is an issue for all seven women, although two of them work and one of them claims to use her own money saved from Russia. One admits that she hangs on to her marriage because of the financial security her husband offers. Five women plan divorce 'as soon as circumstances permit', one is 'going to see', and the seventh is determined to 'make it work, no matter what'.

Besides dissatisfaction with their husbands, all of the women express dissatisfaction with certain social and cultural aspects of their environment – be it their husbands' boring friends or the lack of 'true high culture'. Six women express nostalgia and one says she wants to return to Russia. All of them see British culture as somewhat deficient in comparison to Russian culture, or find British people difficult to get along with (or even incomprehensible). These are also conversation topics the women share when assembling frequently at each other's homes (when husbands are absent) or parks and cafes. Being with each other provides them with company, sympathy, distance from their own problems, and a chance to learn coping skills by sharing and comparing their experiences. Also, through socializing, these women create a little world of their own. As one woman, Daryma, put it: 'We live in our own little Russia'. Interestingly, all seven women come from different places in the CIS and almost all of them admit that they probably would not have known each other – or wanted to know each other – were it not for their present circumstances. Daryma, formerly a school teacher, explains:

> I arrived here in 1995. In Uzbekistan, where I come from, I used to enjoy conversing with my colleagues. I had a good big family too. I had the respect of friends. We had a summer house, and we had relatives in Bashkyria, Azerbaijan and Turkmenia. In retrospect, I don't know why I left it all behind. And I guess that's what all of us are wondering about, that's what brings us all together: this sense that we are stupid women who left something good behind. (Daryma)

Another 'Russian wife', Zora, has been married for seven years (having met her husband in her native Kiev) and used to live in Liverpool with her husband until a year ago when he got a job in London. She used to be a textile specialist. Now she is unemployed and unwilling to work. She has a different explanation:

The truth of it is, we all hate our husbands. Just others wouldn't admit it. And the fact that we're friends here – well, it has nothing to do with immigration; it has all to do with the fact that we are not happily married. I had exactly the same conversations with other women when I was married in Russia. It's all the same ... (Zora)

Zora is interrupted by another woman, Agniya, who is married and has been living in London for two years. Agniya is studying English and taking courses in bookkeeping, her former occupation in Russia:

Of course it has all to do with immigration! We complain of our husbands because we're dissatisfied with everything else. Food is bad here. Climate is bad here. People are cold as frogs. But you know, we're all going to make it. We help each other to climb out of this mess and occupy a respectable place in this society ... (Agniya)

Respectable place! As if we're not respectable! I feel respectable. I felt respectable back home, why should I not feel respectable here? I still have my education, my son that I'm proud of, my looks, my wit – what are you complaining about? (Zora)

Such arguments frequently arise; new perceptions are offered and discarded, making for a lively and at times passionate conversation. Ira, another woman from Ukraine, formerly a hairdresser who works as an informal barber in London, sums up the feeling of belonging to a subcommunity, which the other three women present silently agree on:

Yeah, it's these conversations we're having, arguments and all: it helps somehow, it makes us feel at home again, pouring our souls out like that. It's not like we solve anything, but it ... it just feels good, talking things out and thinking that somebody understands. (Ira)

In a sense, these women create a 'subculture' based on common complaints.[4] Although their subcommunity is exclusive, it is almost 'assigned' (as most of them admit to 'being stuck with each other' for the lack of better options) and 'open' as the seven women would not mind expanding their social circle to include non-Russians or anybody who would be interested in their lives. However, when Ira brought in her British lover, the group rejected him as he 'did not fit in', possibly because this subcommunity had a strong gender base.

Sometimes, subcommunity members find themselves among their compatriots 'by accident' as in the case of teenage Russian rock musicians in

Amsterdam. Their band includes five members, all Russian, all under 20, all listening to particular kinds of music and attending the same musical events, gathering in particular bars, speaking in shared slang, sharing drugs. They see themselves as more innovative and open-minded than the older musicians they know, and more determined than their non-musical Russian peers. Although these teenage rockers have friends outside their own circle, these are rarely invited to participate in important events of the rockers' lives. The Dutch or the older generation are considered as outsiders as they do not share the groups' values and standards. Yet, all five come from diverse backgrounds: two have arrived individually – one after a period of country-hopping and street performing, another one straight from Russia. The three others came with their families at different times and from different cities. One of them, Sanya, explains:

> We came together as a kind of accident. First I met Goga: his mother and my mother were friends, found out that he also played guitars. We rehearsed together in the park when these two guys approached us, started talking to us in Dutch – one played drums, another one well, something he invented himself [laughs] … Turns out, they were Russian too, lived here for a while … They played well, so we decided to form a kind of band. Then we started looking for the vocalist and a lyrics writer and placed an ad in *Via Via* [Dutch advertisement newspaper]. Only two people replied and one of them was Shurik, he had a better voice. That's why we're all Russian, it just happened. Of course being all Russian makes it more fun too. We even wrote one Russian song, just for the kick of it … (Sanya)

Most exclusive subcommunities are formed less accidentally. Within exclusive subcommunities, most Amsterdam Russians admit to sharing a 'culture', although their definitions of this 'culture' are highly subjective and context-bound (see the chapters on culture and ethnicity). However, Russian culture is understood, be it through a 'high culture' of art and music, or because of common customs and habits, such as food or the organization of social events. It is compartmentalized into small 'circles' of friends, divided along the lines of class, age, gender or ethnicity.

Exclusive subcommunities can be quite large and can include an entire (perceived) class. Within such subcommunities, there are divisions that break this mega-subcommunity into smaller groups which nonetheless acknowledge belonging to a larger category. In the case of inclusive subcommunities, such formations are only possible when social class in the receiving country is perceived and accepted from both sides as similar to that in Russia (such as 'proletarian' or 'blue collar worker'). In the case of exclusive subcommunities, the reference point is Russian class (as discussed at the beginning of this chapter). An example of such an exclusive subcommunity is the intelligentsia.

The intelligentsia, members of which identify themselves as such, are present in both London and Amsterdam and share a number of values that give this large group a degree of coherence. Generally speaking, condescension towards 'lower art' is a hidden vice of the modern Russian intelligentsia. The intelligentsia in Russia tends to perceive itself separately from the proletarian, poorly educated masses[5] on the one hand, and from the corrupt bourgeois government elite which provides 'bread and circus' for the 'bottom' on the other hand. Russian intellectuals are averse to simple tastes and thoughtlessness which, as many intellectuals believe, are found in popular culture.

Intellectuals' ideals can best be understood in opposition to what used to be called Soviet ideology. These intellectuals proclaim liberal freedom, or Western style democracy, as an alternative to a faceless bureaucracy, the dullness of official 'communist goals', material wealth of those in power and their spiritual poverty, and the domestic routine of the 'simple Soviet family'. They value individualist as opposed to collective effort in the form of educational achievement, as well as political and moral commitment. Civilian duty for intellectuals comes not from an imposed sense of patriotism and pride in their land, but from a deep individual attachment to it. Love of the country comes through appreciation of the freedom and justice it issues, not because of its greatness. Intellectual dissidents (who composed a large proportion of the previous wave of migrants to the West in the 1970s) became known for their opposition to the Communist regime.

Migrants who are not considered intellectuals, however, may have a different opinion of the intelligentsia. As mentioned in the chapter on community, social antagonism is particularly sharp between members of the old (largely consisting of the intelligensia) and the new (generally branded 'economic') waves of migrants. Also, as will be further explored in the chapters on culture and ethnicity, strong mistrust exists between more 'integrated' (and often more educated and professional) members of inclusive subcommunities and exclusive members who try to maintain Russian values. It is not the case that the intellegentsia is always found within 'old waves' or 'integrated and professional' groups; but common perception among the migrants often places intellectuals within these categories and blames them for being arrogant, snobbish and unpatriotic. Aleftina, a housewife from London, reflected:

They [intellectuals] think they own Britain. Well, you know, I can tell you, they'll have no friends here if they need friends – they probably think they don't, they can do everything on their own, you know, like they are the kings here 'cause they have good jobs and stuff. They don't talk to us, simple mortals, they are ashamed of having come from the same country, they say, Russia's full of shit. Everybody's shit except for them, they are like diamonds in the rough, and now they'll sit with other diamonds, you know, all shiny and stuff. They say they like it here, like they are buddies with the Brits, you know, they don't need no Russians – they don't even drink. (Aleftina)

Intellectuals themselves may have experienced a sense of social isolation among the migrants during most of the 1990s and the beginning of the twenty-first century. Ruslan is a history professor working at the University of Amsterdam who arrived in The Netherlands in 1990 after spending ten years in Israel as a self-defined 'refugee for freedom'. He describes his sense of belonging to the intelligentsia:

At the time when I left Russia, my friends warned me that I might never find myself in the West as I'll lose touch with the ideals I stood for. What they meant was: I'll lose touch with them. And indeed, first months in Israel I felt lost, not just because it was Israel and it was different from Russia and there was no 'enemy' (at least, no Communism to fight) and my profession wasn't needed, but because I felt completely cut off from the social milieu which supported my work, my ideas, my ideals. After a while, I found a job teaching history, met other [Israeli] professors, but you know, still I didn't feel at home. These professors, educated, interesting, often admirable people – but they looked at me like I was some poor Russian villager who learned grammar by counting crows; and I looked at them – listened to their stories about Likud and Avoda [Israeli political parties] – and realised how foreign they were. Same here. I mean, I very much respect my colleagues and their work, I just feel that the only environment where I can be myself – except for the room where I study or teach – is with my old friends. That's why my friends here are few but dear. (Ruslan)

Grisha, a biologist from London, also recalls his Russian circle of friends as 'individuals truly committed to certain ideas and values'. He says this is something he cannot find in the West. Although the West provides freedom for intellectuals, it does not provide a context in which their 'subculture' is understood and valued. This is because, Grisha reflected, the West is 'oriented towards the future and does not reflect on the past'.

Exclusive subcommunities in general have a strong connection with the past and measure the present according to Russian standards. Even though nostalgia, dissatisfaction with the present, or aspirations for the future might not be shared by subcommunal members, the sense of deprivation or need created by migratory circumstances is conducive to the creation of close bonds.

Not all Russians are members of subcommunities, or at least not full members. In the previously mentioned group of Russian artists working for a private gallery in London, Lyosha is a self-proclaimed loner. He is nostalgic about his Russian past and tends to view his present social life more pragmatically if not cynically. In Russia he had a 'circle of soul mates' with whom he could share his ideas about art and life.[6] It is hard to assign Lyosha to a subcommunity as his interest in others shifts depending on his practical aims, and there are no central values around which his commitments are organized. Lyosha's social affiliations do not last since he keeps changing jobs and residences. Thus, he keeps hopping from one subcommunity to another. He chooses not to have Russian friends because, according to him, they are as badly off, being uprooted, as himself. Lyosha's position might exemplify a rare case of 'assigned' unstable membership:

> If I'm here I adapt; I speak English, I eat fish and chips. I don't really have friends, more like acquaintances and people I need, clients and such. I just get along with whomever I need to get along with. I do have a group I go out with. Yesterday I went for drinks with my [British] boss, his wife and a couple of their friends, non-artists. What did we discuss? Local ales, marriage ceremonies, I don't remember ... Ask Zhora. He also goes out with them ... Sometimes I get invited by people from [the studio]. So I go ... (Lyosha)

Most migrants, however, find themselves at least partially involved in subcommunities. The following section on boundaries aims to show how subcommunities are sustained over time, and how they recruit or exclude individuals 'from the outside'.

4.3.3 How are Subcommunal Boundaries Drawn and Maintained?

Russian and mixed subcommunities represent something of a miniature model of the 'communities' as defined in the chapter on that topic. In the case of exclusive subcommunities, boundary maintenance may require intentional exaggeration of culture and ethnicity to assert a group's values in contrast with those of the receiving society. As I shall argue in the chapters on culture and ethnicity, said characteristics are often reified and magnified in opposition to the host culture or as a reaction to external labelling. To counteract the danger of losing one's cultural or ethnic identity, members of exclusive subcommunities tend to accentuate cultural differences while underplaying the similarities (Verkuyten, 1997: 114).[7]

Boundary maintenance also depends upon self-classification of members of subcommunities. In cognitive theories, every category presupposes the existence of 'ideal types' which are thought to be more representative of the category than less 'typical' members.[8] 'Ideal types' in subcommunities possess a list of 'typical' characteristics while more marginal members possess only a few of the 'representative' characteristics of their subcommunity. As in the above example of the intelligentsia, a subcommunity whose members share a particular set of values and attributes would likely judge others on the basis of possession or lack of those characteristics. Some people may be perceived as more or less 'intellectual' according to the group's standards. For example, those who study medicine and cannot talk about art and poetry might be categorized more as professionals or specialists rather than intellectuals. Similarly, a 'Russian wife' who has married to acquire foreign citizenship, and yet loves her husband, is not representative of the stereotypical 'fictionally married Russian wife' category. In the previously mentioned case of seven Russian women married to the British, only one was formally employed. She felt that, despite the expressed desire of others to find jobs, they thought of her as different. The employed woman felt that it was the 'feeling of envy and the need to complain and be pitied' that united six unemployed women, making them more 'ideal' for the group than her.

No matter how a medic or a Russian woman categorize themselves, they cannot help being labelled by the group they are in or want to be members of. Because they do not share all of the group's values, this group may mistrust them. At the same time, they might be better fit to join another group (like other doctors or other loving spouses). This makes an art-ignorant doctor or loving arranged-marriage spouse into what I call 'liminal members of subcommunities'. By virtue of their intercommunal positioning, these individuals are well suited for crossing subcommunal boundaries. Armen, an Armenian from Ukraine living in London, finds his ethnic liminality frustrating, while admitting that his 'in-between' positioning has helped him in business:

> As an Armenian from Ukraine, I'm already what you might call displaced, and now I'm here, Armenian from Ukraine in the UK, so I'm even more displaced … The funny thing is, neither the Armenians, nor the Ukrainians, nor the Russians – not to mention the British – consider me to be one of them, I'm a refugee in any country. It gives me certain advantages though, as I often serve

as a kind of buffer in business, or a kind of neutral party, a messenger you might say – but now my business is gone, and neither Russians nor Armenians nor British will help me. (Armen)

Liminal members can also become dual members, adhering to two subcommunities at once. We have previously mentioned the case of three Russian friends who share an apartment and occasionally go out together, while two of them play in the band, and a third one has joined a soccer club. When I met them for the first time, they spoke of themselves as 'best buddies' and invited me to 'their home'. But when interviewed individually, they admitted that their 'true friends' were at the sports club or in the band. Such duality is very common as many migrants may belong to professional, neighbourly, religious, or interest-related subcommunities (among others), considering their membership equally important and being considered by other members as more or less committed to their group. Both liminal and dual members can convey information about other subcommunities. But what is the role of 'liminal' and 'dual' members in mediating subcommunal boundaries?

Let us take Slava, a car salesman from Amsterdam, as an example of a 'dual member'. Slava considers himself to be a 'businessman' and says he has 'connections' with other 'businessmen', especially those selling cars supposedly bought (or, more likely, stolen) in Germany. Sometimes, these 'businessmen' drive their cars together to Russia for a sale. This also involves bribing the Russian customs agents, and a couple of other 'business tricks'. 'Businessmen' often help each other with practical advice and 'exchange clients'. This particular group of 'businessmen' is based in Germany. They trade with St Petersburg. Slava lives in Amsterdam and drives to a village close to St Petersburg where he claims to have a special agent. Unlike other 'businessmen', who are in their early twenties and did not have a career before selling cars, Slava, who is in his late thirties, used to be a linguist. Having met me, he got interested in my research, saying that it is related to his own interest in bilingual migrants. He knows some linguistic lecturers at the University of Amsterdam. Indeed, through Slava, I met two linguists – one Dutch and one Russian – who assured me that Slava was, indeed, quite knowledgeable in their field. They confirmed that sometimes Slava attends linguistic seminars and enters into academic discussions. Slava also goes out for drinks with the Russian lecturer who states that they have 'interesting intellectual discussions' about the specifics of their subject. I have also interviewed two of Slava's business acquaintances and found out that he is quite knowledgeable in their line of work as well. So, which subcommunity does Slava belong to? As he himself says, to neither one completely and to both at the same time. Both the university lecturers and the 'businessmen' know about Slava's divided loyalties. Neither of the parties knows much or has much interest in the other, except for Slava himself. Once Slava invited both a Russian linguist and his 'business partners' to his birthday party which, he admits, turned into a disaster:

> The guys ['businessmen'] like talking rough, they use slang, they are young, you know, they leave their beards to grow. And there's this cleanly shaved neat university professor who spent half of his life here [in The Netherlands] and doesn't even understand their slang. So he just sat there in the corner eating his chicken … But I thought it was worth trying … (Slava)

Similar to the case of Egor's 'guys from the fitness club' and his neighbours, Slava's birthday party shows that social classes and subcultures upon which 'academic' and 'business' subcommunities are based refuse to mix. Through coming into direct contact with each other, members of subcommunities reinforce and exaggerate the boundary, as Slava continues his story:

> You'd think: all of them Russian, here's vodka, just drink to the bottom. But no, no. After a while the guys started cracking jokes about smart professors and the like, and my friend whispered to me that he couldn't stand those types any longer and had to excuse himself and left. It's like they represent the worst of the uneducated masses for him. And for them, I guess, he was a kind of social bore, an arrogant ass in thick glasses who hates working people. It was like a revolution in my very apartment [laughs], only here the proletariat didn't join the educators. (Slava)

Slava may be described as more of a liminal rather than dual member, unlike Egor, whose friends on both sides do not seem to be openly antagonistic to each other and do not try to dissuade him from associating with members of another group. However, both liminal and dual members act as mediators by bringing together divergent subcommunities and unwillingly causing discomfort or even confrontation, which may affect their own standing in the group. Generally, liminal or dual members stand little chance of being seen as 'ideal types' since their loyalties are conspicuously divided. Subcommunity boundary is maintained through social distancing and no mediation from the 'liminal' or 'dual' members can erase the gap. Instead, the gap is accentuated by forced contact. Antagonism, which is both caused by and expresses itself through mutual mistrust, gossip, social class, and ethnic and generational rivalries, helps to maintain subcommunal boundaries.

Dual members can also serve as sources of information about another subcommunity. Seen as shuttling agents, dual members may also be asked to deliver messages or arrange practical deals across subcommunities without actually dissolving or blurring the borders. Social networks between subcommunities become operational through dual members. Once, Egor was asked by Vassily, one of the illegal, working Russian artists exhibiting at his gallery, to find him a British 'sponsor' who would falsely certify that the Russian artist was temporarily working for him. Egor contacted his British fitness club friends and his neighbours and soon found a sponsor willing to vouch that Vassily was in London for temporary business. Egor reflected that Vassily (who did not speak English) was normally condescending towards Egor's British friends and did not understand why Egor spent time with them. After the arrangement, he realized that such friends can 'come in handy', while remaining personally aloof from them. When Vassily gave a birthday party, inviting all of his Russian friends (mostly artists), Egor brought Vassily's British 'sponsor' along. Vassily was so displeased that he refused to offer the man a drink and did not introduce him to any of his Russian company. Later, Vassily reflected that he did not like to 'mix business with pleasure'. He felt that the presence of somebody from the 'business world' at his 'personal party' was a definite violation of boundaries. Boundary maintenance can thus include social exclusion. In Vassily's case, his lack of hospitality backfired, as the 'sponsor' took offence and refused to 'extend' the fake contract to Vassily. At that point, the Russian artist proudly departed back to Ukraine, only to reappear in Britain a few weeks later. This time, he was travelling on a French visa. Vassily, a stubborn member of an exclusive subcommunity of Russian artists, continues to maintain contact with Egor, considering his friend 'confused' at best, and at worst, a 'traitor to Russian values'.

Vassily's extreme nationalism is rare, but many members of exclusive subcommunities do find it more difficult to maintain their boundaries without harsh measures of social exclusion. Another popular method of maintaining the boundary is through the previously discussed example of fostering a subculture within an exclusive subcommunity. Close contact with the country of origin is the main source of maintaining and renewing subcultures. Since exclusive subcommunities often retain old hierarchies, contact with the CIS assures its members of their group's authenticity. It therefore reinforces the boundary with other exclusive subcommunities. Such contact may counteract external assignment when the migrants are lumped together as 'Russians', while they might prefer to distinguish themselves along ethnic or regional lines. In Amsterdam, I knew of a group of Georgians who would assemble together (excluding other 'Russian' friends) to consume food and beverages brought over by one of their commuting friends and family members. They gathered 'to dance and sing and joke' the way they used to do in Georgia. Practically all of these Georgians were also dual exclusive members as they also had non-Georgian 'Russian' friends with whom they socialized on less ethnically coloured occasions.

For exclusive subcommunities, the belief in the authenticity of their group might be the only mechanism that keeps other exclusive groups from blending together. Thus, continuity between groups in Russia and subcommunities abroad is maintained and continuously reinforced. This ensures safe passage for new arrivals through trusted promises of work or other forms of social support by members of the resident subcommunity. Commuting between the CIS and the receiving country has an important social function, as the constant flow of information ensures that friends and family members visiting from the CIS are introduced into the subcommunities and easily accepted.

All subcommunities share a preoccupation with boundary maintenance. They uphold their boundaries by accentuating the internal coherence of the group, by essentializing its values, and by asserting its own uniqueness. At times, they also employ social exclusion. Although individual members may try to bridge the divides, their efforts usually have the opposite effect, bringing constructed differences between subcommunities into sharp relief.

4.3.4 Note on Comparison between London and Amsterdam Subcommunities

In the Introduction, I outlined a number of similarities between the Russians in London and Amsterdam, including their relatively small numbers, lack of established communities, geographical dispersion and social distance. Yet, there are also significant differences between the Russian populations in both cities. Not surprisingly, subcommunities in London tend to be larger than those in Amsterdam, apparently because of the relatively greater number of Russians present in London (see Appendix 1 for statistics in London and Amsterdam). While many of London's subcommunities have exclusive membership, those in Amsterdam tend to be more inclusive. Subcommunities in London may therefore be described as more negative towards outsiders and internally more coherent. The latter phenomenon might be caused by the fact that there are fewer Russians living in Amsterdam, thus encouraging those present to 'mix' more. There are also more institutions conducive to exclusive socialization in London (such as Russian clubs, churches, Russian discos, etc.), while in Amsterdam, the largest Orthodox church, as well as two Russian café/restaurants, welcome an international public.

I found that Amsterdam Russians exhibited more 'negativity' in their relationships, especially between exclusive subcommunities. I find it plausible to speculate, on the basis of my interviews, that this has to do with paradoxical effects of geographic proximity: the closer the contacts between members of sub-communities, the more enmity and irritation they generate. It is also possible that since the all-Russian 'pool' in Amsterdam is so small, members of subcommunities know each other and cannot avoid unlikely contacts as easily as in London. There is also a larger proportion of liminal members in Amsterdam.

Social networking among exclusive subcommunities is minimal in Amsterdam, while particular kinds of networking – practical or functional – are very much present in London. In most cases in Amsterdam, when my informants needed practical help (such as finding a job or looking for housing) they addressed the Dutch responsible authorities or their friends (since most subcommunities in Amsterdam are inclusive, friends are often non-Russian). Only a very few exclusive subcommunities, particularly in London, can afford to be self-sufficient. In Amsterdam, these subcommunities are not large or powerful enough, and have to depend, at least in part, on outside assistance. In London, many of my informants obtained information about 'where to start, where to go, whom to ask, what to do'. They were even able to find housing or employment directly through members of the subcommunity they belonged to, or through other subcommunities which they contacted via liminal members. As my London informant put it: 'It's not my city – how would I have known whom to go to for a job if my friends didn't help me?' One possible explanation for such a difference might be the same geographic distance. In London, greater space might be conducive to more tolerance between the groups. Secondly, in London – the larger city – competition for jobs and housing is more spread out and Russians (as the same London informant put it) 'do not feel like they are stepping on each other's toes'. A third explanation may lie in the fact that the Dutch social services are more comprehensible and helpful than those in England. Although I find this explanation most plausible, my informants' statements seem to indicate that they are dissatisfied with social services both in London and in Amsterdam.

It appears that subcommunities are more relevant than 'community' when describing the Russians in London and Amsterdam, as subcommunities are more revealing of the diversity and stratification of the migrants. Subcommunities allow us to visualize geographically and socially dispersed groups of migrants, simultaneously specifying characteristics, interests and social relationships that hold these fractured groups together. Subcommunities also reveal the way Russian migrants fit within the host society. Subcommunities often function as miniature communities (insofar as the term is understood by the Russians themselves). Subcommunities do not constitute a community, but replicate and imitate it by which they simultaneously reaffirm and negate a community.

Subcommunities are not unique to Russian migrants (for example, Egor's British middle-class neighbours not willing to socialize with his British friends from the fitness club) or to other migrant groups (for example, the case of Hindu Punjabis described by Raj (1997),[9] where the presence of 'smaller social groups, cliques or "circles of friends"' challenges the unity of 'community'). Yet, Russian subcommunities exhibit a number of unique features, such as their strong emphasis on occupational subcultures (perhaps inherited from the Soviet *kollektiv*), and their sharply pronounced antagonism between Russian social classes (such as the broadly defined intelligencia and those seen as non-intellectuals – categories generally seen to divide members of the 'old political and cultural' and 'new economic' waves of Russian migrants).

Notes

1   These changes will be further explored in the chapters on culture and ethnicity and social networks.
2   Hechter speaks of 'intentional communities' where 'retaining members in succeeding generations is a different task because, unlike their parents, the children do not voluntarily choose to become members ... Perhaps the most common mechanism of preference-formation in such communities is the systematic limitation and distortion of information about alternatives existing beyond the group's boundaries ... The status and style of life of parents in all such groups depend on the continued existence of their communities ... Most urban ethnic and racial groups do not persist for these reasons. Few parents in such groups are as strongly motivated to keep their children by their side as are parents in the intentional community' (Hechter, 1996: 96–7).
3   There are many articles in anthropological as well as popular literature about the 'Russian wives': 'Russian women in search of security, especially those with young children, for whom prospects are particularly bleak, are in demand as accommodating, non-feminist wives to predominantly aging, divorced Western men. Declaring their solvent financial status, men such as these seek attractive women ten, twenty, even forty years their junior. In the West, men in their fifties and sixties with glamorous companions in their twenties are usually in possession of a very fat wallet indeed. The fact that Mr Average from an uninspiring provincial town feels he can aspire to a partner such as this, especially when so many of these potential Russian brides are highly educated, says a great deal about the buying power of Western currencies in Russia and gives the lie to all the talk of romance

which surrounds this issue' (Bridger and Kay, 1996: 34–5); 'In the post-*interdevochka* era, however, the revelation that a large number of women (who have had no choice but to carry on living with their former husbands in the same flat for years after divorce) dream of finding a foreign husband and leaving, are tempered by warnings that such marriages do not always bring the happiness they promise. One woman, it was reported, returned to Russia after marrying an Englishman who taught her English politeness by hitting her every time she forgot to say "thank you", while a woman who married a Canadian was subsequently abandoned …' (Pilkington, 1992: 208). Darieva (1998) discusses Russian wives in Germany, O'Connor (1997) in Britain, Siegel in Israel (1998). Most of the articles on Russian wives, however, are written from a feminist perspective, blaming Western men for their presumed misery and presenting Russian women as innocent victims.

In my experience, 'Russian wives' in the West openly advertise the fact that they have married 'that old goat' for money and most of them are eagerly waiting to receive their 'papers' (permits to stay in the West through marriage) to divorce their husbands – granted that they could also inherit a bit of the wealthy lifestyle with the divorce settlement. There might well be other cases I have not recorded because of the selection bias.

Nor are most Russian prostitutes lured into the West by false promises of work in cafes, as the media has it – most of them are well aware of the kind of work awaiting them. There is indeed a very serious problem of human trafficking. Yet, my research did not reveal patterns of domination and abuse usually associated (at least in the media) with this phenomenon. I have had a number of heated discussions with (mostly Western female) scholars about the motivation and prior awareness of Russian women who become (or continue to be) prostitutes in the West. I was asked by a few of my learned opponents to acknowledge the fact that there exists an inherent inequality in the relationship between the Western client and the Russian woman. I can only say to that that there also exists an inherent inequality between *any* prostitute and her (or his!) client, as well as between any (illegal) migrant – female or male – and a 'resident' employer. In the case of my respondents, I did not find any explicit evidence of the fact that these individuals were either misinformed, victimized, abused or misused (I did not question the truth value of their narratives or the accuracy of their prior motives any more than I did in the case of other respondents). The opposite might well be the case of those I have not interviews – the cases of suffering victims of human traffickers need to be further explored (although they *are* already widely represented in the media. Feminist interpretation of Russian gender often uses vocabulary evoking oppression, domination and injustice, thus revealing the researcher's ideological bias and leading to sloppy empirical work.

4   'The crucial condition for the emergence of new cultural forms is the existence, in the effective interaction with one another, of a number of actors with similar problems of adjustment. These may be the entire membership of a group or only certain members, similarly circumstanced, within a group' (Cohen, 1997: 48).

5   Although historically we see that the intelligentsia, educated elite, was often seen on the side of the poor and oppressed, as seen through the writings of great Russian writers, such as Tolstoi, Dostoevskii, Turgeniev; and through political movements fuelled by the intelligentsia, from Decembrists and Populists to the Red October.

6   For a more extended discussion on friendship, see the chapter on social networks.

7   Examples of these exaggerations are given in the chapter on culture and ethnicity.

8   Thus, if flying is one of the central characteristics of birds, a pigeon might be more representative of the category 'birds' than a penguin or ostrich.

9   See the chapter on community.

Chapter 5

Social Networks and Informal Economic Activity

Introduction

This chapter aims to address the issue of informal ties and networks created by migrants who bring expectations from one social context to another, and have to devise new strategies to cope with new situations.

Economic sociology theories, particularly those based on the works on Granovetter (1973), suggest that concepts such as the 'strength of weak ties' and 'social embeddedness' work for social formations in developed capitalist countries. However, these terms may also be applied to those with a Soviet past. The 'social embeddedness' of Russian migrants rests in part on (Soviet) state-enforced policies, and both the individual and collective reactions to them. Russian migrants, having learned that economic survival can be provided from social channels outside a state control apparatus, also found their new country of residence as conducive to developing ties that help them overcome a lack of state provisions. This is especially true in the illegal migrants' case. Bauböck (1994), Portes et al. (1999) and Kloosterman and Rath (2002) have pointed out that migrants resort to extensive use of social networks to compensate for the lack of official support channels. They also use these networks to recreate the type of social embeddedness known in their home country, thereby creating security nets and informal support channels necessary for survival in a foreign country. We may also speak of migrants involved in global or transnational networks, involving not only the countries of origin and destination, but other locations as well. This would include, for instance, places where the migrants' friends or family (or even the migrants themselves) may have been. As Rouse (2002) argues in his study of Mexican migrants in the United States, modern migrants do not simply abandon one country for another. Rather, they form a community that stretches across national boundaries due to continuous circulation of people, capital, goods and ideas. Rouse terms these migrants 'cultural bifocals' who belong simultaneously to more than one home and to no home in particular (Rouse, 2002: 157).

Transnationalism, a godchild of globalization, is often metaphorized ('Disenchanted world', 'Age of Connexity', 'Runaway world', 'Global village/ pillage' etc.) and described as a state of global interconnectiveness in spatial form of social relations, involving a new form of organization and exercise of power at a global scale (Held, 2000: 15), has an influence on global labour movements. Vertovec (2003) defines *transnationalism* as a set of sustained, border-crossing connections. He specifies a number of previously identified typologies, based on binary distinctions such as 'transnationalism from above' and 'transnationalism from below' (Smith and Guarnizo, 1998); 'narrow' and 'broad' (Itzigsohn et al., 1999), etc. Vertovec discusses transnationalism mostly in terms of migration, particularly addressing the question of what is new about transnationalism. Vertovec relies on Portes et al. (1999), arguing that movements of migrants and the networks they built 100 years ago were not truly transnational in terms of 'real time' social contact. 'Rather, such earlier links were just border-crossing migrant networks that were maintained in piecemeal fashion as best as migrants at that time could manage' (Vertovec, 2003: 3).

There is, increasingly, a process of globalization of specialty labour. That is, not only highly skilled labour, but labour which becomes exceptionally high in demand around the world and, therefore, will not follow the usual rules in terms of immigration laws, wages or working conditions (Castells, 2000b). As a result, new categories of transnational migrants have emerged. Among others, these are unskilled labour migrants, undocumented migrants and highly skilled workers (Vertovec, 2002) – particularly IT workers employed through global 'body shopping' as termed by Xiang (2001). Also included are trained occupational specialists drawn back from their diasporas to contribute to the development of their homelands (Meyer and Brown, 1999). In my sample, Russian migrants exemplified such transnational networks, but also added somewhat of a 'typical Russian' flavour to the concept of social network.

In the present-day CIS, following the Soviet heritage, Russians often rely on informal relations enacted through *blat* (connections), bribes and gifts instead of using official or legal channels, as these channels are usually ineffective or untrustworthy in Russia (Gray, 1994; Humphrey, 1996/97; Ledeneva, 1996; Pilkington, 1996a). When Russians arrive in Britain or The Netherlands, they are initially inclined to use these informal methods for obtaining legal status, education and medical care, or housing and employment. The experience of living in a Western country, however, often proves that these informal methods are ineffective, especially when long-term provisions, like legal status or professional employment, are sought. Still, some of these informal methods prove useful in providing the migrants with lesser benefits like social support, short-term housing and employment. It is these methods and networks that I analyse in this chapter.

For the illegals, these benefits may fully provide them with means of subsistence and with the motivation to stay on, despite the lack of long-term prospects (Engbersen et al, 1999; Van der Leun, 2000). For legal migrants, informal social relations may offer emotional support for those who experience social isolation, like professional individuals or families staying on a work contract, senior citizens or spouses of Western nationals. These informal support channels are not necessarily exclusively Russian, and may also be used to facilitate integration into the receiving country.

Thus, while some informal methods inherited from the CIS are used by illegal migrants, most legal migrants have learned not to rely on *blat*, bribes and the informal economy. They do nonetheless participate in social networks. Social relations and the informal economy are culturally important to Russian migrants. Yet while some of these informal methods become obsolete under Western conditions, others remain vital, and still others evolve to fit new situations. This evolution is exemplified by the changing patterns of gift-giving within the informal economy, expectations of friendship, and rules of reciprocity within social networks.

I shall start this chapter with a description of informal economic activity, focusing upon the differences between economic activity in the CIS and Western Europe in practices of business, bribes, barter and gift exchange. Discussion of informal economic activity leads into the sections on social relations and networks used by the migrants. Sections on typology of migrants, based on Doomernik's (1997) classification of migrants according to their level of integration and Bourdieu's (1992) theory of social capital, reveal individual differences in the use of the informal economy and social networks.

5.1   Informal Economic Activity

5.1.1 Business, Bribes and Barter

In order to understand the significance of economic activity for Russians in London and Amsterdam, we must first look at the informal economy's place in Russian culture.

Consistent with the heritage of the Soviet past, when Russians experienced a deficit of goods and services, the present-day CIS lacks political and economic stability. This breeds mistrust of its citizens in the government's provisions (Humphrey, 1996/97; Ledeneva, 1996; Malia 1994). People learned to adapt to the unpredictability and harshness of their everyday existence through exploiting their social connections in order to obtain necessary goods and services. Having developed moral and practical ability in the private sphere in opposition to the strict rules of the public sphere, cheating the system by resorting to deception and manipulation of official rules was common for Soviet, as well as contemporary, CIS citizens (Yurchak, 1997).

Most of the newly emerging businesses in the CIS are not officially registered in order to avoid taxation and other forms of government control. Often, a kind of 'security tax' is paid to semi-criminal organizations for 'protection' from both competitors and other criminals. Many small Russian businesses are privately owned and self-regulating.

During my fieldwork in Russia and Belorussia, I noticed that, despite the fact that money could buy anything (and the assortment of goods on sale was just as wide as in London and Amsterdam), people still traded goods (which were, for example, stolen from the factories they worked for) and services (for example, by unofficial payment to ensure successful medical procedure). While Russians in the CIS are wary of barter as an archaic form of transaction necessitated by economic hardship, they also look at barter as an acceptable and sometimes desirable form of 'goodwill exchange'.[1]

Bribery is equally widespread and involves literally every layer of society. In Minsk and Grodno, Belorussia, I recorded a number of interviews about the bribes given to plumbers, doctors, university administrators, police, military school officials and others in order to insure the quality of service these professionals or officials are supposed to provide, or to manipulate official rules in one's favour. Bribery was considered commonplace and absolutely necessary in the harsh economic conditions and general state of corruption. These kinds of informal transactions are not officially registered, and are thus control-free and tax-free. They persist in London and Amsterdam, but their scale and influence are subject to change.

Informal business Informal business in London and Amsterdam ranges from criminal smuggling operations (including women and refugees) to flower sales. Most informal business functions like any other business, except that it is unregistered and its owners do not pay taxes or officially advertise. Instead, they find their clientele by word-of-mouth. Initially, some migrants become encouraged by the success of certain Russian informal businesses and speak of grand plans for opening firms and providing services for all sectors of the population. But, after a couple of months in the receiving countries, very few of them hope to realize their ambitions. The businesses that do take off are usually small and inconspicuous, and it took me months of fieldwork to actually talk to the owners of some of them. Some of these businesses are informally owned by illegal migrants who either invest money in them or personally run the business (although it is registered in the legal name of a Russian or non-Russian who gets part of the profit).

In London, I encountered a number of individuals offering unregistered services, ranging from beauticians to acupuncturists. The clientele for these services, both Russian and British, was recruited by recommendation and by word-of-mouth. The largest unregistered business involved a massage parlour, whose anonymous Russian owner (employees refused to give me his or her name) employed five Russian masseurs and received supplies, such as cots, towels and massage oil, from Russia. Masha, one of the employees of this business, complained of a lack of security:

> We work normal hours, we get paid regularly … The problem is, you never know when the axe is going to fall … In Kazan you could just bribe a couple of guys [criminal protectors and police] and you had nothing to worry about, business is business. Here I have to wonder when we'll close [using the word *nakryty*, meaning both 'covered' or 'closed' and 'discovered']. (Masha)

In Amsterdam, some of 'Russian cafes', registered in the names of Dutch 'sponsors' and run by Russians, were temporarily opened only to close a few months later (apparently after police warnings, as most of them also ran drug businesses). A recently failed venture (1999) included the ostentatious opening of a wine bar in the cellar of a coffee shop (soft drug retailer). The shop was rumoured to be 'sponsored' by two Armenians who operated the business from their own country, having employed local Armenians to actually run the business. The bar relinquished its wine selection within weeks of opening, turned into another coffee shop, and was closed soon thereafter. Pavel, a former wine/coffee shop employer – presently unemployed and illegal – remarked:

> I knew it wouldn't end well. The Dutch are too sneaky; they smell these things out in no time … We should have opened up somewhere in Utrecht [smaller Dutch town], here in Amsterdam they [the authorities] are trained like beagles in airports [to sniff out drugs] … On the bright side, I've got more money in two months working there than in a year doing the Dutch peoples' wallpaper [working in home repairs]. (Pavel)

The insecurity expressed by Masha and Pavel is reflected in most of the informal business employees' stories. It stems from both their mistrust of the owners who might 'bail out' at any time, and the authorities, who might discover illegal employers or operations. This situation is often in contrast to the relative ease of running an illegal business in the CIS, provided one pays for 'protection' and bribes the authorities.

Nikita, a legal owner of an antique shop in London (specializing in Russian icons and czarist memorabilia), told me that the only way to do 'serious business' in the West is to do it 'the Western way' – unless you are a 'downright criminal', which is an 'altogether different category'. Nikita admitted to having bartered and bribed in Russia in order to acquire his collection of Russian antiques, but was proud to have a 'clean business' in London. Nikita also reflected that for Russians without a legal status, 'clean business' may not be an option. Among the legal Russian businessmen he knew, all of them have chosen the 'straight road'.

Vitya, a travel agency co-owner in Amsterdam, complements this view. He testifies that, while in his native Kiev, he could make profit by 'organizing informal tours abroad' (working for an official domestic travel agent in Ukraine). He could only start earning 'serious money' in Amsterdam after receiving a work permit and taking on legal business.

Bribes   Many Russians reported trying to approach English or Dutch officials 'informally' – by offering gifts. They were surprised by the 'lack of understanding' in the best cases, and a 'call for authorities to intervene' in the worst. Still, some migrants reported success with bribes in matters of relatively small significance, like getting first class tickets on overbooked flights or raising their child's exam grade at school.[2]

However, significant matters, like getting political status or legal protection in the receiving countries, could not be solved by a bribe. Most Russians gave up bribery after living in the receiving country for a number of months. Aleftina, a former accountant and presently a housewife from London, noted regrettably:

> Connections worked in Russia, but they don't work the same way here. I cannot just ask my friend Manya the name of her [immigration] lawyer and the amount he'd like to receive in order to get me a [permanent] status here and a divorce from my husband … Here, lawyers have established fees and give no guarantees of success. (Aleftina)

Bribery is still used within exclusive subcommunities, but it is also modest in scale. Bulat – a former garage owner in Georgia, now unemployed in London – bribed his Georgian friend Erik to introduce him to an 'eligible British woman' (for a fictitious marriage). Bulat referred to the sum of one hundred pounds as a bribe, not a 'gift'. Yet Erik spoke of it as such (the woman in question knew about the arrangement and the money did not induce Erik to act dishonestly, as the bribe would). Bulat felt that it was a bribe since 'this woman was Erik's business associate, and I paid in money, and when you offer money for something related to business it's a bribe'. Since the match did not work out, Bulat asked for his money back and Erik refused, which ended their friendship.

The borderline between gift-giving and bribery is not always clear, even when the transacting parties are both Russian. In my consequent conversation with Bulat, he insisted that Erik 'would be put to shame' in his own country. He implied that Erik's refusal to refund the money for an unsuccessful transaction would not be socially acceptable in Georgia.

Because of the migratory experience that influences expectations and patterns of reciprocity established in the CIS, social relations and expectations become confused. Generally, attitudes towards bribery seem to change as the migrant spends more time in the West. Still, the habit remains, and proves useful in certain cases involving petty transactions.

Barter Like bribery, barter is used only in small-scale transactions in London and Amsterdam. They involve non-Russians as well as Russians. A housewife from London, Aleftina, recalls:

> When I came here, I didn't know too many people and missed company. One day my [English] neighbour noticed that I was knitting, so she asked me whether I wanted to knit a sweater for her son. I refused to take her money, because I did it just for the sake of friendship, so she gave me a box of Christmas cards that her friend makes for her charity … That gave me an idea and I started knitting for more people I knew, refusing money but getting something else in return …

Aleftina herself reflects that this arrangement is 'good enough to provide me with something to do and an opportunity to meet new people'. In Russia, she knitted in exchange for other goods. This provided her with basic necessities, especially at the beginning of the 1990s when the Russian rouble completely devalued and food shortages became commonplace. In London, Aleftina depends on her husband's income and considers barter a social rather than economic activity.

In Amsterdam, I met a woman who became an 'informal barber', as she called herself. Instead of charging her clients (mostly Russians), she accepted their 'gifts', which ranged from chocolates to perfume. She had a paid job in the café and 'earned enough to afford to do some services for the community' (Sofia). Having come from the small town of Uglich, Sofia remembered the time when money 'just wasn't around' and her barber skills 'provided food and clothing' for her family.

I have heard of a group of small businessmen in Amsterdam who exchange their products (car parts and mobile phones, all supposedly 'imported' from Russia) and were thinking of opening a 'joint company'. However, the group diffused within a year when, according to local gossip, a violent fight broke out among the barter partners. In my interview with one of the 'close associates', I was told that he 'would give up barter all together' seeing it as archaic and unsuitable for 'modern conditions'.

5.1.2 Reciprocity and Gift Exchange

Offering favours Informal exchanges take place between the migrants themselves, and between the migrants and members of the host society. The latter sometimes creates room for misunderstanding and 'teaches' the migrants about Western values and expectations.

Generally vulnerable and dependent, many illegals cannot get an asylum seeker's status in the receiving country nor temporarily return to the CIS because, having once been illegal, they will not be allowed back into the receiving country. Dina, an engineer from Georgia who now does odd jobs in Amsterdam, found herself unable to visit her family in Tbilisi even for her father's funeral. She was afraid that she would not be able to return to The Netherlands, and that she would lose the only source of income she could provide for her impoverished family. Dina describes *okaziya* (literally, 'a chance to transfer something abroad' – a person travelling to the CIS willing to take on luggage or money for the migrant's family), a Dutch friend who went to Georgia and transferred a package of goods to her family.

> I bought a tape recorder and a number of new clothes for them … It's not something they really need, but it's very different from money I've been sending. They complained that instead of money they wanted to see me … I recorded a tape, like a letter, so that they can listen to it – they sold their

record player a long time ago … I bought more tapes – beautiful music, should cheer them up. And clothes – they sent me their pictures, they are still wearing the same old rags. They say that since there's no electricity most of the time, nobody would see them during the evening, and during the day they stay at home […] The fact that Richard [Dutch friend] is going – well it's like a miracle. It's the first time somebody I trust goes to Georgia in four years. It's so noble of him! (Dina)

Richard reported that Dina's family was indeed in dire financial need. They were touched to tears when he made his delivery, which 'took up two thirds of his entire luggage'. He brought another recorded tape back for Dina – her family was afraid to send it by mail. Dina offered to take Richard for dinner but he refused saying that he 'enjoyed knowing people in Tbilisi' and transferring the goods was a way for him 'to get to know a nice Georgian family'. Dina felt that her personal gesture of gratitude was rejected.

Armen, an Armenian 'unemployed businessman' from London, sent money to his family through the bank but allegedly the Armenian bank 'lost it'. Armen waited for three years before his English employer, Mr Jones, went to Armenia with a 'very large sum of money' for Armen's family. Mr Jones received a bottle of Armenian cognac from the family and a stack of photographs for Armen. He reported that Armen's family thought he had forgotten about them and were so touched that they organized a lavish feast in Armen's and Mr Jones' honour, after which he felt 'truly welcomed in Armenia'.

The relationships between Dina and Richard, and Armen and Mr Jones, remained friendly but distant. Dina and Armen felt that they 'owed' Richard and Mr Jones, and tried to express their gratitude. Richard and Mr Jones, on the other hand, were 'glad to help'; they did not view the transfer as a large favour.

Perhaps the misunderstanding lies in the fact that material or other favours are usually granted in the CIS by friends, and not acquaintances that one trusts. Illegal migrants are in a weak position of having to rely on people they hardly know. 'Befriending' them by granting generous return favours makes their weakness less conspicuous. As I shall further discuss in the sections on gift exchange and friendship, the Western counterparts may take a very different view of social relationships and obligations.

Gifts   Russian words associated with 'gifts' are similar to those used in English: *podarok* (gift), *dar* (gift, as in talent), *odarenniy* (gifted). But the Russian word *podarok* may have wider connotations, ranging from bribes to tokens of appreciation. While the gift economy is present but not essential in West European countries, traditional gift-giving is a more salient feature in the CIS, even after the collapse of communism. The pattern of informal exchanges of goods and services is a significant characteristic of the former life in the Soviet Union (Humphrey, 1983; Ledeneva, 1996/97; Malia, 1994; Ries, 1997). In the present-day CIS,

> large parts of the population were active in distributing by means of exchange the products and services they had access to as a result of their occupation *... Social networks were as a result much more important than they are in Western capitalist society and of much greater significance for a satisfactory existence.* (Doomernik, 1997: 63)

Yet, migration alters this pattern. Gift-giving has become more 'Western', in a sense of becoming socially important instead of practically necessary (as in the case of the barter and exchange of products which could not otherwise be obtained).

Ron, a Dutchman married to a Russian, noticed that Russians 'tend to give less second-hand gifts the longer they live in Holland'. Galya, a bank teller from London, also noticed that the gifts she used to receive in Ekaterinburg tended to be functional, like 'something to eat or to wear'. Therefore, giving somebody a second-hand sweater was considered a 'gesture of sharing' rather than a hand-me-down. Galya noticed that if her Russian friends in London gave her clothes, they tended to be 'cheap but new'. Galya attributed this to the Western habit of throwing old clothes out and buying a new set of cheap but fashionable clothes each season. Galya also reflected that perhaps Russian fashion did not change as quickly, but in London one had to give clothes which had to be worn the same year.

> Still, Russians tend to give more clothes than the British. The British tend to give me decorative, impersonal things, or even gift vouchers. I guess, the Russians like more personal gifts ... (Galya)

Galya implies that together with the functional value of the gift, it is also the personal value that constitutes a good Russian gift. It is not the monetary value of the gift but its symbolic and personal value that 'counts'. In this sense, giving a second-hand sweater satisfies both the functional and personal requirement in Russia, but is seen as a hand-me-down by the Westerners.

My London informants, who celebrated their fiftieth anniversary and received 'an enormous amount of precious gifts', valued their grandchild's drawing of a 'grandma and grandpa holding hands' the most. Children in Russia are often encouraged by their parents to submit original pieces of their own work or to recite poetry. Nastya, a mother of two in Amsterdam, compared this to the alleged tradition amongst Dutch children of saving their pocket money to buy small gifts for their parents. Nastya confessed to giving money to her elder son to buy a present for his father's birthday, because she sensed that her Turkish-Dutch husband would not be as appreciative of a child's drawing as his Belorussian grandmother would. Nastya still encourages her children to submit 'personal effort' gifts to her Belorussian family members.

The personal element of Russian gift-giving can cause misunderstandings in the host society not only in the case of second-hand sweaters and children's drawings, but also where general social relationships are concerned. Armen sent money to his family in Armenia through a non-Russian *okaziya*. After the delivery was made by his British employer, Armen tried to reciprocate by offering Mr Jones the gift of cigars. Mr Jones refused the gift, saying that he had already been rewarded by Armen's family in Armenia. Armen complained to me that his English employer 'cut him off', keeping their relationship strictly business. Armen could not understand why Mr Jones would not accept the token of gratitude on a personal level. When Mr Jones went to Armenia for a second business trip, Armen refused to send money to his family since he felt he already owed Mr Jones a favour. Mr Jones, when I interviewed him about the matter, 'could not understand what the fuss was about'. He said that it 'wouldn't be any trouble for him' to deliver the money again. Mr Jones felt that Armen did not trust him anymore, which has further strained their relationship at work. Although it is hard to generalize from this singular case about the Armenian and English understanding of gift-giving and reciprocity, Mr Jones' choice not to accept the gift of cigars clearly had a negative effect on Armen's willingness to use this *okazya* again.

I have observed Russians in London and Amsterdam giving different gifts to each other than they give to the British or the Dutch to avoid confusion. Russians often give each other 'traditional' Russian gifts, such as food or drink items (caviar or vodka), while presenting less 'national' gifts to their non-Russian acquaintances. Zoya, an agriculturist from Krasnoyarsk and a member of the Orthodox Church in London, reflects on her learning experience:

> Once, I brought vodka, which I brought from Russia, and marinated mushrooms my mother sent to me [from Krasnoyarsk] to my [British] friends from the church. I noticed that although they opened a bottle and offered me a glass, they did not drink themselves. They did not even open the mushrooms. I directly

asked them why and they said they didn't drink vodka and gave me a very long story about mushroom poisoning in the suburb of Manchester. I think they thought they'd be poisoned by Russian vodka as well … Next time, I bought them a bottle of red wine which they poured out instantaneously. (Zoya)

Thus, gifts sometimes change in London and Amsterdam as soon as the Russians become conscious of their 'native' hosts' or compatriots' different expectations. Some Russians continue giving each other 'traditional' functional and personal gifts, while giving different gifts to the non-Russians. Others abandon 'second-hand sweaters and children's drawings' altogether. Few Russians, like Armen, persist with the old patterns of gift-giving, showing either a lack of observational skills or a calculated insistence on doing things the way they have always been done.

We have seen that the informal economic activity known to the Russians in the CIS does not always 'work' the same way in Western Europe. The skills of running an informal business and the habits of gift-giving learned in the CIS may prove to be useful to certain migrants in particular situations abroad, but damaging to others. It is usually those migrants who can afford (due to their legal status or personal flexibility) to adapt to the 'Western way of doing things' that succeed the most.

The success or failure of the informal economy is also dependent upon the social and institutional context of interaction. As the following section aims to show, social network structures inherited from the CIS are used with a different rate of success by the migrants.

5.2   Social Networks

5.2.1 Svyazi *and* Kontakty

I shall use the term 'social networks' to loosely define 'any form of social interaction among the Russians or between the Russians and the members of the host society'. The Russian networks are often seen as informal support channels, adapted to using every loophole in the official system to advance one's aims.

> … Network notions seem particularly useful as we concern ourselves with individuals using roles rather than with roles using individuals, and with the crossing and manipulation rather than the acceptance of institutional boundaries. (Hannerz, 1980: 175)

Social connections in Soviet times could also act as a counterbalance to the cruel political system:

> Close human connections were vitally important to Russians in their homeland because of the often abusive political and economic system that dominated their lives. (Hardwick, 1993: 13)

The most instructive way of looking at Russian social networks in this context is the concept of *svyazi* – links. In the singular, *svyaz'* may be translated as tie, bond, connection, relation, liaison, communication, and postal system. The word *svyazat'sya* means both to 'get in contact' and to 'be bound' (by the relationship one regrets but has to maintain). *Svyazi* may involve a number of persons designated as friends, acquaintances or useful individuals.

A jargon term *nuzhnik*, originated in the 1980s, stemming from the word *nuzhda*, 'need', means both 'toilet' and 'useful person' (meaning, somebody you use only for practical needs). More 'altruistic' terms used for people involved in relationships are *drug* (friend), *znakomiy* (acquaintance), *priyatel* (buddy) and the best known *tovarish'* (comrade). The latter term is rarely used among migrants, while *znakomiy* is often used to designate anybody from *drug* to *nuzhnik*. *Nuzhnik* implies a limited practical capacity (somebody who can always repair your car but will not walk your dog or take your messages) while *drug* may be used for all those functions, granted a certain amount of reciprocity. At the same time, *drug* can be 'saved' for emergencies since less important people may be used for petty help. Interestingly, nostalgic migrants often refer to their CIS friends as *druzýa* (friends) but present ones as *znakomiye*.

Friends, acquaintances or useful persons use *svyazi* to come into contact with each other. The term *kontakt* means not just the contact person but also the mediator in the transaction and generally 'the person one knows and can use'. The idea of *kontakt*, in the sense of 'social contact', may be a form of *svyazi*. The term *kontakt* is sometimes used interchangeably with the term *svyazi*. *Kontakty* are often based on rules of reciprocity, and are often linked with *blat* (profitable connection). The expression *po blatu* translates as 'on the quiet' or 'illicitly'. It implies hard-won favouritism, a widespread survival technique in Soviet Russia (Ledeneva, 1996).[3] I have observed *blatnye* relationships in the present-day CIS as well.

Like any other resident, a migrant may need a whole array of functionally diversified *kontakty*. A sociologist from London summed up Russian *kontakty*:

There are two main forms of social contact: that on a verbal level, and that on the level of shared interests and ideas. The verbal level of contact means chatting, small talk, superficial interaction, *posidelki*. This is difficult here as people are mostly self-sufficient; they are reluctant to let the newcomers join their established circles. As for the common goals: in most cases, the longer we know these people, the less common ground we find. It is also a problem of age; older people are not as interesting for the younger, more active and practical generation. At this age, acquaintances are distant and intimacy is avoided. We host guests but it seems to be an effort to reciprocate; one has to cook, to prepare, and it can be a burden in these busy times. It's the absence of common interests that makes it hard: even dog owners have more in common than some Russian-speakers. It would be nice to meet some Jewish or non-Jewish intellectuals who'd share our views. Generally, I've noticed, the lower your intellectual level, the easier it is to find friends, and the less choosy you are. We have a kind of indirect circle of friends: for me it's English and Russian books and Russian TV for Alina [my wife]: a kind of surrogate of impersonal communication. Just speaking Russian isn't enough for friendship. (Michael)

What may start as *kontakt* may or may not grow into *druzhba* (friendship). Despite Michael and his wife Alina's claim to social self-sufficiency, expressed on other occasions, they clearly miss the more personal *kontakt* and friendship. It seemed that they often rejected Russian *kontakty* because of a perceived lack of substance, and were rejected by the British because of the lack of common ground or understanding.

Stepa is a retired schoolteacher from Minsk, who has been living in Amsterdam for eight years. He drew me a diagram of his *otnosheniya* (relationships), using different colours to designate friends (red), acquaintances (blue), and those he comes into daily contact with, like a boy neighbour, the baker, the lady who feeds the pigeons, etc. (designated in pencil, intensifying the colour depending on his perceived dependency on that relationship). He clarified:

I made the baker dark black because I cannot live without him. Don't laugh, I literally cannot. I hate the bread that other bakers sell; this one is just divine … He sells great sandwiches too that pull me through the day. I learned my first Dutch word from him: *broodje* (sandwich) … Now, this lady with the pigeons is a nut case, but I also made her dark [in pencil] because without her my Dutch would have never advanced beyond *broodje*. She talks about her birds; I use the same words for my neighbours. Like this boy, he's always impatient, flying off whenever his mother isn't watching … He runs past me down the stairs, shouting 'sorry' as he tumbles down, without even noticing what he's hit ... He's light grey [on my drawing] because I don't talk to him, but I do like him all the same. I like children. I need at least one child per day to make me feel good about humanity. (Stepa)

Aside from his unfailing humorous style, Stepa is suggesting that social relationships need not be functional or even clearly defined. Some contacts are fleeting and superficial but nonetheless important, especially for the 'lonely old migrant', as he calls himself. Arguably, a neighbourhood boy can hardly be seen as a *kontakt*, and yet the personal importance of the non-verbal communication with him (arguably even 'social contact') cannot be underestimated. Stepa hardly knows any other Russians (although he speaks of his friends back home or his vague 'acquaintances' from Rotterdam), and these minute contacts constitute for him a 'picture of Dutch society', as he puts it.

Another story of a 'fuzzy network' comes from London, where a lonely, elderly Russian couple 'communicates' with their English neighbours about a TV serial:

> Since we moved into this apartment and started watching *Chicago Hope*, we've noticed that our neighbours across the street were watching it too. We don't speak a word of English, but having seen *CH* in Russia, we know what it's about. So, sometimes we greet our neighbours with 'Quick, to the paramedics room!' or 'Don't worry, he is stable'. They just laugh ... Once our TV was broken and we didn't know whom to call, so they called for us ... Another time, they were weeding their garden and I showed them that they shouldn't weed near the daisy's roots – they were grateful ... (Vasya)

Such *kontakty* expand beyond the lonely and the elderly and include large categories of young Russians, ranging from street bums and prostitutes to musicians and artists. The people they come into contact with are not only 'clients', 'buyers', 'listeners' or 'spectators' but also 'just people with whom we live'. A seasonal artist in Amsterdam explained:

> The whole day I stand here, exhibiting my pictures and watch the people. They study my paintings, I study them. Only a few of them will actually provide me with my livelihood, many others will just pose for a while, make a comment, ask a question – first about the price, then about where I get the inspiration, then – where I come from, then – how interesting, etc. In a way, they place me into their own landscape, if you will pardon my pun ... Once I was invited to submit my work to this guy's gallery ... he said he'd come back – but I never heard from him again ... (Dima)

Social contact is thus important in the lives of many migrants. As in the case of a retired schoolteacher or a seasonal artist, migrants often see themselves living among and yet standing at the margins of the host society. A neighbour boy brushes by, a pedestrian casts a passing glance at the painting, and one feels lonely, or one feels welcomed into the world of strangers.

Many Russian women married to English or Dutch spouses (especially the cases of 'mail order brides' prevalent in London) expressed their desperation at feeling isolated: not knowing the language, having no job, making no friends, feeling lonely and bored.

> The Russian woman … moves to her husband's home … where there are few if any Russians living. Her chances of finding work are limited, especially if her English is poor. She does not own the house; she is entirely financially dependent on her husband. He is out at work all day; she is bored and lonely. She pines for friends and family, and experiences *toska* (yearning) for the company of other Russians; lack of communication with her husband and living in a completely different culture take their toll, and resentment on both sides sets in. (O'Connor, 1997: 9)

Presently, institutional support channels are emerging to provide moral and social support for those seeking the company of other Russians. *Londonski Kurier*, the largest Russian newspaper in London, has set up a monthly column which publishes housewives' letters and serves as an informal contacts forum. Internet newsgroups have a broader focus that includes business and employment-seeking ads. The 'Russians in London' newsgroup serves as a contacts medium among Russians. But unlike the housewives, most of the Internet users are professionals, so the types of contact they are seeking ranges from personal ads to seeking business partners. In Amsterdam, the Internet newsgroup 'Russen in Nederland' has an extensive 'ads' section that advertises anything from refrigerator sales to lonely hearts seeking contact from Russia with The Netherlands. Unlike 'Russians in London', 'Russen in Nederland' has only around 100 'Dutch Russian' subscribers and many ads are posted by Russians from the CIS and Dutch seeking Russians for services.

Thus we have seen that *svyazi* and *kontakty* among Russians are highly diversified. While some groups seek friends (like the elderly and the Russian wives), other groups, such as young professionals, seek business contacts. These contacts are mostly necessitated by the migratory context which cuts the Russians off from their social environment. They attempt to fill in the gaps by means of heightened sociability, advertisement, joining clubs and the like.

5.2.2 *Friendship*

Friendship is an obvious bridge between a migrant and his surroundings; it can separate migrants into exclusive groups or allow individual migrants to get closer to the host society. Often, friendship sets the entire process of finding and maintaining *kontakty* and consolidating *svyazi* in motion. A friend's help, although often crucial to finding *kontakty*, is considered by the Russians to be 'above the game': it is something 'pure' that can only be accepted as a gift (rather than 'used'). The Russian saying, *drug poznayetsya v bede* (a friend reveals himself in time of trouble) implies that helping someone out of trouble is the only sign of real friendship. Friendship is valued above money, as another saying suggests: *ne imey sto rubley a imey sto druzey* (you don't need to have 100 roubles but a hundred friends).[4]

Druzhba – friendship itself – is often said to have changed as a result of migration. Mercantile transitions between friends, mentioned in the section on informal economy, are often seen as corrupting. Slava, a car salesman from Amsterdam, reflects:

> I came here with my best friend; we were both involved in a car business [smuggling cars from Germany]. I worked with him in St Peters[burg] [supposedly, in a gas station] for five years. We were very close (*nerazluchimiye* –inseparable). I trusted him with my money, and I could always borrow money from him – or he from me, or from my wife. We even tried to open our own business [gas station] but failed [because of racketeers]. My friend knew some people who were working in Germany and Holland, and he said they earned a lot of money … By that time I was divorced, so I said, why not, and off we went. That's when it started. We were supposed to take all our money, and so I did, but as I later found out, he left a fat bank account in St Peters'. He later relocated it to Berlin. But at the time, I didn't know it, so suddenly it was like he was poor and I had to pay his bills, and pay his gasoline, and he was living in my apartment [in Amsterdam] for seven months, and I was paying rent … All the while, he was hiding his money and putting whatever he earned into his [German] savings account! … I think it's the West, the Western psychology that's affected him. Everything for himself! Back home we'd share the last crumb of bread; here he felt he was his own capitalist … (Slava)

In a sense, Slava suggested, his friend betrayed not only his friendship but himself, forsaking his values by becoming more 'Western' and 'capitalist'. The same perceived 'Westernness' is evaluated as positive by Zhora, a London street artist. Zhora values his friendship with non-Russians, because he sees it as less binding, more liberating and allowing for greater privacy than Russian *druzhba*.

> In Moscow, people could knock at your door in the middle of the night, bring in a bottle – or expect you to produce one – and just camp in your kitchen. It was fine when I was a student, living in a student hostel, but when I had a job and had to get up at 6 in the morning, and every morning I couldn't even use my own toilet because somebody was puking in it – that has gone too far. Here [in London], you see, there's a notion of privacy. Nobody comes in without an appointment. If you want a party, you call for a party. The party doesn't drop on your head two hours before your alarm goes off. (Zhora)

Reflective of Zhora's sentiment, Sergei, a Russian theatre director, is unhappy about his Russian friends in London. Sergei is referring, particularly, to the Russian 'culture of envy' when others' success is criticized instead of being emanated. He is also critical of the Russians' hypocritical use of friendship for their own benefit:

> First time in England I had nostalgia, sought [Russian] friends, met with them; forged friendships … felt that many were envious of my theatrical career, when things were going well … Other people, while singing praise, wanted to free-load on the wagon of my success, to cash in on my benefits. Many people use friendship for their personal benefit, especially in Russia, and they continue doing it here. (Sergei)

Usually, younger London and Amsterdam Russians referred to their party guests as friends. Friends are invited *v gosti* (literally, 'to be guests'), *an vecherinku* (to the 'evening party'), or *na tusovku* (to the youth gathering). Anton, an artist and amateur businessman, is probably the most successful in amassing Amsterdam Russians, inviting 'all his friends', who number in the hundreds, to the Vondel Park for his birthday party. Some of Anton's guests are commuters and seasonal workers who work in Amsterdam in the summer but disappear a month later. Despite the unprecedented success of Anton's park party to amass the largest number of Russians in Amsterdam, these Russians are rarely seen in as large a group throughout the year. Here are my notes from my first park party or *tusovka*, which I went to with an anthropologist friend of mine:

> Anton organized his birthday party in the largest park in the centre of Amsterdam. Loud Russian rock music told the guests where the party took

place, where, under a tree, a carpet with an assortment of alcoholic beverages and stylized Russian snacks (herring, potato salad, beet salad, cuts of salami, caned fish sprottes, etc.) attracted more than a hundred Russian and a couple of Dutch friends. The age of the invited ranged from 15 to 50, and by the time we arrived most of the guests were conspicuously drunk. We were welcomed by a young man with a bottle of vodka who insisted that we kiss him first in order to get a glass. 'Only friends are invited!!!' – He proclaimed. Soon we were surrounded by a school of young men with drinks and asked to dance. A few guests called themselves artists and poets, and instantaneously offered to paint our nude portraits or began reading poetry which could best be characterized as drunk. Other guests asserted that they are 'doing business' and looking for Russian partners, while others related to us that they were secret spies for the Russian government and their task was to get secret information about this gathering. At least seven guitars were present and seven times this number of self-proclaimed musicians competed for their use. Russian popular songs brought tears to some guests' eyes and sentiment to their stories of the past. Friendship was probably the most popular topic, and its value in a strange country could not be over-emphasized. Even Dutch guests were drawn into the circle of sentimentally inclined Russian friends ... (Notes, August 1998)

Russian parties, like the one described above, are usually smaller in scale and take place in people's homes, their focal point being either the kitchen or the living room table. These are occasions when exclusive subcommunity ties are re-asserted and an atmosphere of conspicuous 'Russianness' is consciously boosted through food, music and jokes. It is also a time when proclamations of mutual friendship and loyalty are made. Sergei, the theatre director from London, laments:

> Russian gatherings are a sad spectacle (*grustnoe zrelishe*), fun as something exotic; I usually avoid them. Many of my friends refrain from these gatherings, avoid contact with the Russians. For example, *Aquarium* disco: proletariat, Comsomol youth ... These Russians are not interested in arts ... In the summer, when Maliy Teatr came, a few people showed up. (Sergei)

Mixed parties, however, are often more restrained. One such party was given in Notting Hill by a young Russian architect from London, Lena.

> Guests started arriving an hour and a half after the official starting time, 9 p.m. They came in small groups, well dressed, slightly tipsy, some brought champagne. A group of five Russians entered, with flowers and CDs, soon dispersed among others whom they apparently knew through work or from

previous parties. Most of the guests present, including the Russians, were either architects or lawyers, like Lena's German roommate. Except for a small number of middle aged apparently well-to-do but 'alternative looking' men with tattoos, among whom were two Ukrainians, supposed businessmen who allegedly knew Lena's parents in Moscow, guests were in their mid-20s and early 30s. Although Russians were in a minority, British guests insisted on listening to Russian music and consuming only cocktails with vodka to create the atmosphere of a Russian theme party. Lena and the Russians participated reluctantly, and by midnight nobody cared about cultural themes but danced to house music. I asked the Ukrainian businessmen how they were enjoying the London party; they said they were at a very similar party in Kiev just a week ago. A Russian architect, working for the same company as Lena, complained that the food was a bit 'snacky' – chips and small sandwiches. A Russian lawyer, speaking impeccable English, resented not knowing many people since 'When I'm drunk I like to be carried out by friends'. His Russian girlfriend was intent on 'seducing at least a dozen British blokes'; her friend, visiting from Moscow, was interested in 'learning English'. Generally, both the Russians and the British seemed to have enjoyed the party that went on till dawn. (Notes, May 1998)

Friendship with the members of the host society may give a migrant a sense of belonging and provide him with deeper insights into the receiving culture and society. An IT worker, commuting between London and Amsterdam, reflects:

I appreciate my [English and Dutch] friends. I still don't get their jokes or references to films I've never watched or books I've never read, but if they are real friends, they don't mind explaining things to me ... Although I prefer spending time among my own [Russian friends], I feel that having contact with the locals while you live abroad is the only way to actually *live* abroad. (Sasha)

Note that in the above quotes, the notion of friendship varies from being functional – as in doing business together – to recreational. Some of the network theories, both new and old, appear to lack distinction between the qualitative types of networking and those characterizing relationships in terms of their strengths and weakness, or closeness and distance. Yet, specifying what each relationship consists of reveals the way people think of and use their social connections. Friendship is one important type of social interaction that ties subcommunity members together. It can be used for functional purposes such as obtaining employment or for providing sustenance in the case of illegals not qualified for social benefits.

Through the example of friendship, we can also see that it is referred to and enacted differently among different groups of Russians. Older migrants and intellectuals, like the retired sociologist Michael and his wife Alina, or the theatre director Sergei, are more cautious about embracing all other Russians as friends. Migratory situations may render people both lonely and vulnerable. Yet many Russians, like the car salesman Slava, apply a high friendship standard, extended from the Russian reified *druzhba*, to choose the select few to be their friends. Younger, more sociable and integrated Russians, like the artist Anton or the architect Lena, organize large parties embracing all the people they know as 'friends'.

As discussed in the chapter on subcommunities, the choice of friends is often self-conscious; while some contacts are carefully avoided, others are actively sought. These choices have to do not only with the general Russian understanding of what friendship is meant to be, but also with migratory context.

We have seen that although ideas about *svyazi* and *kontakty* are generated in the CIS, they are interpreted differently by Russians living abroad. While the standard of 'Russian friendship' gives a base of moral judgement to one migrant, it is mocked and resented by another. This interpretation depends on both the personal characteristics of the migrants, and on their level of integration in the host society. We shall now look at both of these factors to determine their responsibility for the differential success rate of the migrants involved in the informal economy and social networks.

5.3   Typifying the Migrants: Who Interacts with Whom?

5.3.1 Doomernik's Classification

Doomernik (1997: 59–73) divided his Russian informants in Berlin into two major categories: achievers and consumers. These categories are subdivided into 'conservative' and 'innovative' types, thereby presenting a set of four simplified but revealing characteristics measured according to their success in adapting to the receiving society.[5] Specifically, these four types are: innovative participant, conservative participant, innovative consumer and conservative consumer.

The most successful group of 'assimilators' are 'innovative participants' who are characterized by their high level of education and energy. They rarely rely on Russian social networks and approach the receiving society's government agencies, housing associations, real-estate agents and [German] acquaintances directly.

Less successful immigrants are the 'conservative participants', who 'endeavour to retain their old professional and societal status, and combine the wish to do so with long term planning'. This segment falls back upon 'Russian' networks when a direct approach to the receiving society's institutions and acquaintances seems unsuccessful:

> In a number of cases the accompanying status devaluation leads to a phase of lethargy and a falling back on strategies known to be effective in Soviet society; i.e. the reliance on social capital. Social capital has currency among fellow immigrants and within the established 'Russian' community. These contacts not only serve to offer some comfort but also to find piecemeal work. (Doomernik, 1997: 70)

The third type of immigrant, 'conservative consumer', is said to 'rely on compatriots to find them a job instead of looking for one independently'.

> In almost all cases conservative consumers found their accommodation through the mediation of the 'Russians'. In summary, these strategies are characterised by a short term perspective and a strong reliance on social capital, in this case relations with compatriots. (Doomernik, 1997: 71)

The last type of immigrants, 'innovative consumers', have 'strong ambitions of achieving material wealth and seek to do so by the quickest means possible'. These means are often illegal. Doomernik admits that his knowledge of this group is limited to second-hand stories and newspaper articles. It appears through my own superficial communication with the partners of 'shaky' businesses[6] that they rely heavily on both 'Russian' and 'native' social networks, both for sponsors and clientele.

These types of migrants are also present in London and Amsterdam. However, Doomernik uses a classification system based on the perceived level of integration into the host society which is more limited than the system of migrant classification exemplified by the more holistic subcommunity approach I advocate. Also, Doomernik's 'types' represent only some of the subcommunities I have encountered in London and Amsterdam, and do not give a good description of groups such as the 'Russian spouses', 'single entrepreneurs', temporary or seasonal workers and visiting families of 'established migrants'. Doomernik's classification, however, throws light upon the question of 'who interacts with whom'. Members of both exclusive and inclusive subcommunities might belong to any of the above-mentioned types.

A large proportion of migrants in London and Amsterdam can be classified as 'innovative participants'. Both legal and illegal, they are usually young and energetic, having arrived in London or Amsterdam alone or with a single partner, determined 'to make it' in the receiving country. These migrants, at least initially, avoid contact with their compatriots, trying to come into contact with officials and regular 'native' residents instead. Nastya, a young mother from Grodno, married a Turkish Dutch citizen. She started off by helping her husband in his Turkish restaurant, simultaneously taking Dutch language courses and preparing for the exams to study computer science at the Free University in Amsterdam. Although Nastya has many Russian friends, she believes that the only way to survive in a strange country is 'by doing what the Dutch do'.

Grisha, a middle-aged biologist from Moscow working on a temporary contract in London, gives priority to *kontakty* that promote his successful integration into British society:

> It's not that I'm not interested in Russians … But I'm more interested in extending my contract here which may enable my family to join me and my sons might have a better future … I'm trying to learn English better, talking to my colleagues and neighbours … If I need anything practical – to find an apartment, to buy cheap furniture, I just look through ads in the newspaper or call the real estate agent … I know some Russians address each other for these sorts of things, that's the way it used to work in Russia, but here the country is different, so I try to adapt. (Grisha)

'Conservative participants' within a Russian network are usually older professionals, seeking to retain their former social and professional status through official channels (or, and if that fails, informal ones). Marina, a former Russian university professor presently unemployed in London, has attempted to find a job by applying for a position at the British academic centres. After two years of trying to 'get back up to where I came from' Marina felt a failure, 'sitting at home with nothing to do but cook for my [English] husband, whose friends regarded me as something of an exotic misfit'. Marina forged a friendship with another Russian unemployed professional, Aleftina. Together, they posted an ad looking for a Russian-speaking secretary in order to open their own Russian translation agency. Having found a young Russian secretary, Marina and Aleftina's business took off only to fail shortly after – a failure they blame on the dishonesty of the secretary. Presently, they are looking for another Russian partner. In the meanwhile, the two are enjoying 'London cultural life', going to theatres and concerts, and feeling generally happy about their newly acquired circle of Russian friends.

Unlike 'conservative participants', 'conservative consumers' are more reluctant to start their own business. Partially, this is due to the fact that most 'conservative consumers' are illegal. They are usually less educated and less motivated to find prestigious jobs. Andrei, a musical technician from Ekaterinburg presently working at private construction sites in Amsterdam, never tried to find work through official channels. He explains that 'they wouldn't even interview an illegal, plus I don't speak a word of Dutch or English'. Andrei, with his opera singer wife Dusya, spent their first three months living with an artist named Anton. Anton hosted both of them in the hope of gaining interest from (mostly Dusya's) expected career success. After a month of co-residence, Anton complained that the couple was not making any progress approaching potential employers. Except for a number of concerts they gave in cafes or once on the leisure boat (which Anton organized), Andrei and Dusya 'remained passive and depressed about their future prospects' (Anton).

> They were afraid to approach Dutch employers, and it wasn't just because of their lack of status – I believe that talent, at least in Dusya's case, goes a long way. They just … I don't know, they wanted to be comfortable, they couldn't earn anything back home, but they didn't want to go to much effort here either … They also complained of being lonely and bored, so I had to provide friends and entertainment to keep them from running away … It's not like I'm their sponsor, but I did lend them some money and they promised to pay it back as soon as they found a job … (Anton)

Finally, Andrei was offered a job by a Russian friend of Anton's, helping build a private office on the outskirts of Amsterdam. Within a month, the couple was able to move out and rent a small room of their own, sharing it with another Russian construction worker.

Most of the Russians in London and Amsterdam combine the characteristics of Doomernik's four types. 'Conservative consumers', who normally belong to exclusive subcommunities, often use outside connections, since exclusive subcommunities are usually small and rarely economically self-sufficient. Both conservative and innovative consumers in London and Amsterdam depend, at least partially, upon members of the receiving society. In only very few exclusive subcommunities, are the networks, to a large extent, self-enclosed and self-sufficient. They form a unified system of relationships where Russians occupy all levels of functional necessity in the receiving society and are able to accommodate its members with little external help. Here is an example of such an 'innovative consumers' network from London, having at its core five illegal entrepreneurs with connections to at least a hundred others. Tolya, one of the employees of the firm, tells about its functions:

> We are small, what you might call an NGO or private firm specializing in accommodating Russian tourists. We [five core employees] use outside information [from other illegal Russians who get temporarily employed by the 'agency'] to locate and contact new arrivals. Some of our colleagues work from Russia and have established travel agencies there[7] who advertise our services... We help them to get to know the city [by organizing tours with temporarily employed Russian guides] and, if desired, bring them into contact with 'Russian London' [for the purpose of finding business contacts, buying real estate, etc.] ... Some of them take English lessons from Russian tutors. This is much cheaper than formal English courses ... So, we are a tour agency who employ, target and help our own people. (Tolya)

Members of inclusive subcommunities may partially use ethnic networks to draw other Russians into their circle of friends or to initiate them into business, thus creating 'exclusive pockets' among the inclusive membership. As mentioned in the chapter on ethnicity, there are few specifically ethnic circles (Ukrainian or Armenian)[8] – most 'exclusive pockets' are formed by Russian-speakers of various ethnicities. An example of such an 'exclusive pocket' in Amsterdam is given by Igor, who may be classified as a 'conservative participant' – an enterprising young man from Orel with a large circle of Russian friends.

> I entered the country [illegally] as a technician but quickly ran out of work. I had odd jobs here and there but as soon as my individual contract was finished – usually after a few days – I was eating spaghetti again [meaning, lacking money]. Luckily, one of my [Dutch] employers was an architect, with his own building firm. He said he needed a technician, as he had plans for expansion. But he didn't want just a technician, he wanted a whole set – construction workers, painters, you know ... So I asked my [Russian] friends who were also doing odd jobs at the time – some of them had no experience in construction – and of course there they were ready to work the following morning ... Well, he [the Dutch employer] figured we were cheap labour but then he figured we weren't professional, and fired some. He fired me too [reasons unexplained] ... So my friend went to his [Russian immigration] lawyer and since by that time I had a status [and work permit] he said that I could take this architect to

> court. So he [the architect] got scared and took both of us [me and my friend]
> back and now we work as a nice team ... If it wasn't for my friend's lawyer,
> I'd still be eating spaghetti. (Igor)

We have seen, thus far, how the level of integration into the receiving
society depends upon the choice of social networks by the migrant. More
business-oriented Russians, like the 'Travel NGO' employer Tolya, actively
participate in the building of such networks; while less active ones, like the
musicians Dusya and Andrei, rely on their compatriots to help form, and
integrate them into, a network.

Doomernik's classificatory system reveals certain particularly Russian
types of modern migrants, but it is limited insofar as it presents a rather
simplified scheme of how these migrant types operate within networks.
Doomernik discusses levels of integration as an indicator of the migrant's
success and a determining factor as to the kinds of networks a migrant uses in
the receiving country. However, other such factors may include the migrant's
character, level of ambition and ability – qualities that differentiate individuals
in the CIS as well. Migrants' individual backgrounds play a large role in the
choice of adaptation strategies as well, including their use of social networks
and the informal economy.

Aside from the social capital embodied in networks, migrants also use
other types of 'capital' to integrate into the receiving society. Social capital
is interrelated with cultural and economic capital as we shall discuss in
the following section. Our understanding of social networks is therefore
complemented by exploring the types of capital different migrants bring with
them and exploit in the receiving countries.

5.3.2 Capital and Networks

Bourdieu (1992: 123, 170)[9] discusses three types of capital: social, economic
and cultural. In a migratory context, social capital consists of the types of
social relations discussed in the previous section.[10] Economic capital refers
to financial capital accumulated in either the CIS or the receiving country.
Cultural capital consists of a person's upbringing, and his educational and
professional achievements. Migrants may aspire to convert cultural capital
acquired in the CIS into economic capital in the receiving country.

> Some ex-Soviet citizens have used their cultural capital – knowledge of
> language, culture, customs, and social contacts – the knowledge dormant

during the Soviet times – for generally economic purposes, taking part in the increasingly frequent connections between The Netherlands and the countries of the CIS. (Snel et al., 2000: 62)

The Russian case demonstrates how the three types of capital are used interchangeably by different groups of migrants. While in this chapter we are mostly interested in social capital, and in particular social networks, we observe that some migrants prefer to use economic capital (for example, 'new Russians' who would rather buy products and services than go through the messy and time-consuming process of social networking and gift-giving). Others consolidate social capital on the basis of cultural capital (for example, by choosing friends who have the same educational background or professional status).

Older, better-educated migrants belonging to the Soviet 'class' of the intelligentsia (as discussed in the chapter on subcommunities), have few social contacts outside their own 'circle' and usually not much economic capital. As a retired sociologist in London reflects: 'In Russia, we didn't get paid for the knowledge we had, and all we could bring with us was our experience and education' (Michael).

Younger migrants generally have more social connections in the receiving country and more money brought over from the CIS. Their social and economic capital is fundamentally important for finding jobs. A young Russian entrepreneurs like Slava, who is involved in the car business in Amsterdam and Germany, found it initially easy to 'find his own niche' by employing his friends to work with him and covering initial expenses using the funds accumulated in St Petersburg. Gosha, a 25-year-old tyre shop owner from London, reflects:

> If you have money and friends prior to coming to England, as far as work goes, I'd say you're all set … Those who come here individually, hoping to get rich on the streets and not knowing anybody usually end up unemployed. (Gosha)

Those who arrive with substantial amounts of money are usually not seeking employment but looking for investment and residential opportunities. Most of the wealthy Russians I have found in London used England as a 'summer residence' rather than a place for business. 'New Russians' in Amsterdam referred to the 'diamond season' – the time when diamond prices dipped and attracted seasonal Russian buyers. Some 'new Russians', involved in money laundering, invested in Russian or the receiving country's businesses (famously, the case of Amsterdam's only current Russian club/restaurant, *Kalinka*) and, while residing either in the CIS or elsewhere abroad, visited their 'investment sites' occasionally while staying in London or Amsterdam hotels. In a few rare interviews and through second-hand information channels, I was able to deduce that these Russians referred to their activities in London and Amsterdam as a 'side business' or 'second jobs', seeing themselves as managers, coordinators, co-owners or sponsors. A London businessman who actually resided in France founded what he calls a 'cultural entertainment firm' (inviting Russian artists and musicians to give concerts, organize exhibits, etc.). He referred to himself as the 'benefactor', provider of employment for a dozen London-resident Russians working for his firm, while asserting that his enterprise 'does not really pay' and rather functions 'as a gift to the Russian community'. The same individual has bought an English noble title and considers himself to be a member of the 'new aristocratic elite'. As such, he 'needs to elevate himself above purely mercantile interests' (Valentin).

Thus in the case of the 'new Russians', economic capital does more than generate more funds or launder the ones already acquired. It also turns into morally praiseworthy and invariably conspicuous 'charities' and 'good enterprises'. These enterprises do indeed provide employment to mostly young professional Russians, some of them illegal, who may themselves become independent businessmen or join the receiving country's workforce when the 'good enterprise' fails after less than a year of operation (which is usually the case, especially in London).

5.3.3 Brief Note on Employment

Legal status enabled the migrants to approach official channels through which they had a greater chance of obtaining long-term employment. Illegals, settling for black jobs, had less of a chance to ensure continuous employment and little hope of finding higher status jobs and resisting the sliding scale (working below their educational qualifications or professional level).

Aside from legal status, generational and educational factors played a role in the success or failure of employment-seeking strategies. Social networks were less helpful to the older, higher educated migrants who experienced the sliding scale in the receiving countries. Most of these migrants became members of exclusive subcommunities and, if legal, often found themselves 'hooked' on social benefits; if illegal, they survived with the sporadic help of their compatriots. Younger, less-educated, usually single Russians with significant social capital were more successful, at least in terms of short-term provisions. Their professional ambitions and expectations were usually lower than those of the older professional Russians. Their higher energy and their desire to learn the language and new skills rendered them more attractive for the Western job market.

Notes

1   My interviews in the village of Smena in Russia (1998) show that barter is used not only between individuals but whole firms and corporations, trading raw materials for ready-made products, etc.
2   Both cases recorded in London.
3   Ledeneva (1996) argues that in present-day Russia *blat* is replaced by money payments. My own short fieldwork in Russia and Belorussia shows that this might be true in large cities and with established institutions or corporations, while people in smaller towns or villages still very much resort to *blat.*
4   This saying is reversed in present-day Russia: 'You don't need 100 friends, you need 100 roubles'.
5   Doomernik includes such features as employment, command of German, personal satisfaction, social and cultural associations, etc.
6   Particularly, I have talked with the owner of an [admittedly stolen] car business and one of the masterminds behind prostitute trafficking. Interviews were conducted informally and without 'getting into too much detail'.
7   Which I was unable to locate on my visit to Moscow.
8   With rare exceptions such as small groups of older Russian Jews or family-based circles of Georgians.
9   P. Bourdieu (1992), *Distinction. A Social Critique of the Judgement of Taste*, London, Routledge.
10 Aside from social relations, social capital includes obligations and expectations, information channels, and social norms (J. Coleman (1994), 'Social Capital in the Creation of Human Capital', *American Journal of Sociology*, S95–S120).

Chapter 6

Cultural Discourses

Introduction

The following two chapters on culture and ethnicity are devoted to expanding upon the ideas presented in previous chapters. They will draw the topics of community, subcommunity and social networks together, while explaining why Russian migrants present an ethnographic case which is both instructive to the study of other migrant groups and original in its contribution to the above-mentioned theoretical topics.

As in the case of general cultural debates in anthropology, the early studies of migrant cultures came under attack for presenting cultures as reified closed entities, within which migrants were 'exoticized' and even 'tribalized' by anthropologists (Akhbar and Shore, 1995; Frankenberg, 1994; Macdonald, 1993). Consequent studies in migration, following general culture de-essentializing trends, argued that modern migrants are in fact 'transnational' or 'hybridized', most of them being 'men of at least two worlds' (Benmayor and Skotnes, 1994; Grillo, 1985;[1] Hutchinson, 1996). Moreover, the idea of migrants as culture carriers became suspect as the very notion of 'culture' in a (post)modern world, along with 'ethnicity', came to be seen as a subjective construct – imagined, invented and easily manipulated by the 'culture carriers' (Mandel, 1994; Tonkin et al., 1996). It has been argued that in the modern world, with its ever-expanding information technology and opportunities to travel and work abroad, people cross geographical and symbolic boundaries with an ease previously known only to elite cosmopolitans. Migrants, it was argued, are no longer 'migrants' in the traditional sense of the word. Instead, they are commuters, temporary workers and true internationals. While attention was called to the power relations between the rich and the poor nations (north and south, west and east), which lie at the root of the 'new' migration, migrants were presented as more or less free agents choosing to inhabit the worlds of perceived opportunities (Fischer et al., 1997; Hammer et al., 1997; Havinga and Boker, 1999; Petronoti, 1995). Migrant identities were said to shift easily, being subject to constant negotiation, challenging the old ideas of 'roots', 'belonging' and 'tradition' (Melotti, 1997; Ong, 2002). In this context, cultural adaptation to the host society in the form of 'acculturation' or 'assimilation' appears irrelevant as the migrant gains independence from the bounds of 'his culture' or 'his ethnicity', freely floating in a (post)modern world of his fellow transnationals.

In the following chapters on culture and ethnicity, I want to investigate whether this condition is true of Russian migrants. I shall ask whether Russian discourse does in fact reflect a lack of 'cultural' or 'ethnic' constraints, and whether Russians' everyday lives demonstrate that 'culture' and 'ethnicity' have become redundant notions in their migratory experience. In other words, does 'being Russian' or 'being from the CIS' matter to the migrants? Are Russian migrants 'men of two worlds', feeling equally 'at home' in the CIS and abroad, or are they still psychologically or practically bound by their experience and identity as Russians?

Instructed by the discovery of group and individual variation in the Russian use of social networks and informal economy (discussed in the previous chapter), I shall also ask whether my conclusions about the Russian discourse on culture and ethnicity can be generalized to Russians as a group; or, are there individual differences in the way migrants speak of and feel about their 'Russianness'?

I shall start this chapter with a brief theoretical overview of the term 'culture' as it is used in anthropology, with special emphasis on the contemporary criticism of culture as a reified entity. I shall show how, at least initially, cultural stereotypes help the migrants make sense of the host society, and help members of the host society relate to the migrants. A discussion of stereotypes will be followed by examples of cultural discourses expressed through different contexts, such as religion, language and literature, behaviour, or as a heritage to be passed on to the children. I shall then turn to the topic of acculturation and assimilation which, although largely discredited in academic discourse, remains of concern for migrants.

6.1 Culture: Brief Survey of Contemporary Debate

Similar to the term 'community', the term 'culture' has accumulated an enormous amount of semantic baggage. Criticism of 'culture' is similar to that of 'community' and is triggered by the realization that 'cultures' are neither homogenous nor closed; that reified and essentialized notions of culture are outdated.

Wolf addressed this problem in the 1960s, rejecting treatment of culture as a 'singular, highly bounded, self-maintaining and self-correcting system' (Wolf, 1974: xi).[2] Wolf's observations sound strikingly (post)modern:

> Having long seen cultures and societies as isolated and distinctive, we must learn to see them in interchange and cultural synthesis. Having learned to visualise cultural boundaries as fixed and stationary, we must now learn to see them as shifting and evanescent. (Wolf, 1974: xii)

In line with the idea of shifting boundaries, the term 'transnationalism' has gained popularity in recent migration studies. Staring (2001), an anthropologist studying illegal Turks in The Netherlands, cites the pioneers of transnationalism who observed that migrants build social fields that link together their countries of origin and destination. The migrants

> ... take actions, make decisions, feel concerns and develop identities within social networks that connect them to two or more societies simultaneously. Strongly improved communications technologies as well as improved means of transportation, support the development of transnational networks, and shape the opportunities for immigrants to maintain close-knit ties with other network members in other parts of the world. (Staring, 2001: 2)

As a description of the real-world changes that affect the migrants, transnationalism seems to give an accurate description of large numbers of people who, due to intensifying economic inequalities between countries, move to places of greater opportunities. These individuals commute between countries of origin and receiving countries, maintaining links with their friends and relatives abroad. However, transnationalism has also inspired theoretical debates on culture, implying that the people have not only become more mobile and connected to countries other than their own, but have, as it were, stripped off certain constraints of culture and become 'transcultural'. In a widely shared consensus at present, culture 'is understood not as a reified entity but in terms of processual identity, as a constantly changing aspect of people's lives which is ascribed and inscribed by their experiences' (Raj, 1997: 129).

Part of the reason that the traditional 'culture' concept has come under attack has to do with an ideological shift related to the 'discovery' of power and inequality inherent in the relationship between an anthropologist and his subjects. From the arguments about anthropology's colonial roots, to the critique of the present-day distancing practice ('exoticizing' or 'orientalizing' the 'other'), anthropologists have become acutely self-conscious about their positioning within the 'field'. Self-awareness led to a re-examination of questions in regard to representation and meaning.[3]

Abu-Lughod (1991) argues for writing 'against culture' as a way of dealing with the built-in inequalities of fieldwork.[4] In essence, she suggests that one should write about the everyday lives of people and not their 'culture', concentrating on common human rather than 'peculiar' behaviours.

> And the particulars suggest that others live as we perceive ourselves living, not as robots programmed with 'cultural' rules, but as people going through life agonising over decisions, making mistakes, trying to make themselves look good, enduring tragedies and personal losses, enjoying others, and finding moments of happiness. (Abu-Lughod, 1991: 158)

Aside from the apparent difficulty of separating the notions of culture and everyday life (where does one end and another begin; are they not expressed through each other?), I find Abu-Lughod's approach particularly useful. Migrants identifying as 'Russians' tells us little about their mundane concerns, which might be very similar to those of the English and the Dutch.

However, culture remains important insofar as it is seen as such, both by the migrants themselves and by members of the host society. Culture and cultural differences in particular enter prominently into people's own discourse (Verkuyten, 1997: 99). To examine this discourse's significance in the everyday life of the migrants, we shall question what 'culture' and indeed 'Russian culture' mean to the migrants.

6.2 Discussing Culture

In this section I shall argue that although cultural differences are commonly perceived as important by the migrants, there is little consensus on what 'culture', and particularly 'Russian culture', entails.

'Culture' may be understood differently by the migrants and the host society. Russians often speak of 'high culture', meaning arts and sciences, while the Dutch and the British often use the term to speak of traditions and customs. Hardwick (1993: 5) notes that 'Russians have ... been slow to assimilate into American life because of the cultural baggage they brought with them'. She is referring to the incompatibility perceived by the Russians of their own great historical traditions with the 'popcorn Mickey Mouse' host culture, or lack of it. The Russian word *nekul'turniy* (uncultured) or *beskul'turniy* (devoid of culture) implies 'uncultivated' or 'ill-mannered'.

Although Russians see themselves as representatives of Russian culture, they are well aware of the fact that they are separated from it. Lev, an unemployed doctor from Amsterdam, contrasts what he terms 'African culture' in The Netherlands (including festivals, shows and other colourful events defined as 'cultural' by Dutch organizers) with a lack of Russian cultural spirit. The situation in Amsterdam is described as 'devoid of culture':

> For us [Russians] Amsterdam is a cultural void, a desert if you will. The only culture around is Dutch culture. Whatever we bring with us – books, films, and memories – it remains in our rented flats … You will not find anything Russian in Amsterdam except for whatever they organize for local tourists: like we had an exhibit of treasures of Catherine the Great, or – whatever it was called – something with weapons from the Kremlin storage house … There's no Russian *duh* (spirit) in it. This has little to do with us. (Lev)

My London informants referred to 'imported', 'lost' or 'transplanted' Russian culture, which appears as an artefact in a historical museum, objectified, viewed under the glass, taken out of context. As such, culture 'can be exhibited for tourists or presented to [non-Russian] friends' (Petya). Petya, a retired accountant living in London for two years, disapproves of such 'fossilized' culture. He also admits that his Russian friends, who have lived in London longer than him, have begun to view it 'as something they've imported from home, like vodka and matryoshkas'. Living culture, supposedly existing in Russia, may also be found in London, but in a 'limited capacity' (Petya).

Petya is reifying Russian culture – magnifying it in opposition to his non-Russian surroundings. In my interviews with recently arrived migrants, Russian culture did become explicit, conspicuous and exaggerated in contrast to more muted reflections by the Russians or Belorussians in their native countries during my fieldwork in the CIS. Most of the indigenous Russian or Belorussian informants did not know what I meant by asking them about culture, while the migrants spoke of culture as a self-evident category. It would appear that the migratory situation makes culture serve as a kind of defence against a strange environment, something used as a fortress against an invasion of foreign influences.

However, as I shall discuss in the following sections, this Fortress Culture is not unitary; in other words, the very notion of culture is understood and used differently by the migrants in various contexts. The following section addresses Russian discourse on cultural differences in which the uniqueness of cultures is seen as self-evident, while concrete examples of cultural differences reveal a range of views as to what Russian culture actually entails.

6.2.1 Cultural Differences and Similarities

As Richmond (1969) suggests, cultural differences might not really be that great, especially in the case of structurally similar countries of origin and destination. The case can be made that modern Russia, with its capitalist ambitions and greater openness to the rest of the world, is no longer producing a breed of citizens completely foreign to the Western world. Thus, Russian migrants are not necessarily experiencing culture shock or cognitive strain once in the receiving country.

> The greater the similarity between the culture and the way of life of the former place of residence and the new one the less likely a migrant will experience cognitive dissonance or role strain ... Classical studies of immigration have tended to exaggerate the problem of 'marginal man' torn between the irreconcilable demands of different cultures and socially unable to establish his legitimate membership in either. Contemporary migrants are frequently 'men of two worlds' able to move easily from one to the other. (Richmond, 1969: 266–7)

Writing in the late 1960s, Richmond's statements are reflective of the debates on transnationality and locality that followed critique of cultures as reified entities. Migrants came to be seen as well-informed autonomous agents rather than limited culture carriers unable to adapt to or understand the host society (Benmayor and Skotnes, 1994; Hammer et al., 1997; Hutchinson, 1996). But does the Russian discourse reflect this ease of oscillation between two worlds?

While it might be wrong to conceive of migrant cultures as homogenous, self-contained wholes on a theoretical level, it has been noted that the people themselves use reified notions of their own cultures and of foreign cultures as well (Baumann and Sunier, 1995; Calgar, 1997). In the common discourse, like in earlier anthropology, compatibility or similarity of cultures (often implicitly enclosed by nation-states) is often taken for granted or even overlooked in favour of more conspicuous cultural differences. My ethnographic data suggests that very few migrants are 'shocked' by cultural differences between themselves and their English or Dutch hosts. However, as we shall further discuss, migrants do tend to emphasize cultural differences and operate with cultural stereotypes, often ignoring the similarities.

Once a migrant finds himself in the receiving country, he looks for similarities in order to adjust to new conditions, avoiding radical changes within himself. At the same time, he also looks for differences, which could explain problems of adjustment. Dina, a former engineer from Georgia, tells of her desire to find 'things in common' with the Dutch, a process happening simultaneously with her evocation of differences:

> I don't think the Dutch are creatures from another planet; they understood most of my basic needs. When I was lonely, I could say to Karen [Dina's Dutch friend]: I'm lonely, and she understood I needed company; or I could tell her I missed my family [in Georgia] and she would say: I miss mine too [they live in the extreme north of The Netherlands and Karen does not get to see them as often as she likes]. Of course it's not the same – I cannot go back, because I'm illegal. I can only write letters, and she can visit any time – but still, she understands my feelings … But I don't think she can understand what a family means to me … Karen grew up differently – like all the Dutch, her family is used to keeping distance from each other, allowing privacy, not interfering … A Georgian family is so tight it can be suffocating at times, but a sister is always there for a brother, a grandmother is always there for a grandchild … (Dina)

Dina acknowledges that there are basic similarities between her and Karen's ways of feeling and understanding. She also points out differences that stand in the way of complete understanding. However, in a recently conducted interview with Dina, she told of Karen's loss of a grandfather and how Karen felt 'like a part of her was missing' – a feeling Dina had about her family in Georgia. That human link of bereavement made Dina think that perhaps her Dutch friend is not so dissimilar in the way she feels about her family, despite the fact that she expresses her feelings differently.

> I almost felt guilty for once thinking of Karen as cool and distant, that her family didn't matter for her as much, that she'd talk to them about money or just visit socially and live her independent life … I thought Karen, like all the Dutch, did not want to get emotionally involved. [When her grandfather died] I saw a different side of her – she became vulnerable and opened up and I realized that perhaps she wouldn't acknowledge her love for her grandfather the way I would about mine not because she didn't feel it but because she wasn't taught to express it this way. (Dina)

As Dina herself spent more time in The Netherlands (the last abstract from an interview was recorded almost two years after the first one), she came to realize that the stereotype of the Dutch being 'cool and distant' in emotionally charged matters might not lie in the way the Dutch and the Georgians 'feel' about their families, but in the way they learn to express their feelings. I find this interview particularly instructive as, in the course of my fieldwork, I have encountered a number of migrants who, proportional to the length of stay in the receiving country, remained aware of cultural differences but were willing to acknowledge the underlying similarities.

The discourse on cultural differences tended to be more extreme ('they are not like us') for those migrants who were unemployed, socially isolated or illegal. We shall further discuss the example of an IT consultant Sasha who makes negative generalizations about Westerners. Although professionally and financially successful, Sasha suffers from low self-esteem and shyness which, he admits, makes it difficult for him to forge friendships and fit in with his colleagues. Zhenya, a more sociable and personally open computer specialist from London, is much more positive about his colleagues in particular and Western mentality in general:

> I cannot really tell how my [British] colleagues are different from us [Russian specialists] – except for they tend to be more punctual and they also leave on time, while we tend to work through the night ... I don't have much contact with the British people in general, but it's my impression that they aren't that different ... After work, they hurry to their families, and if I didn't have to do my absolute best to get an extension [of a work permit] I'd also leave at 5 p.m., not a minute later ... I know some Russians think the British are completely different creatures, but I guess if you actually work side by side with them, they are just like any other colleagues ... (Zhenya)

Generally, more integrated Russians addressed similarities between Russian and Western culture. However, migrants consistently acknowledging cultural similarities were in a minority, and most of the spontaneous discourse I have recorded focused on cultural differences. In order to answer why this might be the case, I shall first look at different ways cultural differences are evoked in migrant discourse.

Migrants often speak of culture on the basis of broad national generalizations, using the stories of the people they personally know to illustrate how the culture differences are concretely enacted. In an interview with a Dutch newspaper, a young Russian athlete, who arrived in The Netherlands in 1994 with his mother, makes some judgement-free observations:

> If you meet somebody in The Netherlands for the first time, he asks you about literally everything. After that, you might not see him for months. In Russia, it's the other way around: few questions asked the first time, but the second meeting will soon follow. (Kirill Poltavtsjov, 5 May 1997)[5]

Usually, cultural differences are discussed more cautiously in mixed groups in order to avoid offence, and tend to be less judgemental. Concrete examples are usually avoided and national generalizations tend to be more neutral. However, when Russians and non-Russians know each other as friends or find themselves in an informal relaxed atmosphere, opinions on culture can be less guarded. Most of the 'mixed' discussions I have recorded take on a joking tone. Although 'outside' opinions are often dismissed in favour of the 'natives know better' perspective, the tone of these discussions tends to be reconciliatory, with the involved parties attempting to either explain their own culture or to deal with irreconcilable differences in an amiable way.

Richard, a Dutch student of Russian language and a volunteer for Russia-based charity projects, likes to contrast Russia with The Netherlands. He begins with Russia's formidable size and ends up with generalizations about the openness and generosity of Russian homes as opposed to the cold and closed nature of Dutch ones. Once, Richard joined a discussion in the Russian cafe, *Oblomov*, Anton, an artist and dilettante businessman from Ekaterinburg, and Igor, an unemployed young man from Orel, were debating the meaning of Russian culture. I initiated the discussion, posing the question, 'What is Russian culture?' The mood at the table could be described as 'drunk and sentimental'.

> *Igor*: I miss Russian culture here [in Amsterdam]. I don't miss the hardship
> …
> *Anton*: I don't know – what's there to miss … I just miss my friends … What do you mean by 'culture'?
> *Igor*: I also mean – friends, and kissing a girl in a park and just dropping by without invitation …
> *Richard*: People behave more informally in Russia, I also miss it here …
> *Igor*: But you miss it differently, because you're not Russian. You have to be Russian to miss Russian culture. You may like Russian girls, but … They are more interesting for you, right? But you cannot behave like a Russian guy – no offence intended [They all laugh] …

The two Russians, Igor and Anton, dismiss Richard's modest contribution to their discussion on Russian culture on the grounds that he is Dutch; although he can sympathize with Russian culture, he does not understand it. The Russians, however, claim to 'understand' the Dutch, enabling them to judge their culture and their character. While the tone remains amiable, cultural differences are assumed to be beyond negotiation. Although this discussion carried on for another hour, the opinions remained fixed.

Another subject that came up in the above-mentioned exchange was that of gender, when Igor said that Richard 'cannot behave like a Russian guy'. Cultural differences become particularly prominent through gender discourse.

Ellen, a British employee at the Russian-British Centre, finds gender relations particularly revealing of the way Russian culture is lived out. She finds it understandable that many Russian women choose British men because 'Russian men don't know how to treat women'. Ellen paints a poignant portrait of Russian men in London: short and podgy, wearing Adidas trainers with pouched knees, black leather coat on top, behaving like the world belongs to them while – even if they've lived in Britain for years – they do not learn English. Russian culture has, according to Ellen, spoilt these men. It has allowed them to become lazy and mean, while women do all the work – both in the house and outside. No wonder, Ellen concludes, that Russian women are more attracted to British culture which aspires to treat the two sexes more equally.

In contrast to the spoilt Russian men, Western men are said to be more egalitarian and to share domestic responsibilities. A former medical professional, now the wife of the former Russia correspondent of the Dutch newspaper *NRC Handelsblad*, Hubert Smeets, recalls her husband's visit to her Moscow family in her interview with a Dutch newspaper *Trouw*:

> Her Moscow family had a hard time getting used to the position of a Dutch man in the house, says Frantova: 'If Hubert cooks, my mother feels indignant. But it irritates the Dutch if she shoots straight to the kitchen to prepare the table, being 75 years old'. (Olga Frantova)

However, views on the subject of gender differ as widely within 'cultures' as between them. Sergei, a theatre director from London, likes to muse on the nature of Russian-English social relationships. He tells many anecdotes from his personal life, blaming Russian women for being spoilt:

> Some Russian women want to get the best of both worlds – being independent and demanding respect and yet assuming that men should pay for everything, even for their girlfriends they bring on a dinner date. Men should refuse softly. Russian men are not emancipated yet, they are used to both paying for everything and acting like teddy bears ... Many different Russian women thought they'd be going out with the lords, and some of them do. There are some mysterious women, some princesses; others are simple country bumpkins or money bags ... British women – it's difficult to generalize; those from

mixed marriages are generally more temperamental. They can be eccentric, alert, feminist, changing. My students, 22–25, are all from different countries, reflect this diversity … It depends on social rules of conduct they've learned, a Spanish woman is somehow different from the Russian one. (Sergei)

Sam, British husband of a Russian waitress, observes differences in dress and attitude comparing Russian and British women:

First of all, Russian women dress up for everything. Going shopping, going to a museum, visiting a doctor, climbing a mountain – you can always expect them to be meticulously groomed, clothes starched, body perfumed. High heels are a must … My wife thinks British women are prudish and have no sense of style, the only ones that wear make-up are under 20, going to a disco. She wonders how British men can find them attractive. (Sam)

Galya, a bank teller from Ekaterinburg working in London, frequently visits her home town and finds her own attitude towards gender roles in Russia changed:

I like it in England, but I'm still Russian; Russians understand me best. Still, when I go back to Ekaterinburg I find Russian men's attitudes towards me rather odd. It doesn't bother them whether I'm married or not interested in conversing with them – they take my reluctance to talk to them personally, they can even get in a physical fight with my boyfriend. Still, I think that Russian men are more gentlemen than the British, treating you like a woman, paying for everything, opening doors for you, helping you put your coat on. You want to look good in Russia, it gives you confidence. Here I also make a point of making my British boyfriend pay for everything. (Galya)

Gender discourse is a good example of how culture differences are discussed as conflicting, while the difference itself may be perceived subjectively. While Ellen talks of the Russian men as boorish in comparison to more refined Englishmen, and Olga Frantova recalls her Russian family's surprise at the 'domesticated habits' of her Dutch husband, Galya sees Russian men as 'more gentlemen than the British', and Sergei blames them for not 'being emancipated' and 'paying for everything and acting like teddy bears'. Russian women, in the words of the Russians themselves, might also be seen as being anything from soft and feminine to hard and calculating. Although the gender roles of Western and British men and women are clearly perceived as different, the content of this difference is not fixed. Another example of this paradox is the Russian and Western ideas of 'fun'.

Olga, my key London informant, married to an Englishman, observes:

> Russians can really enjoy themselves to the full potential (*veselitsya na polnuyu katushku*), while the British, like my husband, like to discuss work and drink beer. My husband's friends would go to pubs every evening and drink buckets of beer but their jokes wouldn't improve from it. The British sense of humour is dry and can be hurtful as it intends to outsmart people, to make them feel stupid. (Olga)

Ironically, Sam, an English man married to a Russian, refers to the Russians in social situations as 'rather grim'. Russians 'drink in order to forget' and 'their jokes are rather sad' (Sam). A similar view is expressed by Margarita, a St Petersburg poet from Amsterdam:

> [A Russian party] usually starts with laughter but ends in tears. In comparison to the more sophisticated Dutch humour, our fixated fascination with political failures, adultery, and other's wealth seems rather pathetic. 'Fun' consists of getting drunk, not having a good time per se. (Margarita)

Clearly, Olga and Margarita both perceive Russian and Western ideas of 'fun' as contrasting, but while one sees Russian fun as 'enjoyment to the full potential', another one refers to it as 'pathetic'. Olga sees English jokes as dry and hurtful, while Margarita sees Dutch humour as 'sophisticated'; in both cases Western humour is directly opposed to Russian humour. Sam's view of Russians as sad drinkers also generalizes perceived cultural habits while making an implicit comparison in favour of one's own culture.

Negative generalizations about 'representatives of other cultures' are quite common in migrant discourse. I have often heard generalized statements like 'they don't know how to work', 'they are all so distant', etc. from the migrants. Sasha, an IT consultant from London, reflects on the differences in the Russian and Western mentality:

> The Americans and the British have different points of view from the Russians. One can talk to them about events, concerts, prices in the store, but these conversations don't touch the soul. What binds the Russian community together here [in London] is not the language but culture: deep Russian culture. In three years I have learned English well enough to discover how different we really are – despite understanding each other's language. Our mentalities don't cross. If he talks or makes a joke the British ask: What is it about? What is he laughing at? Despite common physical needs, the Russians and the British have a different view of life. Main continent Europeans and especially East Europeans are closer

to us in values. These are common human values such as family, friendship, empathy and sympathy for other people; as opposed to American values, such as getting a discount on good food, picking up a cute chick. Some Russians here absorb the worst of the British and American cultures. What is an obvious humanitarian value to the Russians has to be proven in court in the US. The Russian intelligentsia doesn't need a talk show host to tell them how to live. When they are sent to hell by the Russian bureaucrat, it feels better than the polite denial of a British official which is cold and impersonal. Noble feelings or any real human emotions are absent in the British and Americans. Not that they are worse than the Russians: just different. (Sasha)

Sasha's final conciliatory note does not conceal the clearly judgemental tone he uses to describe cultural differences. Sasha also acknowledges that 'some Russians' absorb [bad] Western values, while others reject them in favour of retaining 'common human values' which are supposedly inherent in the East European culture. In the face of Western culture, he suggests, Russians with their openness and sincerity present a united front, collectively standing for 'family, friendship, empathy and sympathy for other people'. This is described in stark opposition to the clearly inferior Western values, such as 'getting a discount on good food, picking up a cute chick'.

In direct contrast to Sasha, Sergei, a theatre director from London, speaks of Russian mentality as 'petty and mercantile', evoking the 'culture of envy' and Russian inferiority complex. Russian pettiness is seen in opposition to the Western 'capitalist system that has taught people to be more broad-minded and accepting of different views and styles' and which has 'influenced them to think in bigger terms' (Sergei). Here, again, we witness simultaneous reification of the difference between Russian and Western mentality without consensus as to what this difference entails.

At the beginning of this section I asked why dialogue on cultural differences is more prominent than discussions of cultural similarities. Through examples of concepts such as gender and 'fun', we have noticed that 'Russian culture' is not always consistent and examples of 'cultural behaviour' can be mutually contradictory. Social behaviour, manifested through interaction with non-Russian colleagues and friends, is also not 'fixed' in the sense that it is being interpreted on the basis of subjective experiences (such as length of stay in the receiving country or exposure to the members of 'other cultures'). In this respect, I disagree with Barth (1969) who says it is the boundaries, not the content, that matter. In my opinion, observing how opinions change over time, content appears to be more significant. Since neither the cultural nor the social behaviour of the migrants comes across as 'consistently Russian' in migrant discourse, perhaps cultural differences are 'constructed' rather than objectively observed, and indeed 'fluid' rather than 'fixed'. This observation, however, stops short of explaining why cultural differences are evoked in the first place.

Cultural differences are expressed most strongly through stereotypes. We can learn a lot by examining the function of stereotypes, and asking who uses them the most and why. Such a study may reveal to us the importance of stories of cultural differences and teach us how these stories function in the context of the receiving country.

6.2.2 Stereotypes

There are many possible reasons why migrants, along with the members of the host society, use cultural stereotypes. As McDonald notes, much of the discourse on 'construction' and 'invention' of stereotypes possibly emanates from 'philosophical and literary traditions which do not always take the sometimes messy trivia of daily events into account' (McDonald, 1993: 232). Stereotypes might be more than just imagined, since 'after all, people have the opportunity to observe directly that a number of "alleged" differences are meaningful differences, for example, with regard to gender roles, the upbringing of children, religion, customs, norms, and opinions' (Verkuyten, 1997: 102). As discussed in the previous section, most of my informants felt that the differences they were observing were 'real' and 'objective'. They would have been offended to learn that they have 'imagined' or 'constructed' these differences.

This is not to say that these 'real' stereotypes cannot be used and manipulated by migrants for ideological or practical purposes (Al-Rasheed, 1995; Baumann, 1995; Verkuyten, 1997). For example, stereotypes may be used as a psychological defence mechanism by migrants who feel socially or legally vulnerable in the receiving country.

> Migrants are concerned about 'fitting in' the new world around them and making sense of new situations and challenges. Perhaps at initial stages of migration cultural stereotypes help the migrants to deal with new situations by explaining hosts' behaviour and justifying their own failures. (Bowie, 1993: 170)

As with discussions of cultural differences, stereotypes may serve to familiarize the migrant with the new society, or familiarize members of the host society with the migrants. Gerda, a friend of Oksana (the Russian restaurateur from St Petersburg), admits to not knowing 'anything about the Russians' before meeting Oksana. Remembering this first encounter, Gerda self-consciously reflects:

> I met Oksana through work … Rather than approaching her as an unknown entity, I tried to dig out all the knowledge of Russia and Russians I had stored … I was very surprised to find out later that Oksana was not a communist, didn't drink vodka and found winters in Holland [which were supposed to be much milder than in Russia] freezing cold. (Gerda)

Gerda reflects that individual Russians may not fit into a stereotype but she also admits that 'whenever I meet another Russian, like yourself, I cannot help wondering whether you drink vodka or find the Dutch winter warm'. 'Stereotypes,' Gerda continues, 'also have to do with what you've learned in your own society about others.' In school, Gerda learned that 'Russians were different from the Dutch' and these differences, although not always carrying positive or negative connotations, are often presented as contrasting and absolute. But as Gerda's Russian circle of friends expanded, she started thinking of them in individual terms ('This friend is easy-going, that one is shy but caring') rather than collectively.

Generally, in London and Amsterdam, the Russians' stereotypical opinion of themselves in contrast to the hosts does not differ much whether the host is the Dutch or the British. I have often heard the following oppositions mentioned:

Russian	Dutch	British
Open and warm	Direct and cold	Indirect and cold[6]
Women: feminine, attractive	Coarse and rude	Coarse and distant
Men: strong, supportive	Mild, indifferent	Weak, treacherous[7]

In the previously mentioned example of Dina, a Georgian engineer, continuous exposure to the Dutch has made her realize that the 'cool and distant' stereotypes are not always individually applicable and may be generally suspect 'once you get to know the Dutch better'. The idea that more contact with each other broadens the mind and abolishes certain stereotypes is also voiced by Helen O'Connor, an employee at the British/Russian Centre in London, who sums up the stereotypes of the Russian women in Britain:

We all know what the Soviet stereotypes of old were: Russian women were bulky shot-putters or tractor drivers, or else fragile ballerinas or even occasionally heroic types such as cosmonauts. These images have been replaced with stereotypes of Russian women as prostitutes, or down-at-heel *babushki* standing in the cold holding up one object for sale. Travel broadens the mind, they say, and the number of British citizens visiting Russia for work, leisure or other activities has vastly increased which has to some extent served to mitigate the stereotypes; on the other hand, media representations continue to dwell on the sensational and so those who have not had the experience of visiting Russia and getting to know individuals there have little choice in what to take on board. (O'Connor, 1997: 12)

Indeed, as we further discuss the role of external labelling in creation of identity, media representation has an important role to play in maintenance and replication of stereotypes. Those Russian informants who had easier access to information about their country of destination in the CIS (either through the media, or through travelling friends) generally used fewer stereotypes.

In regard to stereotypes and cultural differences, although cultural uniqueness and homogeneity are asserted, migrant discourse challenges these assertions by giving concrete examples of cultural conduct. Whether through behaviour, religion or language, culture is shown to be 'more than one thing'. I shall now turn to the discussion of the different contexts in which the concept of 'culture' is used by Russians.

6.2.3 Culture as Behaviour

The statement, 'Culture is expressed through people's behaviour' (*kul'tura byrazhaetsya v povedenii*) was a common response of my Russian informants to the question of what culture meant to them. As mentioned in the sections on cultural differences and stereotypes, Russians often saw British and Dutch behaviour at home, on the street, or at work as manifestations of their culture. The way the Russians behaved in London and Amsterdam also elicited 'cultural observations' from the Dutch and the British. Returning to the question of 'living culture', Sergei, a theatre director, had this to say about the English meaning of culture (as custom):

The only time when you get some true living culture here is at the [Russian] party ... Drinking, jokes, deep conversations, remembering the past – that's what I mean ... Anybody can spot us [Russians] by the way we behave. (Sergei)

Asya met her Dutch partner, Jan, in Moscow. After only three months in Amsterdam, Asya already had many observations about the 'Dutch way of doing things' and, implicitly, Dutch culture. During their conversation in a cafe, Jan and Asya spoke of 'institutional differences of behaviour', when Russian or Dutch officials, or the service sector, operated differently and thus enacted culture:

> *Asya*: You go to a doctor here and he asks you a few questions and just sends you home with one prescription. No X-rays, no urine or blood samples – no problem, you're alive and moving, so move on.
>
> *Jan*: I was surprised how many samples I had to bring and how many prescriptions I ended up having [while working] in Moscow. Here, you don't normally even go to your doctor if you're not seriously ill. In Russian you'd be in the hospital with a common cold.
>
> *Asya*: With a chronic cold perhaps. At least there you get the idea that doctors care about your health …
>
> *Jan*: Or exaggerate your illness …
>
> *Asya*: It's our custom to be caring.
>
> *Jan*: [Half jokingly] It's our culture to be efficient.

Jan and Asya usually end up complimenting each other's 'customs' but remain loyal to the ones they have learned in their own country. On another occasion, Jan and Asya were discussing traffic regulations and adherence to the law, concluding that the Dutch were generally 'law-abiding' but also 'occasionally frivolous' (especially in the case of the bikers ignoring street lights). Russians, on the other hand, 'had no general respect for the law and could break it any time they could afford it' (meaning, avoiding police fines). The discussion was concluded with the admission that the Dutch police and public both behave according to their 'culture of respect and tolerance' (Asya) while the Russians 'have a more cynical, pragmatic culture stemming from general corruption' (Jan).

'Being Dutch' has different implications for different Russians, but is generally understood as a way of behaving in a particular way. In this respect, Russians admit that culture can be learned, not inherited. For example, one can 'become' Dutch if one acts Dutch. But there is also a sense of limitation, as when one is dreaming 'if I only could'. The Internet newsgroup 'Russen in Nederland' published an essay by a Ukrainian migrant, called 'If I was Dutch':

> … I would have faithfully paid my taxes and not cursed my government. Would have gotten myself a big dog to walk down the canals in the evenings. In the

summer I would have lived on a yacht, in the evening drinking Portuguese Port with friends of all possible nationalities, sexual orientations and world views … Every morning I would have gone to the flower market to buy different kinds of flowers … I would have driven to the airport to meet my Ukrainian friends in the small car. Why do I need a big and cool one? I would have tried to save money on gasoline and looked for free parking. But I would have offered my guests the most expensive and old varieties of cheese … ('Russen in Nederland', September 1999)

Conversations between Jan and Asya, and the above quote from 'Russen in Nederland', are examples of public or institutionalized behaviour becoming 'culturalized' and thus treated not just as institutional differences but as manifestations of culturally conditioned behaviour. A British electronics retailer from a chain store frequented by Russians told me that Russians have a particular style of shopping which irritates his colleagues. He claims to understand this behaviour, since he has 'read a lot about their culture' and 'can understand Russian behaviour':

> When a Russian walks into the store he already knows what he wants and he goes straight for it. He asks: 'Do you have such and such model phone?' Our response is normally: 'Yes, but let us first hear about your particular needs and tell you which phone best suits them.' Now, the Russian becomes agitated and says: 'No, I want THAT phone.' 'But,' say my colleagues, 'we also have …' At this stage the Russian stamps his foot and leaves the store unless I stop him and say: 'But of course we have THAT phone.' Then the Russian asks for a reduction. So I raise the price by 10 per cent and give him a reduction of 10 per cent. He is happy, I am happy … He knows very well what I'm doing, but it's a game he wants to play and he leaves with his phone – one happy customer … Knowing other cultures is good business, I can assure you! (Jim)

Jim's statement shows how people can 'think themselves' into another culture. When I shared Jim's observation with my Russian friend Sveta, she laughed: 'I don't think he's too far off!', confirming the fact that a foreigner really can learn culture by observing behaviour.

Culture is assumed to be expressed through behaviour both by Russians and by members of the host society. As we have seen, 'behaviour' is a broad category that includes all aspects of living or 'active' culture. Cultural behaviour reveals itself through interactions between people of the same 'culture' and people 'across cultures'; as well as through interactions between institutions and individuals. Cultural behaviour can also be extended to include customs and beliefs, as discussed in the following section.

6.2.4 Culture as Religion

Religion is often mentioned by Russians equivalent to Russian culture. Religious worship offers an opportunity to enact culture. This can be done through (traditionally Russian) Orthodoxy, Christianity or any other religious affiliation that sets a group apart by demarcating its area of belief and action, and by defining a group on the basis of this demarcation ('We believe/do things that way, therefore we are …').

In both London and Amsterdam, the largest gatherings of Russians, outside of the occasional Russian club or disco, takes place in churches. The congregation members mention both Russian community and culture in connection with their church. In Amsterdam, there are two Orthodox churches – the Moscow Church and the Orthodox Church Abroad. While the former is the 'popular church', the latter attracts a few members of the older waves. The Moscow Church also houses one of the two Russian schools in Amsterdam and has a modest library and book shop. Aside from these churches, a few Russians have joined local Catholic or Protestant churches and synagogues.

In London there are three Orthodox churches – the two Moscow Orthodox churches and the Russian Church Abroad – and a number of Anglican or international churches (notably St Luke's Church in Redcliffe Gardens, which has Russian-speaking pastors and services, and offers free English courses and Sunday school for Russian children; and Church '*Slovo Vechnosti*' – 'The Voice of Eternity' – which also includes a school for children and audio-videotheque). A small number of Russians have joined the Jehovah's Witnesses, and a very small percentage go to Baptist churches. There are a few Russian Jews in Munks synagogue.

In both London and Amsterdam, Moscow Orthodox churches attract a regular congregation of over a hundred members, while on holidays, such as Easter or New Year, there might be up to a thousand visitors in Amsterdam and a few thousand in London. Congregations are not exclusively Russian but include other Orthodox worshippers, including British and Dutch.

Even if not all Russian churchgoers in London and Amsterdam are religious in any strict sense, the church functions as a magnet for those who feel alienated from Russian culture. For occasional church attendants, the Orthodox church seems more of a social club than a religious organization. Russians in both London and Amsterdam often referred to the Moscow Orthodox church as 'our church', and spoke of it in connection with Russian culture. Many occasional attendants admitted to going to church 'to meet other Russians' or 'to talk Russian' or to 'share common concerns'. Church notice boards were usually used for secular advertisements of Russians looking for work or apartments, seeking Russian-speaking nannies or offering translation services.

A Greek priest at the Orthodox church in London reflects:

> Who are these Russians? There are different forces at play, and language alone cannot bind them together. Even within one family one gets different languages being spoken, such as second generation children using English. Some immigrants come to the church while others don't. Some newer members come to church led by stereotypical ideas of Orthodoxy; some are put off by the elaborate service and manifest religiosity of the ritual.
>
> Most of the Russian-speakers come to our church for special ceremonies or celebrations. In the past decade about five or six thousand people came to us, the majority coming for events like Easter service. Up to three hundred come for Sunday services and the flow increases. Some people coming from Russia wait for a couple of years before coming to us, because of something happening in their life or because they suddenly awake. People don't come here for material goods as we can rarely offer such help. One feels awkward coming to church for anything but contact with God. (A. Fostiropoulos)

A group of five Orthodox church attendants in London – among whom were two British, one Greek and two Russians – also spoke of the 'living culture', enacted through Orthodox worship and conduct. While a Russian member of the congregation, retired doctor Vasya, asserted that 'Orthodoxy is part of Russian culture', his Greek friend clarified: 'But it's not exclusive to Russia'. This prompted a question from the British Orthodox: 'I wonder whether Russia would be the same without Orthodoxy?', to which Vasya replied: 'I don't think Russia would be what it now is without Orthodoxy, no'. Unfortunately, the conversation, which took place outside the church, stopped there. Perhaps this was due to the fact that my religious informants felt uncomfortable discussing such matters in my secular presence. On another occasion, one more Russian present during the above-mentioned discussion – a former accountant from Kiev named Aleftina – reflected:

> Culture comes from religion. Religion is not just about believing in God, it's also about following the path of the righteous, and living in particular way … Morality is also part of culture. (Aleftina)

Anna, who lost her job as a surgeon in Moldova after migrating to Britain, has regained something she feels she lost living in the CIS – ironically, her 'Russianness'.

> I became a religious person here [in the Anglican church with services in Russian]. I also became more Russian ... I mean in a sense that Russians are religious people, also Christian, although their branch [of Christianity, Orthodoxy] is different, they still believe in Jesus. In Kishinev [Moldova] I lived without religion, now Jesus has brought me back to my roots ... There are more of us here; we all came from the godless country, having forgotten our roots, where our people came from ... Thanks to the church, I'm Russian now. (Anna)

Religion, thus, is often seen by migrants not just as a passage into the domain of God but also as a bridge to Russian culture itself. Orthodoxy in particular may be seen as a cultural heritage transferable outside its country of origin. Yet, as we have seen from the above quote, 'Russian religion', similarly to 'Russian culture', can be expanded to encompass more than just Orthodoxy. By implication, although Russian culture is felt to be linked to religion, it is not defined by one type of religious worship. Like language and literature, discussed in the following section, religion is one way of talking about Russian culture without necessarily defining what culture concretely entails.

6.2.5 Culture as Heritage

Since 'Russians' are socially and ethnically diverse, language is sometimes the only common link between Russians in the West and their culture. An article about the fledgling Organization of Russian Artists in Britain (whose first meeting and one-day exhibition took place in March 1998 in Hampstead, London) recognized the fact that the art and the artists assembled were so diverse that their only link with Russian culture, albeit mystified and reified, was their shared language:

> Russian culture being powerful, distinctive, and with deep historical roots, a Russian artist in the West remains still a Russian artist. This Russianness is hard to define, but could be as simple as sharing of a common language. (Rogers and Lipskaya, 1998: 28)[8]

During my interviews with the British and the Dutch, who have either personal or professional contact with Russians, Russian culture was often spoken of as a self-evident category. It was described as something the migrants bring with them, both as 'luggage' and as an integral part of their personalities. 'Russian culture' can be perceived as both an asset and a limiting factor, as far as the Russians' integration into the host society is concerned. Henk, a

Dutch investment banker married to Tanya, a Russian actress, speaks of his wife as being able to give their daughter 'a little extra', to enrich her life with something that Dutch children would not have.

Some Russian parents try to impart Russian culture to their children by sending them to Russian schools, or buying Russian children's books, records and video tapes. I have also observed some parents trying to 'shelter' their children from certain Western children's TV programmes which they felt were inappropriate ('tasteless', 'uneducational', 'violent', 'simplistic'). Russian cartoons were felt to be of greater intellectual value. Some parents tried to influence the choice of their child's Russian friends to the exclusion of others, thus forming 'intentional societies' (Hechter, 1996) – these usually form the core of exclusive subcommunities. Often, children resist this enculturation and come to see their parents' culture as archaic and unnecessary, as Michael and Alina observe about their granddaughter who grew up in Britain:

> Our granddaughter lacks the cultural background to provide her with the context for participating in Russian children's culture. She doesn't understand the symbolism and the humour of Russian cartoons children's songs and fairy tales don't make much sense to her. She lives in a different world, where her peers listen to their own music and watch their own cartoons, which are different from ours as they stem from a different tradition. She prefers anything British to almost anything Russian. It is necessary for her to survive in the world she lives in, and our antiques are foreign to her. (Michael)

Other parents, especially mixed couples, chose to teach their children only the 'dominant' language. They justified this decision with reasons ranging from 'They won't speak Russian anyway, their friends won't speak it, it won't be taught in school' (Mariana) to 'Russian is the language of my past, the child doesn't need it for her future' (Raisa). Mariana, who admits to 'making a fine living' by ordering deliveries from Russia and selling Russian products in Amsterdam, thinks it will be fine for her children 'to work with Russia' – but if they want to make this choice and learn Russian, they can do it when they are old enough to make a choice for themselves. Raisa, who has a dual Israeli and Dutch nationality, has three sons speaking Hebrew, English and Dutch – 'sufficient to become true cosmopolitans'. Russian, however, is not a 'world language' and since the 'children lack the knowledge of Russia, and what it's like to live there, what's the use of learning the language?' (Raisa).

One parent refused to speak Russian to her son because she felt she needed more practice with English. In all cases, parents felt that it was not just the Russian language at stake, but culture as well. Unlike Raisa, who considers the Russian language useless without the culture reference, Tanya, a young actress from Odessa currently studying Theatre and Performance Arts in Amsterdam, reflects that through language and literature one can actually learn about culture:

> When I read [to my daughter] Russian fairy tales, she looks enchanted … I think these stories become what she lacks here – Russia … When I speak Russian to her, I also try to evoke the country she's never known but will some day visit … since it's part of her heritage. (Tanya)

In the course of my fieldwork I hoped to deduce a pattern that would explain why some parents choose to teach their children the Russian language and introduce them to literature and folklore, while others do not. In mixed couples, the choices made by the Russian parent were sometimes influenced by the British or Dutch spouse, but the eventual decisions of whether to 'give a child something extra' as opposed to 'burden the child with unnecessary weight' were made on the basis of parents' views of the importance of Russian culture as such.

Culture could be underplayed by being reduced to 'just some stories and songs' that children may as well learn in another language. Alternatively, culture could be magnified by exaggerating the importance of those stories and songs as crucial in the formation of the child's innermost thoughts and feelings to be carried into adulthood. Generally, more educated and older parents attributed greater importance to imparting Russian culture to their children. Russian couples found it practically easier and more 'natural' to teach their children the Russian language and folklore, while mixed couples had to make a conscious effort to do so. This might explain why fewer of them chose the 'Russian heritage'. For all those interviewed, however, the question of choosing the Russian or Western approach still rested on the parents' idea of what culture meant, and how important it was for their children.

We have thus seen how culture and cultural differences are talked about through contexts as diverse as language and religion. Culture's very complexity, along with the lack of common consensus on what Russian culture is, negates the notion of culture as a reified whole but does not undermine the importance Russians attribute to their cultural belonging. Despite the lack of common definition, the word 'culture' is used by migrants in connection with practically everything that has to do with their life in the receiving country – to emphasize differences and to assert their own uniqueness. Cultural discourse is also used to bridge the gap between 'self' and the 'other' and to position oneself within the 'new culture'.

6.2.6 *Assimilation and Acculturation*

Similar to the term 'culture', concepts of 'acculturation' and 'assimilation' have sustained academic criticism since the late 1960s, as they were perceived as extensions of the general culture-essentializing fallacy (Richmond, 1969: 280; Macdonald, 1993: 13). Migrant discourse on these processes highlights the question we asked earlier: are migrants 'choosing' and 'negotiating' between cultures – being 'men of two worlds' – or do they feel constrained by their own 'world' of imported culture and tradition? Can Russians adapt to the non-Russian culture?

A migrant is faced with a number of practical dilemmas regarding what might be broadly termed 'integration', 'absorption' or 'adaptation'. Depending on the host country's receiving policies, its welfare system, as well as its cultural and social characteristics, a migrant tries to adapt to his new place (or 'adapt a place to his needs' as a Russian businessman from London put it). At least initially, a migrant is not concerned with contesting his culture or asserting his ethnicity or analysing cultural disparities while questioning stereotypes. Having entered a receiving society, a migrant is concerned with very basic necessities, such as obtaining legal status, learning the language, finding employment, and applying for housing, medical care and education. Cultural and social factors come to the fore only later when migrants feel more confident, having dealt with their practical problems. Thus, assimilation and acculturation are important for migrants as they account for the everyday, mundane and yet very important events in a migrant's life.

A retired sociologist from Moscow, living in London for eight years, reflects upon the issues of assimilation and acculturation:

> I know some Russian people from the Russian BBC station – most of them live between two worlds. They consider themselves to be practically as British as they are Russian and speak of themselves as cosmopolitans. Perhaps this could be explained by the temptation to live two lives in one. Most of the people on the Russian BBC don't read Russian newspapers and distance themselves from Russia, wishing to escape one society and enter another one. They go to local expositions, films, theatres – but this is not enough to become British. They orbit their own planet, they will always be foreigners for the outsiders. When these Russians visit the British they are introduced as 'these are my dear Russian friends'. I've noticed this in relation to myself, as they would characterize me as 'that nice old Russian fellow, he reads books, he is well informed' – and thus we have a semi-learned discussion as one would about the book. People who live here for a few years still have the circle of friends that reflects their

own interests. Russian Jews also don't mix with the local Jewry freely as they represent a sort of unknown breed for the British, there are no associative ties. Russian Jews are not religious, they don't know their own history – even what I've read of Jewish history in the Soviet books is very limited – Russian Jews are neither Russians nor Jews. If you've lived your life in one country and learned its values, you cannot just go to another country and declare yourself its citizen, even when you get naturalized. (Michael)

Michael touches upon the issues of ethnicity and identity that will be discussed further in this chapter. He emphasizes that as much as migrants may want to be 'assimilated', they are often constrained by external labelling and by their membership of subcommunities. This problem is reflected in the discussion of a group of newly arrived migrants in Amsterdam. Marusya and Volodya have been staying for over half a year with Igor from Orel, who lives in Amsterdam sustaining himself by ladies' help and odd jobs. Maxim, a friend of Igor, is 18 years old and rumoured to be an army deserter and a petty thief.

> *Volodya*: All this talk [in newspapers] about acculturation: I guess they mean if you live here for a while you become Dutch …
> *Maxim*: [Drunk] You become like the Dutch …
> *Volodya*: Even if I behave like the Dutch I won't be Dutch. Even with the Dutch passport I won't be Dutch.
> *H.K.*: What do you mean by being Dutch?
> *Volodya*: Like they are … kings of Europe, like they know better, like they can teach the rest …
> *Marusya*: They are cultured people.
> *Igor*: So are the Russians, we are not peasants … We can learn a bit from their culture here, but they can also get something from us…
> *Volodya*: His [Dutch] girl-friend calls it 'cultural exchange' [All laugh].
> *Maxim*: When you become like the Dutch you'll know … When you no longer know what you are, then you are 'assimilated'.

We may recall our discussion of culture as behaviour, when 'acting Dutch or English' may equal being Dutch or English. In the above discussion, the conflict between becoming (being able to learn and adapt) and being (unable to alter one's state) is clearly seen, although the speakers are not addressing the concrete issue of what it is 'to be Russian' or 'to become Dutch'. In contrast to the young Russians' half-joking exchange, Vasya, a retired doctor from London, gives an in-depth example of 'acculturation':

> In a way, I've always been a bit English. From childhood on, I read English books [in translation], like *Winnie the Pooh, Alice in Wonderland, Wind in the Willows* or *Mary Poppins*. Most Russian children were brought up with English books. Later we read more advanced literature, like Dickens and Blake, we watched films, we heard stories … But mostly we read and we created our own England … We imagined how the English take their morning tea and, being prohibited from freedom, we imagined a gentleman's easy stroll across Hyde park; we envisioned the Queen speaking from her throne … So, when I came here I had a bit of English culture in me. But it was my vision of English culture … When I arrived in London I looked for Cherry Lane, I found it, but there was no Banks family living there … Although I was 'acculturated' I felt out of place – my imagination of London had little to do with the real city. (Vasya)

I have noticed that those Russians who attempted to assimilate (by perfecting their knowledge of Dutch or English, by associating with members of the host society, by avoiding cultural or social engagements that may betray their origin, etc.) were disapproved of by other Russians. Their integration in the host society was seen negatively, as a rejection of 'roots', as arrogance in thinking that they were 'above their own people', and generally as 'fake'. 'A real Russian is always Russian, whether he wears *valenki* [traditional Russian footwear] or wooden shoes', as Andrei, a music technician from Ekaterinburg, living in Amsterdam, put it. Bulat, a garage owner in Georgia, presently unemployed in London, speaks of another Georgian:

> I just couldn't believe it when my friend suddenly started acting English, started smoking their cigarettes and 'working on his accent'. He sits at home day and night listening to [English] tapes, repeating words in the upper-class dialect … You should listen to his answering machine … Like he's forgotten his past! (Bulat)

On the other hand, those who did not integrate (not having learned the language, having only Russian social and cultural affiliations and loyalties, etc.) were seen as 'hillbillies' by their more integrated compatriots, and were stigmatized by both the Dutch and the English. As Henk, a Dutchman married to a Russian, put it: 'If they aren't interested in this country and don't make any effort to integrate, why come here?' Margarita, who translated her poetry into Dutch and achieved professional success and recognition in The Netherlands, avoids contact with other Russians 'not because I don't feel Russian myself, but because they are a clan, they live completely apart from the rest of society'. Margarita also admitted that the Russians themselves do not accept her because she 'just wants to be herself'.

The Internet newsgroups 'Russians in London' and 'Russen in Nederland' published observations (bordering on 'jokes') about assimilated Russians. These are two abstracts from their on-line publications:

> *You have lived in Holland for a long time if:*
> – you give a woman a hand to get acquainted, not to help her out of a tram;
> – you understand that the question 'Would you like another cup of coffee' means 'Isn't it time for you to go home';
> – you indifferently throw out in the trash 'the key from your new house' or a questionnaire with the question which bank branch they should transfer your 'won million of guilders' to;
> – when visiting you ask whether it is possible to use the phone;
> – you realise that the lack of a mobile phone does not make you less cool;
> – you realise that old jeans, untidy T-shirt and shaven back of the head does not mean that their owner is a man;
> – you realise that if two men are kissing each other on the street they are not necessarily general secretaries of friendly communist parties … ('Russen in Nederland', September 1999)

> *You've become British if:*
> – of all the world languages you speak only English;
> – you eat your dinner for breakfast;
> – you drink tea for lunch;
> – you address all women as 'love' but get slapped in the face if you hold a door for one;
> – you think that the Russians take the British prime minister seriously …
> ('Russians in London', February 1999)

Although humorous, the above examples bring us back to the question of what culture means to Russian migrants. Both the migrants and members of the receiving society, who use the terms 'acculturation' and 'assimilation', lack the scepticism expressed by academics about the terms' relevance. Like the term 'culture', 'acculturation' and 'assimilation' are understood to accentuate or to bridge some of the perceived cultural differences.

In this chapter, I have argued that 'culture' discourse is evoked in many contexts of migrants' lives, ranging from bringing up children to approaching a host society's institutions and individuals. Most Russian migrants talk about culture in terms of cultural differences, contrasting themselves with members of the host society. Despite their 'invisibility' many Russians feel that their cultural origin matters insofar as it restricts, although does not prohibit, their entry into the host society, or shapes their views, values and beliefs about the society and themselves. Russians do use 'culture' as a reified category, even though they disagree about what Russian culture actually means.

To return to the questions asked at the beginning of this chapter, it appears that although Russians see culture and cultural differences as 'real' and use them to define themselves and to relate to the world around them, their understanding of culture is flexible enough to be used differently in different contexts. On the one hand, Russians do not perceive themselves as 'men of two worlds' and do feel constrained by their culture. On the other hand, this same culture allows them to interact, adapt and learn from the perceivably different culture (as discussed in the chapter on social relations). Depending on a migrant's personal characteristics – such as age, gender, education or level of integration in the receiving society – some feel more or less constrained by 'their culture' and more or less accepting of the 'other culture'.

Notes

1   R. Grillo (1985), *Ideologies and Institutions in Urban France. The Representation of Immigrants*, Cambridge University Press, Cambridge.
2   First edition in 1964 by the Trustees of Princeton University.
3   See my discussion of my own role in the field both as the 'native' and the 'outsider' in the Introduction.
4   I do not find extreme reflexivity and guilty awareness of one's supposed superiority very useful in conducting fieldwork or writing ethnography, but this issue needs to be explored in more depth elsewhere.
5   'Proefwerken gaan voor trainingen', Biography by Paul de Lange, NRC Handelsblad: 17.
6   Kaznina sums up Nabokov's comparison of the Russian soul (*dusha*) to the British character. As it appears in an article titled 'Cambridge', published on 19 October, No. 281 in the newspaper *Rul'*, Nabokov observes: 'Between them and us, Russians, – there is a kind of glass wall; they have their own world, round and solid resembling a meticulously colored globe. In their soul there is no inspired storm, thumping, shining, dancing frenzy, that anger and tenderness that brings us to God knows which heavens and abysses; we have moments when clouds are upon our shoulders, seas are at our knees, – go, *dusha*! For the Englishman it is incomprehensible, new, perhaps tempting. If he drinks and brawls, his brawling is trite and benevolent, and the keepers of public order only smile at him, knowing that he would not pass a certain line. And on the other hand, not even the most liberating intoxicant will not push him to give way to his feelings, open his shirt, throw his hat to the ground ... At any time he shies away from confessions. It happens that you talk to a fellow about this and that, strikes and horse races, and let down your guard, tell him that you could have, it seems, given all your blood to see once again some little marsh near St Petersburg, – but expressing such ideas is supposed to be inappropriate, he will look at you as if you were whistling in the church'.

The stereotypical notion of the 'mysterious Russian soul' in this article is opposed to the commonly assumed image of the 'English wise man'. On the one hand, 'dancing frenzy', 'heavens and abysses', 'sea at the knees', 'go, *dusha!*', 'to open one's shirt', 'to throw one's hat to the ground' ... on the other hand – 'round and solid' world of an Englishman, coloured globe of his imperial self-consciousness ... Of course, even an Englishman can open his shirt, and there are sometimes reasonable and calculating Russians. But the writer is trying to find the common denominator, which makes stereotypes so persistent, and their contrast unfailingly effective. Nabokov is trying to understand why a Russian cannot integrate into the British lifestyle naturally, remaining true to himself (Kaznina, 1997: 290).

7   A more extended observation was made by the Russian newspaper editor in London: 'Russian stereotypes of the British are pretty uniform. The British are funny: both kind and friendly and yet somehow artificial. The British are polite, but not really well-meaning. They might be hypocritical and one has to make sure there is no double-meaning attached to their statements' (Natalya Shuvaeva).

8   'Can you name three Russian artists?', *British East-West Journal*: 28.

Chapter 7

Ethnicity and Identity

Introduction

This chapter is intended to continue and expand upon the questions presented in the previous chapter. We will examine whether modern conditions render ethnic identities, particularly with respect to the ideas of roots and belonging, redundant in the transnationalist world.

In this chapter, I shall focus upon ethnicity, and shall argue that in the Russian case, ethnicity discourse reflects cultural differences, expanding upon historical, political and economic disparities within the CIS and between migrants and the host society. I shall then address ethnicity through the contexts of memory and physical differences, as well as discuss ethnicity as a reaction to external labelling.

In the concluding section on ethnic identity, I shall sum up the themes discussed in the sections on culture and ethnicity. I shall argue that as migrants internalize, reject, or negotiate the notions of culture and ethnicity, their identity changes accordingly. Analysing these changes, I shall draw some conclusions about the relationship between Russian culture, ethnicity and identity in a migrant context.

7.1   Culture and Ethnicity

So far, we have not touched explicitly upon the issue of 'ethnicity' which underlies most 'cultural' discourse. 'Cultural differences' and 'ethnic differences' are often interchangeable in common conversation and in the Western media. While this trend glorifies cultural and ethnic diversity, it also tends to equate 'culture' and 'ethnicity' with 'race' and other politicized forms of difference, thus rendering these terms morally suspect.

Reflecting these trends in common discourse and politics, academic deliberation has put 'culture' and 'ethnicity' under close scrutiny. 'Ethnicity', like 'culture', has come under attack for reifying something that is 'constructed', 'flexible' and even 'negotiable'. Recent works in anthropology attempt to demonstrate that ethnicity, like 'race', is neither objective nor 'real'; that it is 'imagined' and 'subjective'. Lyon (1997) speaks of ethnicity as a pure invention, constructed for the purpose of asserting difference where there is none: 'Ethnicity is a way of *imagining* (sic) peoplehood that ignores everything that makes a people – asserting a boundary that asserts only uniqueness' (Lyon, 1997: 204).

Most contemporary social scientists emphasize that although ethnicity is subjective, it is nonetheless important for people to believe that it has an objective reference to their perceived common roots (Baumann and Sunier, 1995). Weber defines ethnic groups as entertaining a '*subjective belief* (sic) in their common descent because of similarities of physical type or of customs or both, or because of memories of colonization and migration; this belief must be important for the propagation of the group formation; conversely, it does not matter whether or not an objective blood relationship exists' (Weber, 1996: 35).

In the previous chapter on culture, I have argued that although culture is perceived as 'real and objective' and cultural differences are reified, there is no consensus as to what Russian culture entails. I shall now ask whether ethnicity, like culture, is subjectively perceived by migrants and members of the host society. If common discourse is inconsistent in its definition of Russian ethnicity and appears to 'construct' the concept, I shall also ask how, by whom, and for which purposes ethnicity is used.

In the following section, I examine how Russian ethnicity and nationality were constructed under Soviet and later Russian rule. The consequent sections will be devoted to the migrants' discourse on ethnicity, providing examples of different contexts, ranging from memory to physical differences, in which ethnicity is discussed. The section on ethnic identity will explicitly address the questions posed above, and be followed by a conclusion to both the culture and ethnicity sections.

7.2   'Russian' Ethnicity and Nationality

In the chapter on community, I mentioned Soviet communitarianism and socialist hierarchization, which have probably caused fragmentation and animosity between migrants. Also, in the chapter on migration, I discussed how being Russian, that is belonging to 'Mother Russia', is still a common theme and a cause of nostalgia for both old and new 'waves' of migrants. Although spoon-fed to millions of people in the former Soviet republics, the idea of 'common Sovietness' seems to have disintegrated soon after the fall of the Soviet Union for the younger generation, while it still plays a significant role for the older one.

Until the break-up of the Soviet Union and the emergence of nationalism, culture and ethnicity were rarely linked in the USSR. This was due to the restraints of the Soviet and dominant Russian ideology. Russification was a tool for the propaganda of communism, forced upon all the peoples of the Soviet Union. Ethnicity and culture go hand in hand in migrant discourse, as 'being from Russia (or even the CIS)' may be internalized by the migrant as 'being Russian' because of external labelling and perhaps because of the phenomenon of isolation. This phenomenon occurs when an ethnically diverse but numerically small group of migrants from the same geographical region (CIS) clings to whatever they perceive as being common among them: place of origin, language or certain traditions. However, ethnicity is now often mentioned in connection with newly independent states of the CIS and its peoples attempt to revive suppressed cultural and ethnic traditions.

In Soviet Russia, the question of one's 'nationality' (*nazional'nost'*) actually meant the question of one's ethnic origin. Thus, while a Georgian-born British naturalized citizen would answer 'British' to the question of his 'nationality', inscribed in the passport, the same individual in the Soviet Union would have to respond by giving the name of his ethnic group.[1] To avoid discrimination in the CIS, parents of ethnically mixed marriages chose to give their children Russian 'nationality'. When emigrating, proving one's Jewish 'nationality' could thus be difficult. On the other hand, obtaining false papers proving minority status became relatively easy in post-Soviet times, and thus it is suspected that many bogus Germans and Jews departed for the West (Snel et al., 2000: 20). Consequently, the concepts of ethnicity and nationality in the Soviet Union were clearly demarcated, while in Britain and The Netherlands ethnic categorization is usually not required.[2]

Categorizing oneself as part of a large group (for Russian-speakers, presenting themselves as 'Russians') has a practical advantage for a migrant in a strange country: 'In forming of ethnic groups subtle distinctions are overridden; there is an advantage to belonging to a big group, even if it is looked down upon' (Glazer and Moynihan, 1996: 138). Interestingly, the emerging ethnic consciousness and nationalism of different ethnic groups is not reflected in the groups' Western representatives. Russians may adopt the label of their 'common' ethnicity, while cross-cleavages of class, age, education and actual ethnicity, which were so important 'at home', now become obsolete in many of their transactions with outsiders and even between themselves.

Similar to the previous discussion of 'culture', the role of 'ethnicity' in migrant interactions is best revealed through a number of different contexts.

7.2.1 Ethnic Community: the Case of Soviet Jews

The Jewish case is particularly interesting for the study of the Russian diaspora because Jews are said to be a 'prototypical' diaspora group. Their experience as 'eternal migrants' provides an interesting context for the study of Soviet migration, ethnic relations, adaptation and many other migration-related topics.

Jewish migration in itself is a remarkable topic in the study of 'Russian' migrants (Kopnina, 1998; Morozov, 1998; Siegel, 1998). Soviet-time emigration from the Soviet Union has been characterized by proportionally large numbers of Jews who left 'their' country mostly for political reasons. There is, however, a difficulty in classifying these people as 'ethnic Jews', since European Jews have been treated from the outside as constituting a religion and, more recently, as an ethnic group; both these models have been internalized by Jews themselves (Webber, 1997: 25). Describing categories of Soviet 'Jews' in Berlin, Doomernik classifies Jews into three types: those who have at least one ethnically Jewish parent (which already presents problems since Jewish law recognizes only the maternal parent's ethnicity as determinant for that of children, not to mention the issue of 'one-fourth-blood', etc.); those who are not Jewish and arrived as spouses in mixed marriages; and those who claim to be Jewish and use forged documents to prove it (a case legally impossible to detect) (Doomernik, 1977). I have found the same categories present in London and in Amsterdam.

Soviet Jews are often credited for outstanding educational and occupational achievement. Doomernik asserts that immigrants who came to Berlin have 'educational and professional levels which are above average for the entire Soviet population':

> This is not just true for this particular migrant population but also for the Soviet Jewish population in general: '… they are overwhelmingly urban, have a higher educational level than non-Jews, and are concentrated in technical-cultural-scientific occupations, described as upper socio-economic levels in Soviet terms'. (Levin, 1990: 761[3]) (Doomernik, 1997: 62)

This achievement is partially explained by what Armstrong (1992: 231)[4] calls 'mobilized diaspora', which is explained by two forces originating in

Soviet society: the need for the 'high-level skills disproportionately present among its Jewish citizens'; and a striving to eliminate inherent Jewish influence by overt or hidden anti-Semitic measures. Advised by his informants, Doomernik concludes that this situation results in a motivation for the Jews to perform above average to overcome anti-Semitic barriers. My interviews with Jewish informants confirm this conclusion.

It is also argued by Chervyakov, Gitelman and Shapiro (1997: 280–91) that loyalty to the Jewish community or Jewish ethnicity among Soviet immigrants often comes as a reaction to anti-Semitism. They outline the bonding features that bring the Jewish groups within the Soviet Union together:

> Several features set Jews apart from others: the absence of a Jewish territorial identity (notwithstanding the Jewish autonomous region of Birobidzhan, whose population is less than 5 percent Jewish); the experience of exile from the ancient homeland for nearly 2,000 years; the role of Israel and the Jewish diaspora which are promoting Jewish ethnic and religious revivals; ongoing massive emigration; the consequences of Soviet policies which effectively banned religious education and even the preservation of Hebrew and Yiddish cultures; and anti-Semitism, formerly both a governmental and societal phenomenon now exclusively the latter. (Chervyakov, Gitelman and Shapiro, 1997: 280–81)

Most of the authors' informants report that they do not feel particularly Jewish unless reminded of their ethnicity (usually negatively) by non-Jews. Since many Jewish informants felt that they were not really allowed to 'blend in' with the 'Russians' and were always assigned a special category as non-Russian Soviet citizens, this common experience of rejection led them to a relative degree of internal solidarity. Part of this solidarity is explained by what Halbwachs (1960) refers to as collective consciousness and awareness of common history. This history is often linked with the shared memories of the Holocaust and worldwide persecution.

> Thus, the new Jewish identity arises out of the realization that one belongs to a people who, despite persecutions, have contributed much to civilization from biblical times to the present, a people which rose from the ashes of the holocaust and attained its centuries-old dream of statehood. (Chervyakov, Gitelman and Shapiro, 1997: 291)

The very Jewish identity, even when not supported by common ethnic or religious beliefs, can be said to rest on common interpretation of history:

> Hidden behind the surface realities lies a field of historical consciousness
> which in many ways acts to direct how a minority group sees itself *vis-à-vis*
> the outer world. This is especially clear in the Jewish case, where, given the
> particular attitude to history within diaspora culture, the scope offered by
> historicization marked the emergence of a radical internal re-evaluation of
> the Jewish cultural personality ... For many Jews, as indeed for many other
> Europeans today, history has become a new religion, the basis for critical and
> rational re-evaluation of their inherited identity. (Webber, 1997: 274–5)

These observation are relevant to Russian Jews from London and
Amsterdam, but can be also extended to include non-Jews. The mentioned
topics of external labelling, feelings of inferiority and ideas of common heritage
are equally important for other Russian-speakers, whatever their ethnicity.

7.3   Discourses on Ethnicity

7.3.1 Ethnicity through Memory

Speaking of Russian migrants in Germany, Freinkman-Chrustaleva and
Novikov note the social diversity of the migrants. Yet, they find a common
longing for the lost motherland:

> Yet all the emigrants, and especially those of the first generation, share nostalgic
> feelings towards the country they have left as well as reminiscences of their
> childhood and friends; they share, too, the feeling of being spiritually linked to
> the country of their childhood and the feeling that their generation is doomed
> to be somewhere in-between – for they do not feel like other people around
> them. (Freinkman-Chrustaleva and Novikov, 1995: 151)

Memories of the past are often similar among migrants from different parts
of the CIS, be they from small villages in Georgia or large cities in Ukraine. The
national school system, media broadcasts, children's literature, music and films,
and many other state-controlled enterprises were responsible for the creation of
the 'common Russian culture' which transcended local history and ethnicity.

> ... There is a close parallel between communist identity construction and
> ethnicity, for both are processes that involve a complex use of political and
> ideological strategies and the political exploitation of any number of items and
> objects drawn from their cultural situation. (Shore, 1993: 41)

Most of my ethnically non-Russian informants referred to themselves as 'Russian'. Shared memories of a common past involve an assumed 'link with a homeland and a sense of solidarity among at least some of its members' (Hutchinson and Smith, 1996: 6). Some migrants develop nostalgic images of their Russian past. This is especially true for illegal migrants who cannot return home for fear of being unable to re-enter the receiving country, or previous waves of migrants who were either afraid or unwilling to return, even for a short visit, to the country that persecuted them. In isolation from their home country, immigrants develop 'images of their starting points'. They share their memories with each other which soon become undifferentiated and blurred, constituting a shared memory of their forsaken motherland (Halbwachs, 1960: 113). The migrants emphasized their 'common past', be it through celebrating 'big holidays in the Russian way' (such as New Year's), or through telling each other Russian jokes, or evoking stories and songs, which are recognized by all CIS migrants.

Some migrants maintain their links with the CIS, either by direct commute, letters, or simply maintaining their interest in the homeland by reading newspapers or watching Russian television. This reinforces the migrants' sense of continuity with their roots and creates a generalized and often romantic image of 'their country' and, by implication, themselves.

> Wherever the memory of the origin of a community by peaceful secession or emigration … from a mother community remains for some reason alive, there undoubtedly exists a very specific and often extremely powerful sense of ethnic identity, which is determined by several factors: shared political memories or, even more importantly in early times, persistent ties with the old cult or the strengthening of kinship and other groups, both in the old and the new community, or other persistent relationships. (Weber, 1996: 36)

The fact that many Russian migrants in the 1990s are free to move from country to country, easily commuting 'back home' without having to experience the trauma suffered by previous waves of the politically or culturally oppressed, may explain why the new wave of Russians do not seem to form ethnic 'communities'. The situation described by Weber seems to be true of present-day asylum seekers and illegals, for whom memories of the 'mother community' may cause nostalgia and feelings of ethnic isolation. This is true in cases where a migrant is prohibited from keeping in touch with his country (because of fear of persecution at home, or the lack of legal status or financial ability).

Irina, an economics student from Amsterdam who first migrated with her mother to Germany (and later The Netherlands) retorted to my question of why she misses Belorussia:

> I didn't choose to leave Minsk – it was my mother's idea. For years, I wanted to go back but my mother told me she didn't have money to send me, and that I should get used to [life in Germany], and that travelling with my [Belorussian] passport wasn't safe because they might not let me out again … I'm surprised how a Russian cannot miss his country. I mean, if you had your childhood and youth somewhere – even if they weren't always sunny – you kind of grow into a place or it grows into you … And you cannot change what you are and you keep longing for the place you came from. (Irina)

Like many other migrants in London and Amsterdam, Irina suggests that where you grow up and your memories of that place make you, as it were, Russian; and your being Russian, in turn, makes you long for this place and treasure its memory.

Even if memories of the Russian past are not experienced as bereavement, ethnicity is evoked by those memories for all migrants who grew up in the CIS. Aleftina, a 'Russian wife' from London, reflected that although her husband accompanies her on her trips to Russia, he 'experiences it as an exotic holiday' while for her 'every house, every street, every smell and sound brings back memories'. Aleftina concludes that her husband cannot experience Russia the same way as her, not only because he was not born and did not grow up there, but because 'he is not Russian'.

Anton, an artist from Amsterdam, reflects that his Dutch friend cannot understand why he keeps going on about his art school (in Russia) and camping in the woods with his parents. His Russian friends in Amsterdam, however, even though they never went to an art school or camped in the wild, understand his stories.

> In art school, we devised many pranks and infuriated our teachers – something that all Russian kids do … Even though [my Russian friends] hate mosquitoes and have hay fever, they know what it's like being in a Russian forest, making a fire under a birch tree, baking potatoes, drinking and singing … You just have to be Russian to understand those things. (Anton)

Thus, being Russian is equated to growing up in Russia and having particular memories that only Russians can relate to. Ironically, however, these memories are not always shared. Jean, a friend of Anton's from Kazakhstan, who was present during my conversation with Anton, reflected that in his school children were severely punished for practical jokes and the teachers did not tolerate any disobedience. On the subject of nature, Jan also reflected that he lived 'almost in the desert' and never learned how to bake potatoes. 'But you're still Russian!' exclaimed Anton, patting his friend on the shoulder, to which Jan readily agreed.

It would thus appear that, like with the case of culture discussed at the beginning of this chapter, memories of Russia may differ, but a sense that the common past binds all migrants together is persuasive. The assumption of commonality creates a sense of 'being Russian' – thus being constructed in opposition to Western outsiders.

7.3.2 Ethnicity through Physical Difference

As mentioned in the chapter on community, present-day migration is often discussed in the media in ethnic or racial terms both in Britain and in The Netherlands. As such, migration is turned into a problem connected with the issues of racism and discrimination. The Russian case is particularly interesting because Russian 'ethnicity' is not linked to 'race' and therefore is not necessarily conspicuous as might be the case with other migrant groups in Western Europe. Being a Russian American myself, I have not encountered open discrimination in my personal or professional life; neither have I heard of such stories from other Russians. This brings us to an interesting question: how much does ethnic discrimination have to do with apparent physical differences and whether a 'white' migrant actually gains advantages in the receiving countries?

Brass defines ethnic groups on the basis of three criteria: 'in terms of objective attributes, with reference to subjective feelings, and in relation to behaviour' (Brass, 1996: 85). Russians may be said to 'blend in' with the receiving society at the level of the first criteria, while their own and their hosts' subjective feelings (being foreigners or being different) and behaviour (the case of conspicuous consumption by new Russians) might jeopardize their invisibility.

Nash speaks of the surface pointers of ethnic groups, such as 'dress, language, and (culturally denoted) physical features' (Nash, 1996: 25). While the surface pointers serve to signal difference to the members of the receiving society, Russians themselves do not seem to be acutely conscious of them. Some Russian men in London and Amsterdam still wear old Adidas trainers topped with black leather jackets while women parade in ostentatious mink coats with cross-bearing golden chains. Although most of them are visitors to the cities, some actually do live in the West. These surface pointers may signal an 'I don't care what you think about me' attitude, or indicate a lack of observational skills.

Nonetheless, Russians often speak of themselves as 'European' and 'Western' while other migrants may be perceived as less civilized. Unlike the case of common memories, Russian ethnicity suddenly crosses the borders of the CIS to include the West in opposition to yet another group, that of other migrants. Some Russians express resentment toward other (more specifically 'coloured') minorities, and express their dislike with racist remarks and a refusal to share neighbourhoods with the 'coloureds'. In the following exchange, two young Russian women take a presumably 'Western' perspective on migrants:

> *Katya*: Refugees here are treated like second class people. Look at some Indian streets. The British call them dirty, they don't walk there at night. And you probably have the same streets in Amsterdam, and the Dutch speak as badly about them.
> *H.K.*: Well, not necessarily …
> *Sveta*: Well, I won't live on an Indian street myself. [To Katya] You don't think they are dirty?
> *Katya*: Yeah, but …
> *Sveta*: Well, I mean, look at their children, running around and screaming like that – Russians don't do it.
> *H.K.*: So you think Russians are different kinds of migrants?
> *Sveta*: I don't know … but Russian children don't run around screaming. Russian houses are clean and we don't live on top of each other like that …
> *Katya*: For the British, we are still dirty migrants …
> *Sveta*: How do you know?
> *Katya*: I see their attitude towards us.
> *Sveta*: You see the attitude of your husband towards you, it's a different matter. My boyfriend …
> *Katya*: He isn't British, is he?
> *Sveta*: But that's just the point, [he's Russian] – if you want to be respected, you have to mix with your own kind.
> *H.K.*: Do Russians here respect each other?
> *Katya*: No …
> *Sveta*: They help each other; sure, they respect each other …

We shall discuss possible reasons for this distancing in the following sections on hierarchy and superiority complexes.

Most Russians I have interviewed were surprised that members of the receiving society could 'spot' them, while they have themselves reported recognizing their fellow compatriots on the street. Be it the taste in clothes, or high Slavic cheeks, or the way Russians are said to 'stare into the distance as if they are about to go through the wall' (an observation made by Anna, a surgeon from Moldova, living in London), many Russians seem to 'sense' even the slightest physical features of their compatriots. Zoya, an agriculturist from Krasnoyarsk, living in London, reflects:

> I just know they are Russian or Georgian or whatever … I just feel it … When I just came to London and missed talking Russian, I would stop Russians on the street and ask: 'Are you Russian?' They'd be very surprised, since they thought they'd camouflaged themselves pretty well. (Zoya)

Richard, a Dutch student of the Russian language and a participant in volunteer projects in Russia, told me that he could not 'spot' Russians easily before going to Russia. Seeing Russians in 'their natural environment' he 'sensed a certain commonality' about them. 'It's not just how their eyes are positioned, but how they look', he observed.

Perhaps in the case of Russians, ethnicity through physical differences is really more a question of behaviour, expression and body language rather than anything more tangible. Having met a couple of members of the 'old waves', in most cases I myself have been struck by their physical likeness to either the British or the Dutch. Second generation Russians also seem indistinguishable from members of the receiving society. Thus, although the 'ethnic' features of Russians may be 'spotted' on the street, at closer examination it appears to be 'cultural' differences that betray Russian invisibility.

Russians themselves seem to want to 'blend in', masking their ethnicity by asserting physical similarity with members of the host society. In this context, ethnicity is talked about as something shared with all other Europeans. 'Being Russian' becomes equivalent to 'being Western' – quite a different perspective from the discussion on common memories.

7.3.3 *Ethnicity through a Hierarchical Scale*

Being a cultural or ethnic minority is not a desirable position for most Russian migrants. Although minority status may bring practical benefits, as in the case of lobbying for social services, social status is generally seen to suffer as a result of being perceived as different or 'deviant'. Western media reports in the 1990s were increasingly critical of the economical and political failures of the CIS. Also, migration is clearly perceived in terms of hierarchies and inequalities between the 'rich West' and 'poor the rest'. In the previous discussion of stereotypes, Russians fall into the category of 'poor migrants', a classification that they largely resent.

> When he is in one of these philanthropic countries a refugee who in his homeland possessed some property and social privileges finds himself on an equal footing with a refugee of no particular distinction. The refugee's passport reduces everyone to the same level. And the population of a country that gives shelter to these refugees usually looks upon them, not without some grounds, with condescending contempt. (Shilovsky, in Glenny and Stone, 1990: 291)

One way of fighting against this classification is through invisibility. Russian invisibility, discussed in the chapter on community, is largely self-imposed, and involves cultural and ethnic camouflage. This obscurity is made possible by both the lack of obvious physical differences (discussed in the previous section) and the drift of economic and, to some extent, cultural systems of the CIS towards the West. Being a minority reminds Russians of their perceived inferiority in the West.

> There is ... the fact that with the cultural implosion of the city, people who would rather not want a culture of theirs to be open to anyone's glances are quite sophisticated enough to choose another culture out of their repertoires of interacting with strangers; in conventional terms, something 'mainstream' rather than 'deviant' (Hannerz, 1980: 309).

While on the one hand many Russians prefer to remain invisible by blending in with the host society and thus 'hiding their shame', they are also attempting to boost their self-image. For Russians, both 'at home' and in migration, the feeling of uniqueness as a group is of paramount importance. In talking about the myths of the 'chosen people', Smith states that long-term ethnic survival depends 'on the active cultivation by specialists and others of a heightened sense of collective distinctiveness and mission' (Smith, 1996: 189). This point is interesting not only in respect of the proverbial case of the Jews, but also in relation to Russians. In the latter case, a whole set of ideas has been generated by outsiders and by Russians themselves, having to do with alternating feelings of superiority and inferiority.

Russian migrants used to be viewed as tragic heroes, who escaped the terror of their native country but were received in Europe without special sympathy.

Even earlier in the century, Russians were perceived as somewhat peculiar in the West. Zamyatin, a Russian writer quoted by Kaznina, describes the English attitude towards Russians as curiosity. Russians are seen as 'exotic animals', as 'talking seals'[5] (Kaznina, 1997: 291). As a result, life in exile sharpened the feeling of their cultural uniqueness (Siegel, 1998). The gap between the perception of Russians as people from a backward uncivilized country – drunk and rude 'bears' – in contrast with the idea of a unique 'Russian soul' with great Russian literature, music, strength and spirituality, is very large indeed.

Grisha, a middle-aged biologist working in London on a temporary contract, reflects on this ambiguity:

> We are seen both as something odd and pathetic; and as odd and great ...
> At hearing that I'm a Russian scientist, some people say: 'Ah!' – like this is
> actually something to be proud of, but some others say, 'Ah, Russian ...' as if
> I should be embarrassed of my nationality. (Grisha)

Thus, the question of ethnicity can be personally charged for Russians. Migration suddenly puts economic disparities between the West and the East into sharp relief. This contrast provokes Russians to use their ethnicity as a defensive tool, or to hide it in order to cope with external labelling and set themselves apart from other migrant groups. Russian discourse on ethnicity reinstates ethnicity as a real, objective, and clearly demarcated entity. Although it may be morally and politically inadmissible to use ethnicity as a reified entity in academic debate, it is nonetheless important to acknowledge its significance in the construction of the world-views, and in the creation of self-image for the majority of people who live or migrate within modern nation-states.

As I shall discuss in the following section, identity, formed by both external labelling and internal responses and perceptions, reflects back upon the issues of cultural and ethnic differences. Like cultural and ethnic differences, identity is often perceived as 'fixed' by the migrants although, as contemporary academics may argue, it may be shifting, subjective and fluid.

7.4   Ethnic and Cultural Identity

There are two main factors that make the Russian case of identity different from that of other migrants. The first is the combination of specific features inherited from the CIS (such as the paradoxical mix of mutual antagonism combined with strong dependency on informal economy and networks).

Added to that are the intrinsic features of migrants (such as the tension they experience between their perceived commonality as ex-Soviets and the actual ethnic and cultural diversity which is underplayed when migrants find themselves in the West). Russian discourse on culture and ethnicity reflects these paradoxes and tensions. Most migrants believe that there is something special about them 'being Russian' or 'being from the CIS' while there is no consensus as to what this actually entails. Culture and ethnicity are often spoken of as solid, unchangeable entities, when cultural or ethnic belonging endows an individual with a set of perceivably fixed characteristics, usually contrasted to those belonging to the 'outside' group. However, individuals relate to the issues of culture and ethnicity differently, and their identity as Russians, although often perceived as absolute and distinct, is dependent upon their subjective understanding of what Russian culture and ethnicity means. Torn between feelings of superiority and inferiority, caught between the East and the West, Russians appear to present a case of shifting cultural and ethnic identity.

Ardener (1989) and Macdonald (1993) agree that the most important informants on the question of identity are the people themselves. Russian migrants' discourse on identity confirms some of the contemporary academic theories which describe identity as shifting and contextual.

> ... Just as individuals play many roles in everyday life, so they have many identities each of which will shift according to the position of the actor in relation to others. The pattern that results from this is often a stratified structure of loyalties which corresponds to different levels of perceived community. (Shore, 1993: 37)

The shift does not necessarily occur between equally important or balanced identities, but is issued in response to the interviewer's own perceived identity. For example, a respondent answering in terms of national identity ('Russian') for the outsider, would go into more detail with the friend, specifying that he or she is Jewish. Both identities (Russian and Jewish) serve to categorize oneself in relation to the interviewer's perceived identity (seen as the insider or the outsider). It is almost impossible to ask a direct question in Russian about one's identity (*tozhdestvennost'*) because of semantic difficulties; instead one has to ask indirect questions. The questions of 'What do you feel yourself to be' (*Kem vy sebya oshushaete*) type might initiate a number of contextually determined responses, but if the context is lacking (for example, when I ask this question 'out of the blue', cutting the logical link with the previous subject), the responses tend to focus on geographical or occupational identity. Geographical identification (such as being a Muscovite, or being from Ukraine) would sometimes be elaborated further by ethnic category (such as 'I'm a Muscovite, but I'm Georgian', or 'I was born in Ukraine, but I'm Russian').

Identities can also shift depending on the place or situation a migrant finds himself in. Spatial formation of ethnic identity is apparent through the cultural and religious activities of the migrants. Similar to the 'community' of Hindu Punjabis in London, forged when one enters the temple building and identifies oneself as a Hindu (Raj, 1997: 129), one Amsterdam Russian memorably put it: 'When I'm in a[n Orthodox] church, I'm Russian and I belong there. I step out, I speak Dutch, I bike home – I'm one of them, I'm Dutch' (Andrei).

We may recall the statement by the Moldavian surgeon, Anna, who stated that she 'feels Russian' in the Orthodox Church. Although Andrei 'felt Dutch' biking home, and Anna did not 'feel Russian' in Kishinev, both identified themselves as Russian when speaking with non-Russian nationals. I could not tell whether Anna and Andrei then thought of themselves as 'permanently Russian', or whether they reserved their more private feelings of identity for themselves. But I have often noticed that in more intimate one-on-one discussions, my informants expressed a strong sense of selfhood which, although complex and multifaceted, was internally coherent. Unlike actors who may actually 'feel their part' when playing it, my informants had a sense of what one of them termed 'core values', which were personal, and often rooted in their perception of their culture and ethnicity. Margarita, a poet from Amsterdam who openly admits that she does not miss or need anything Russian in her successful life in The Netherlands, reflects on her identity:

> No, I didn't 'turn Dutch' here. Nor have I lost my 'Russianness'. If anything, I've remained myself ... One can learn a new language, one can travel, change names – but what one *is*, goes beyond simple identification. I am the 'me' of my own experience. (Margarita)

Thus, although ethnic identity does seem to be shifting and contextually defined, it is also limited by a certain sense of selfhood as well as by external labelling. Migrants, who by definition suffer external labelling, such as 'outsiders' or 'foreigners', also have some flexibility in the way they choose to counteract or confirm these labels (for example, by attempting to become 'assimilated' by learning the language, choosing 'native' friends, getting a job; or by asserting their uniqueness and even perhaps superiority). Being identified, or 'named' by others has an important influence on self-identification

(Ardener, 1989). Aside from having personal reasons for being identified as 'Russians', ethnically diverse Russian-speakers may all of a sudden find themselves lumped together as 'Russians' through migration, willingly or not. However, shifts in identity do not alter a sense of self, which both includes and transcends the variety of personas. Migrants' stories of the past and the present reveal a sense of unchangeable self (if inconsistency between 'me then' and 'me now' is detected, it is consciously picked out and explained in terms of evolving personality or circumstances).

Michael, a retired sociologist from London, admits that 'as much as he might want to be Western or English', he cannot shake off his past and change his thought processes which make him what he is. Mr Reed, a British worker at the International bookstore in London, married to a Russian, reflects:

> My wife's lived here [in London] for over 10 years, we have children together … She calls it her home. When we travel to Russia and visit her relatives and friends they tell her that she's no longer very Russian, the way she dresses and speaks. My wife agrees, she doesn't feel like her country is entirely hers any more. But she tells me: 'Even in 30 years, I'll still be Russian'. (Mr Reed)

My experience with Russians in London and Amsterdam shows that people move in search of stability and permanence. Having visited the families of migrants in the CIS, I have discovered that although their lives were affected by the family member's migration (through financial contributions, access to information, or their increased mobility), they had a clear idea of what their 'roots' or 'home' were. Neither did the first generation migrants perceive themselves as 'hybrids' or 'deterritorialized persons'. Instead, they clearly demarcated their ethnicity and/or country of origin, their place of residence and work, their emotional ties and loyalties.

We have learned from this chapter and the previous chapter on culture that while cultural and ethnic identities are perceived as fixed, their very broadness and vagueness leave room for imagination and negotiation. I suspect that the riddle of identity cannot be solved clearly one way or another. The very ambiguity of the migrant discourse underlies the complexity and fascination of this subject.

It also appears that there are significant differences between groups of Russians in the way they use cultural and ethnic interactions and present their identities. As argued in the chapter on social networks, after a period of time in the receiving country, most Russians learn to adjust to the receiving country's institutions and policies, retaining some of the old ideas and methods, and rejecting or modifying others. Similarly, the discourse on culture and ethnicity reveals that while the sense of 'being Russian' intensifies for some migrants (for example, exaggerated as a reaction to external labelling), it becomes more muted or altogether rejected by others (for example, in favour of 'becoming Western'). Some feel that their true identity lies with their compatriots and their home country, while others identify more with their 'new home'. Although 'being Russian' or 'being from Russia' matters to all migrants, some groups – by virtue of the length of stay in the receiving country, age, level of education, legal status, religious affiliation and the like – assign these 'states of being' with different importance and discuss their cultural or ethnic affiliation through different contexts.

Unlike mainstream contemporary academics, Russian migrants want to live in a comprehensible, coherent world where they can make sense of and influence certain events, and where their sense of selfhood is reinforced by cultural and ethnic ties. To most migrants, culture, ethnicity and even identity appear anything but 'shifting', 'fluid' and 'subjective'. Although postmodern criticism of these characteristics as fixed and bounded reveals the way political as well as anthropological discourse has developed, it does not tell us much about the way Russian migrants view their culture and ethnicity. While culture, ethnicity and identity in the (post)modern world are said to be constructed, fluid and shifting, and people's lives are described as transnational and hybrid (Gupta and Ferguson, 2002; Guibernau and Rex, 2003), local realities remain embedded in coherent notions of 'self' and 'other' and of 'here' and 'there'. Russian migrants are not entirely free to choose their own identities. They are constrained by their perceptions of culture and ethnicity, by external labelling and by unchangeable personal characteristics of age, gender and ethnicity.

To return to the questions asked at the beginning of this chapter, as in the case of 'culture', Russian discourse does reflect the presence of 'ethnic' constraints to identity. Russians' everyday lives demonstrate that 'ethnicity' is both meaningful and significant for migrants. Although some migrants are less constrained by their Russian identity and feel like 'men of two worlds', most of them are still affected by their experience as Russians.

Notes

1   Usually defined by father's ethnicity.
2   Most of the documents which require specification of one's ethnic origin state it as an optional category.

3   Levin (1990), *The Jews in the Soviet Union since 1917: A Paradox of Survival*, I.B. Tauris, London.
4   J.A. Armstrong (1992), 'The Ethnic Scene in the Soviet Union: The View of the Dictatorship', in R. Denber (ed.), *The Soviet Nationality Reader*, Westview Press, Boulder: 227–56; quoted in Doomernik (1997: 62).
5   From the Notebooks of Zamyatin, 1916.

Conclusion

The main theoretical objectives and research questions of this book focused on the concept of 'community' and its applicability to the situation of Russian migrants in London and Amsterdam in the 1990s. In the opening chapters I introduce the notion of 'invisible communities'. This serves as a descriptive rather than analytical concept, reflecting the fact that the Russian presence (that by limited definition may be referred to as a community) in both cities is recognized neither by the outsiders nor by the migrants themselves. 'Invisibility' of Russians in London and Amsterdam can be explained by both external (statistical, geographical, historical) and internal (social, cultural) factors. In this book, I have chosen to focus on internal factors, with particular attention to the social and cultural diversity of Russian migrants, and the divisions in their views resulting from this diversity.

Instructed both by my fieldwork data and by contemporary theories in migration studies and anthropology, I have arrived at the realization that the concept of 'community' is inadequate to describe the situation of Russian migrants in London and Amsterdam. Instead, I have looked at subcommunities as an alternative to the concept of 'community'. While the Russian presence in the receiving countries is 'invisible', migrants do 'see' small groups of friends or family members that they associate with. Subcommunities, I postulate, are formed both as a consequence of and simultaneously to maintain social divisions between the Russians. Exclusive subcommunities – that is, those with Russian membership only – are fewer in number but stronger-knit than inclusive or mixed membership subcommunities. Each subcommunity, be it based on personal or professional interests, religion or ethnicity, exhibits different techniques of boundary maintenance and recruitment of new members. Migrants may be members of several subcommunities at once, but 'ideal' types of subcommunity members are usually loyal to one subcommunity. Discourses within subcommunities testify to the diversity of adaptation strategies to the receiving countries' social and economic conditions. These divisions are elaborated upon in the chapters on social relations, culture and ethnicity. Combined, they present a Russian discourse reflective of both social fragmentation and diversity of views on topics ranging from 'ethnic identity' to 'friendship'.

Concerning social relations and informal economic activity among Russians, it appears that unlike other migrant groups in London and

Amsterdam, such as Indians and Turks respectively, Russians do not have a strong dependence on social networks or an informal economy (because of antagonism, low critical mass and other reasons discussed in the chapter on community). Although some groups of migrants initially resort to CIS-style informal methods of obtaining goods and services, most abandon these methods realizing that a direct approach to Western institutions or officials 'pays better'. However, other migrants (especially illegals) have little choice but to rely on informal help, looking for jobs and housing on the black market, or trying to arrange medical care or education for their children. Most Russians, like other migrants, also seek 'non-practical' social contact. Groups that feel socially isolated as a result of migration (such as 'Russian wives' or senior citizens) value friendship significantly. Interestingly, though, while some migrants view 'Russian friendship' as being of a higher standard than the Western forms, others resent 'Russian friendship' as intrusive and overbearing.

Neither are Russians unanimous in their perceptions of their own and their hosts' culture and ethnicity. 'Being Russian' or 'being from the CIS' means different things to different migrants (depending on their actual country of origin, ethnicity, desire to integrate into the host society and other factors). Nevertheless, it can generally be said that most migrants, while denying the existence of a Russian community or their belonging to it, have a strong sense of their cultural and ethnic identity. This self-concept is developed in part as a reaction to external labelling (being identified as a migrant or as a Russian) and as a continuation of the identity that was formed back in the CIS. The strong division between 'us' and 'them' (be it within a group of compatriots, such as 'intellectuals' and 'non-intellectuals', or 'Georgians' and 'Jews'; or between self-defined 'Russians' and the 'British' or the 'Dutch') remains significant for all migrants.

Today's world is clearly more open, rapidly changing and, in a certain sense, globally interdependent. Large-scale migratory movements, although known in the past, have now taken on true global proportions. People move, and most of those who stay have information about the world outside of their own villages. But, perhaps due to some general form of human nature, ideas about 'us and them', 'here and there', 'in the past and now' remain important to people. The postmodern observation that culture, ethnicity or community are socially constructed does not seem particularly profound. Although clearly these constructs are no more 'objective' than the identities of the people who identify with them, they do nonetheless structure the social worlds all of us live in. Despite Russian migrants' social diversity (as well as their diverse views and adaptation strategies), analysis of their discourse demonstrates that the concepts of 'community', 'culture', 'ethnicity', 'friendship', etc. are still talked about as fundamental and self-evident categories.

It is true that Russian migrants' lives have become more cosmopolitan by virtue of travel, and that their world-view may be said to have shifted by virtue of interaction with another society's values. Still, migrants' views of themselves, their country of origin, their past and their future – as well as their evaluation of the present – remain rooted in their particular experiences. Migrants' identities are not arbitrarily chosen. Instead, they are often adapted by imposition or assumed as a result of a belief in their objective nature. Postmodern theory claims that both the lives and the views of the so-called transnational migrants are 'constructed', 'shifting', 'hybrid', 'contextual' and 'fluid'; and migrant discourse does indeed reflect flexibility in the way migrants define their culture and ethnicity. Nonetheless, migrant cultural and ethnic identities remain rather 'fixed' (as opposed to 'chosen' as the postmodern theories imply) by both external pressures and the internal sense of 'self' (having to do with ideas of origin and belonging). 'Globalization', 'deterritorialization' or 'transnationalism' in the modern world do not necessarily eliminate the ideas of community nor greatly influence migrants' identity, as the experience of Russian migrants living in London and Amsterdam shows.

Bibliography

Abu-Lughod, L. (1991), 'Writing Against Culture', in R. Fox (ed.), *Recapturing Anthropology: Working in the Present*, School of American Research Press, Santa Fe.

Akhbar, A. and Shore, C. (1995), 'Introduction: Is Anthropology Relevant to the Contemporary World?', in A. Akhbar and C. Shore (eds), *The Future of Anthropology*, The Athlone Press, London.

Al-Rasheed, M. (1995), 'In Search of Ethnic Visibility: Iraqi Assyrian Christians in London', in G. Baumann and T. Sunier (eds), *Post-migration Ethnicity: Cohesion, Commitments, Comparison*, Het Spinhuis Publishers, Amsterdam.

Alvesson, M. (2002), *Understanding Organizational Culture*, Sage Publications, London.

Alvesson, M. and Willmott, H. (2002), 'Identity Regulation as Organizational Control: Producing the Appropriate Individual', *Journal of Management Studies*, Vol. 39, No. 5, pp. 619–40.

Anderson, B.R.O. (1991), *Imagined Communities: Reflections on the Origin and Spread of Nationalism*, Verso, London.

Anderson, M. (1999), 'Children in Between: Constructing Identities in the Bicultural Family', *The Journal of the Royal Anthropological Institute*, Vol. 5, No. 1, pp. 13–26.

Anwar, M. (1995), 'Social Networks of Pakistanis in the UK: A Re-evaluation', in A. Rogers and S. Vertovec (eds), *The Urban Context: Ethnicity, Social Networks, and Situational Analysis*, Berg Publishers, Oxford.

Appadurai, A. (1991), 'Global Ethnoscapes: Notes and Queries for a Transnational Anthropology', in R. Fox (ed.) *Recapturing Anthropology: Working in the Present*, School of American Research Press, Santa Fe.

Appadurai, A. (2002). 'Disjuncture and Difference in the Global Cultural Economy', in J.X. Inda and R. Rosaldo (eds), *The Anthropology of Globalization*, Blackwell, Malden and Oxford.

Ardener, E. (1989), *The Voice of Prophecy and Other Essays*, ed. M. Chapman. Blackwell, Oxford.

Balibar, E. (2003), 'Class Racism', in M. Gibernau and J. Rex (eds), *The Ethnicity: Nationalism, Multiculturalism, and Migration*, Polity Press, Cambridge, pp. 269–83.

Banks, M. (1996), *Ethnicity, Anthropological Constructions*, Routledge, London and New York.

Barth, F. (1969), 'Introduction', in F. Barth (ed.), *Ethnic Groups and Boundaries*, Universitetsforlaget, Bergen.

Barth, F. (1978), 'Scale and Network in Urban Western Society', in F. Barth (ed.), *Scale and Social Organization*, Universitetsforlaget, Oslo.

Bauböck R. (1994), *The Integration of Immigrants*, Strasbourg: Council of Europe.

Baumann, G. (1995), *Contesting Culture*, Cambridge University Press, Cambridge.

Baumann, G. and Sunier, T. (1995), 'Introduction', in G. Baumann and T. Sunier (eds), *Post-migration Ethnicity: Cohesion, Commitments, Comparison*, Het Spinhuis Publishers, Amsterdam.

Bell, D. (1996), 'Ethnicity in the Modern World', in J. Hutchinson and A. Smith (eds), *Ethnicity*, Oxford University Press, Oxford.

Benmayor, R. and Skotnes, A. (eds) (1994), *Migration and Identity*, vol. 3, *International Yearbook of Oral History and Life Stories*, Oxford: Oxford University Press.

Blockland, T. (1999), 'Privatized Communities: The Coincidence of Individualism and Community: An Essay on Kalb's Solution to the Community Question', *Focaal*, No. 33.

Boissevain, J. (1974), *Friends of Friends: Networks, Manipulations and Coalitions*, Basil Blackwell, Oxford.

Boissevain, J. (1975), 'Introduction', in J. Boissevain and J. Friedl (eds), *Beyond the Community: Social Process in Europe*, Department of Education Science of the Netherlands, The Hague.

Boissevain, J. (1994), 'Towards an Anthropology of European Communities?', in V. Goddard, J.R. Llobera and C. Shore (eds), *The Anthropology of Europe: Identities and Boundaries in Conflict*, Berg, Oxford.

Boissevain, J. and Vermeulen, H. (eds) (1984), *Ethnic Challenge – The Politics of Ethnicity in Europe*, Herodot, Gottingen.

Boissevain, J. and Verrips, J. (1989), *Dutch Dilemmas: Anthropologists Look at the Netherlands*, Van Gorcum, Assen.

Bottomore, T. (1991), *Classes in Modern Society*, 2nd edn, HarperCollins, London.

Bourdieu, P. (1977), *Outline of a Theory of Practice*, Cambridge University Press, Cambridge.

Bourdieu, P. (1992), *Distinction. A Social Critique of the Judgement of Taste*, Routledge, London.

Bowie, F. (1993), 'Whales from Within: Conflicting Interpretations of Welsh Identity', in S. McDonald (ed.), *Inside European Identities: Ethnography in Western Europe*, Berg, Providence.

Brake, M. (1985), *Comparative Youth Culture: The Sociology of Youth Cultures and Youth Subcultures in America, Britain and Canada*, Routledge and Kegan Paul, London.

Brass, P.R. (1996), 'Ethnic Groups and Ethnic Identity Formation', in J. Hutchinson and A. Smith (eds), *Ethnicity*, Oxford University Press, Oxford.

Bridger, S. and Kay, R. (1996), 'Gender and Generation in the New Russian Labour Market', in H. Pilkington (ed.), *Gender, Generation and Identity in Contemporary Russia*, Routledge, London.

Bruno, M. (1996), 'Employment Strategies and the Formation of New Identities in the Service Sector of Moscow', in H. Pilkington (ed.), *Gender, Generation and Identity in Contemporary Russia*, Routledge, London.

Bryant, C.G.A. (1997), 'Citizenship, National Identity and the Accommodation of Difference: Reflections on the German, French, Dutch and British Cases', *New Community: The Journal of the European Research Centre on Migration and Ethnic Relations*, Vol. 23, No. 2, April.

Buckley, M. (1992), 'Introduction: Women and Perestroika', in M. Buckley (ed.), *Perestroika and Soviet Women*, Cambridge University Press, Cambridge.

Burgers, J. (1999), 'De huisvesting van illegalen', in J. Burgers and G. Engbersen (eds), *De ongekende stad 1: overkomst en verblijf van illegale vreemdelingen in Rotterdam*, Boom, Amsterdam.

Calgar, A. (1997), 'Hyphenated Identities and the Limits of "Culture"', in T. Modood and P. Werbner (eds), *The Politics of Multiculturalism in New Europe: Racism, Identity and Community*, Zed Books, London.

Carruthers, A. (2002), 'The Accumulation of National Belonging in Transnational Fields: Ways of Being at Home in Vietnam', *Identities, Global Studies in Culture and Power*, Vol. 9, Part 4, pp. 423–43.

Castles, S., Booth, H. and Wallace, T. (1984), *Here for Good: Western Europe's New Ethnic Minorities*, Pluto Press, London.

Castles, S. and Kosack, G. (1973), *Immigrant Workers and Class Structure in Western Europe*, Oxford University Press, London.

Castells, M. (2000a), *The Information Age: Economy, Society and Culture*, vol. 1, *The Rise of the Network Society*, Blackwell Publishers, Malden, MA.

Castells, M. (2000b), *The Information Age: Economy, Society and Culture*, vol. 2, *The Power of Identity*, Blackwell Publishers, Malden, MA.

Castells, M. (2000c), *The Information Age: Economy, Society and Culture*, vol. 3, *End of Millenium*, Blackwell Publishers, Malden, MA.

Chapman, M. (1994), 'The Commercial Realization of Community Boundary', in V. Goddard, J.R. Llobera and C. Shore (eds), *The Anthropology of Europe: Identities and Boundaries in Conflict*, Berg, Oxford.

Cheah, P. and Robbins, B. (eds) (1998), *Cosmopolitans: Thinking and Feeling Beyond the Nation*, University of Minnesota Press, Minneapolis.

Chervyakov, V., Gitelman, Z. and Shapiro, V. (1997), 'Religion and Ethnicity: Judaism in the Ethnic Consciousness of Contemporary Russian Jews', *Ethnic and Racial Studies*, Vol. 20, No. 2, April.

Childs, J.B. (1993), 'The Value of Diversity for Global Cooperation', in J. Brecher, J.B. Childs and J. Cutler (eds), *Global Visions: Beyond the New World Order*, South End Press, Boston, pp. 17–24.

Clifford, J. (2003), 'The Nature of Ethnicity in the Project of Migration', in M.Gibernau and J. Rex (eds), *The Ethnicity: Nationalism, Multiculturalism, and Migration*, Polity Press, Cambridge, pp. 269–83 (from *Cultural Anthropology*, Vol. 9, No. 3, pp. 301–38, 1994).

Codagnone, C. (1998), *New Migration and Migration Politics in Post-Soviet Russia*, Ethnobarometer Programme Working Paper No. 2, available from Internet at http://cemes.org/current/ethnobar/wp2/wp2_ind.htm.

Cohen, A.P. (1979), 'The Whalsay Croft', in S. Wallman (ed.), *Social Anthropology of Work*, Academic Press, London.

Cohen, A.P. (1985), *The Symbolic Construction of Community*, Routledge, London and New York.

Cohen, A.P (1997), 'A General Theory of Subcultures' [1948], in K. Gelder and S. Thornton (eds), *The Subcultural Reader*, Routledge, London.

Cole, G.D.H. (1955), *Studies in Class Structure*, Routledge, London.

Conner, W. (1996), 'Beyond Reason: The Nature of the Ethnonational Bond', in J. Hutchinson and A. Smith (eds), *Ethnicity*, Oxford University Press, Oxford.

Courgeau, D. (1995), 'Migration Theories and Behavioral Models', *International Journal of Population Geography*, Vol. 1, pp. 19–27.

Darieva, T. (1998), 'Making a Community Through the Media? Post-Sowjetische Zuwanderer in Berlin', paper presented at the Kongress der Deutschen Gesellshaft sur Soziologie 'Grenzelose gesellschaft'?, 14–18 September, Freiburg in Breisgau, Albert-Ludwig Universität.

Davis, K. (1988), 'Social Science Approaches to International Migration', in M.S. Teitelbaum and J.M. Winter (eds), *Population and Resources in Western Intellectual Traditions*, Cambridge University Press, Cambridge.

Doomernik, J. (1997), 'Adaptation Strategies among Soviet Jewish Immigrants in Berlin', *New Community: The Journal of the European Center on Migration and Ethnic Relations*, Vol. 23, No. 1, January.

Durkheim, E. (1962), *Socialism, The Division of Labor and Professional Ethics and Civic Morals*, Collier Books and Antioch Press, New York.

The Economist (2004), 'The Coming Hordes: Migration in the European Union', 17 January, pp. 25–6.

Ekholm-Friedman, K. and Friedman, J. (1995), 'Global Complexity and Simplicity of Everyday Life', in D. Miller (ed.), *Worlds Apart: Modernity Through the Prism of the Local*, Routledge, London.

Engbersen, G. (1999a), 'Panopticum Europa', in J. Burgers and G. Engbersen (eds), *De ongekende stad 1: overkomst en verblijf van illegale vreemdelingen in Rotterdam*, Boom, Amsterdam.

Engbersen, G. (1999b), 'Patronen van Integratie', in J. Burgers and G. Engbersen (eds), *De ongekende stad 1: overkomst en verblijf van illegale vreemdelingen in Rotterdam*, Boom, Amsterdam.

Engbersen, G., Van der Leun, J., Staring, R. and Kehla, J. (1999), 'Introductie', *De ongekende stad 2. Inbedding en uitsluiting van illegale vreemdelingen*, Boom, Amsterdam.

Eriksen, T.H. (1993), *Ethnicity and Nationalism: Anthropological Perspectives*, Pluto Press, London.

Erikson, E. (1968), *Identity, Youth, and Crisis*, Faber and Faber, London.

Esman, M.J. (1996), 'Diasporas and International Relations', in J. Hutchinson and A. Smith (eds), *Ethnicity*, Oxford University Press, Oxford.

Fedorov, N. (1998), *Problema Etnosotsial'noy Integratsii Immigrantov iz Byvshego SSSR v Germanskoye Obshestvo (Problems of Ethno-social Integration of Immigrants from the CIS in German Society)*, Samoekonomika, Moscow.

Fischer, P.A., Martin, R. and Straubhaar, T. (1997), 'Should I Stay or Should I Go?', in T. Hammar, G. Brochmann, K. Tamas and T. Faist (eds), *International Migration, Immobility and Development: Multidisciplinary Perspectives*, Berg, Oxford.

Flynn, M. (2004), *Migrant Resettlement in the Russian Federation: Reconstructing Homes and Homelands*, Anthem Press, London.

Fox, R.G. (1991), 'Introduction: Working in the Present', in R.G. Fox (ed.), *Recapturing Anthropology: Working in the Present*, School of American Research Press, Santa Fe.

Frankenberg, R. (1993), 'Who Can Tell the Tale? Texts and the Problem of Generational and Social Identity in a Tuscan Rural Commune', in S. McDonald (ed.), *Inside European Identities: Ethnography in Western Europe*, Berg, Providence.

Frankenberg, R. (1994), *Communities in Britain: Social Life in Town and Country*, Gregg Revivals, Ipswich, Suffolk.

Freinkman-Chrustaleva, H.S. and Novikov, A.I. (1995), *Emigratzia i emigranti: Istoria i psichologia*, St Petersburgh Gosudarstvennaya Akademia Nauk.

Gans, H.J. (1996), 'Symbolic Ethnicity', in J. Hutchinson and A. Smith (eds), *Ethnicity*, Oxford University Press, Oxford.

Gardner, K. (1995), *Global Migrants, Local Lives: Travel and Transformation in Rural Bangladesh*, Clarendon Press, Oxford.

Geertz, C. (1996), 'Primordial Ties', in J. Hutchinson and A. Smith (eds), *Ethnicity*, Oxford University Press, Oxford.

Gellner, E. (1992a), *Reason and Culture: The Historic Role of Rationality and Rationalism*, Blackwell, Oxford.

Gellner, E. (1992b), *Postmodernism, Reason and Religion*, Routledge, London.

Gellner, E. (1994), *Nations and Nationalism*, Blackwell, Oxford.

Glazer, N. and Moynihan, D.P. (1996), 'Beyond the Melting Pot', in J. Hutchinson and A. Smith (eds), *Ethnicity*, Oxford University Press, Oxford.

Glenny M. and Stone, N. (1990), *The Other Russia*, Faber and Faber, London.

Goddard, A., Llobera, J.R., and Shore, C. (eds) (1994), 'Introduction', in V. Goddard, J.R. Llobera and C. Shore (eds), *The Anthropology of Europe: Identities and Boundaries in Conflict*, Berg, Oxford.

Granovetter, M. (1973), 'The Strength of Weak Ties', *American Journal of Sociology*, No. 78, 1360–80.

Gray, J. (1994), *Post-Communist Societies in Transition*, Social Market Foundation, London.

Grieco, M. (1995), 'Transported Lives: Urban Social Networks and Labour Circulation', in A. Rogers and S. Vertovec (eds), *The Urban Context: Ethnicity, Social Networks, and Situational Analysis*, Berg Publishers, Oxford.

Grillo, R. (1998), 'Transnational?', paper presented to the Social Anthropology graduates seminar, University of Sussex, 1 October.

Guibernau, M. and Rex, J. (2003), 'Introduction', in M. Gibernau and J. Rex (eds), *The Ethnicity: Nationalism, Multiculturalism, and Migration*, Polity Press, Cambridge, pp. 1–15.

Gupta, A. (2002). 'Beyond "Culture": Space, Identity, and the Politics of Difference', in J.X. Inda and R. Rosaldo (eds), *The Anthropology of Globalization*, Blackwell, Malden and Oxford.

Haan, W. de (1997), 'Minorities, Crime, and Criminal Justice in the Netherlands', in I.H. Marshall (ed.), *Minorities, Migrants, and Crime: Diversity and Similarity Across Europe and the United States*, Sage Publications, Thousand Oaks.

Halbwachs, M. (1960), *Population and Society: Introduction to Social Morphology*, The Free Press of Glencoe, Illinois.

Hammer, T., Brochmann, G., Tamas, K. and Faist, T. (eds) (1997), 'Introduction', in T. Hammar, G. Brochmann, K. Tamas and T. Faist (eds), *International Migration, Immobility and Development: Multidisciplinary Perspectives*, Berg, Oxford.

Hannerz, U. (1980), *Exploring the City: Inquiries Towards Urban Anthropology*, Columbia University Press, New York.

Hannerz, U. (2002), 'Notes on the Global Ecumene', in J.X. Inda and R. Rosaldo (eds), *The Anthropology of Globalization*, Blackwell, Malden and Oxford, pp. 37–46.

Hardwick, S.W. (1993), *Russian Refuge: Religion, Migration, and Settlement on the North American Pacific Rim*, The University of Chicago Press, Chicago.

Havinga, T. and Boker, A. (1999), 'Country of Asylum by Choice or by Chance: Asylum Seekers in Belgium, the Netherlands and the UK', *Journal of Ethnic and Migration Studies*, Vol. 25, No. 1, pp. 43–63.

Hechter, M. (1996), 'Ethnicity and Rational Choice Theory', in J. Hutchinson and A. Smith (eds), *Ethnicity*, Oxford University Press, Oxford.

Held, D. (ed.) (2000), *A Globalizing World? Culture, Economics, Politics*, Routledge, London and New York.

Hughes, E.C. (1958), *Men and Their Work*, Free Press, Glencoe, Illinois.

Humphrey, C. (1983), *Karl Marx Collective: Economy, Society and Religion in a Siberian Collective Farm*, Cambridge University Press, Cambridge.

Humphrey, C. (1995a) 'Introduction', *Cambridge Anthropology*, Vol. 18, No. 2.

Humphrey, C. (1995b), 'Creating a Culture of Disillusionment: Consumption in Moscow, a Chronicle of Changing Times', in D. Miller (ed.), *Worlds Apart: Modernity Through the Prism of the Local*, Routledge, London.

Humphrey, C. (1996/7), 'Myth-making, Narratives, and the Dispossessed in Russia', *Cambridge Anthropology*, Vol. 19, No. 2.

Hutchinson, J. (1996), 'Ethnicity and Multiculturalism in Immigrant Societies', in J. Hutchinson and A. Smith (eds), *Ethnicity*, Oxford University Press, Oxford.

Hutchinson, J. and Smith, A. (1996), 'Introduction', in J. Hutchinson and A. Smith (eds), *Ethnicity*, Oxford University Press, Oxford.

Itzigsohn, J., Dore Carial, C., Hernandez Medina, E. and Vazquez, O. (1999), 'Mapping Dominican Transnationalism: Narrow and Broad Transnational Practices', *Ethnic and Racial Studies*, Vol. 22, No. 2, pp. 316–39.

Jackson, J.A. (ed.) (1969), *Migration*, Cambridge University Press, Cambridge.

Jackson, P. (1995), 'Manufacturing Meaning', in A. Rogers and S. Vertovec (eds), *The Urban Context: Ethnicity, Social Networks, and Situational Analysis*, Berg Publishers, Oxford.

Jansen, C. (1969), 'Sociological Aspects of Migration', in J.A. Jackson (ed.), *Migration*, Cambridge University Press, Cambridge.

Jordan, B., Stråth, B. and Triandafyllidou, A. (2003), 'Contextualising Immigration Policy Implementation in Europe', *Journal of Ethnic and Migration Studies*, Vol. 29, Part 2, pp. 195–224.

Kaznina, O. (1997), *Russkie v Anglii: Russkaya Emigratsiya v contexte russko-angliyskih literaturnih svyazey v pervoy polovine XX vek*, Nasledie, Moscow.

Kelly, C. (1998), 'Russian Culture and Emigration, 1921–1953', in C. Kelly and D. Shepherd (eds), *Russian Cultural Studies*, Oxford University Press, Oxford.

Kirichenko, E. (1995), *Russkie Emigranty v Amsterdame*, Masters dissertation, Institute of Cultural Studies at the Russian Academy of Sciences, Moscow.

Kloosterman, R. and Rath, J. (2002), 'Working on the Fringes: Immigrant Businesses, Economic Integration and Informal Practices', in *Marginalisering eller Integration. Invandrares foeretagande I svensk retorik och praktik*, NUTEK, Stockholm, pp. 177–88.

Knoppers, J.V.T. (1976), 'Dutch Trade With Russia From the Time of Peter I to Alexander I', Occasional Papers, No. 1, Centre Universitaire d'Études Europeennes, Montreal.

Kopnina, H. (1998), 'Exploring Russian-Jewish Community in London', paper presented and published at the International Conference of Personal Absorption in Netanya, Israel.

Kopnina, H. (1999), 'Russian-speakers in London: A Community?', *British East-West Journal*, No. 112, pp. 10–13.

Kopnina, H. (2004), 'Cultural Hybrids or Ethnic Fundamentalists? Discourses on Ethnicity in Singaporean Small and Medium Enterprises', *Asian Ethnicity*, Vol. 5, No. 2, June, pp. 245–57.

Kotovskaya, M. and Shalygina, N. (1996), 'Love, Sex, and Marriage – The Female Mirror: Value Orientations of Young Women in Russia', in H. Pilkington (ed.), *Gender, Generation and Identity in Contemporary Russia*, Routledge, London.

Lane, C. (1981), *The Rites of the Rulers: Ritual in Industrial Society – The Soviet Case*, Cambridge University Press, Cambridge.

Lange, W. de (1997), 'Te groot, te wild, te anders en te dichtbij: hoort de Rus bij oost of bij west?', *Trouw*, 26 July, p. 10.

Ledeneva, A. (1996), 'Formal Institutions and Informal Networks in Russia: a Study of *Blat*', PhD thesis, University of Cambridge.

Ledeneva, A. (1996/7), 'Between Gift and Commodity: The Phenomenon of *Blat*', *Cambridge Anthropology*, Vol. 19, No. 3.

Lee, E.S. (1969), 'Theory of Migration', in J.A. Jackson (ed.), *Migration*, Cambridge University Press, Cambridge.

Leun, J. van der (2000), 'Embeddedness and Exclusion: Undocumented Immigrants in the Netherlands', *Bulletin of the Royal Institute for Inter-Faith Studies*, Vol. 2, No. 1, pp. 71–95.

Leun, J. van der and Kloosterman, R. (1999), 'Loopbanen onder het legale plafond', in J. Burgers and G. Engbersen (eds), *De ongekende stad 1: overkomst en verblijf van illegale vreemdelingen in Rotterdam*, Boom, Amsterdam.

Macdonald, S. (1993), 'Identity Complexes in Western Europe: Social Anthropological Perspectives', in S. Macdonald (ed.), *Inside European Identities: Ethnography in Western Europe*, Berg, Providence.

Malia, M. (1994), *Soviet Tragedy: A History of Socialism in Russia, 1917–1991*, Free Press, New York.

Mandel, R. (1994), '"Fortress Europe" and the Foreigners Within: Germany's Turks', in V. Goddard, J.R. Llobera and C. Shore (eds), *The Anthropology of Europe: Identities and Boundaries in Conflict*, Berg, Oxford.

Marshall, I.H. (1997), 'Introduction', in I.H. Marshall (ed.), *Minorities, Migrants, and Crime: Diversity and Similarity Across Europe and the United States*, Sage Publications, Thousand Oaks.

Marshall, T.H. and Bottomore, T. (1996), *Citizenship and Social Class*, Pluto Press, London.

McDonald, M. (1993), 'The Construction of Difference: An Anthropological Approach to Stereotypes', in S. Macdonald (ed.), *Inside European Identities: Ethnography in Western Europe*, Berg, Providence.

Melotti, U. (1997), 'International Migration in Europe: Social Projects and Political Cultures', in T. Modood and P. Werbner (ed.), *The Politics of Multiculturalism in New Europe: Racism, Identity and Community*, Zed Books Ltd, London.

Meyer, J.B. and Brown, M. (1999), 'Scientific Diasporas: A New Approach to the Brain Drain', UNESCO-MOST Discussion Paper No. 41, Paris.

Miller, D. (1995), 'Introduction: Anthropology, Modernity, and Consumption', in D. Miller (ed.), *Worlds Apart: Modernity Through the Prism of the Local*, Routledge, London.

Miller, J.R. (1987), *Politics, Work, and Daily Life in the USSR: A Survey of Former Soviet Citizens*, Cambridge University Press, Cambridge.

Mitchell, J. (1969), 'The Concept and Use of Social Networks', in J. Mitchell (ed.) *Social Networks in Urban Situations: Analysis of Personal Relationships in Central African Towns*, Manchester University Press, Manchester.

Modood, T. (1997), 'Introduction: The Politics of Multiculturalism in New Europe', in T. Modood and P. Werbner (ed.), *The Politics of Multiculturalism in New Europe: Racism, Identity and Community*, Zed Books Ltd, London.

Morozov, B. (1998), *Evreiskaya Emigratzia v Svete Novych Documentov*, Ivrus, Tel-Aviv.

Moutsou, C. (1998), 'Handling "Food for Thought": Greek and Turkish Hybrid Representations in Brussels', PhD dissertation, University of Cambridge Department of Anthropology and Archaeology.

Munter, E. (1992), 'Culterele betrokkingen', in E. Munter, B. Naarden and T. Witte (eds), *Voorzichtig en met Mate: DeBetrekkingen van Nederland met de Sovjetunie (1942–1991)*, Oost-Europa Cahiers No. 9, Universiteit van Amsterdam.

Naarden, B. (1992), 'Inleiding: Nederland en Rusland voor 1942', in E. Munter, B. Naarden and T. Witte (eds), *Voorzichtig en met Mate: DeBetrekkingen van Nederland met de Sovjetunie (1942–1991)*, Oost-Europa Cahiers No. 9, Universiteit van Amsterdam.

Nash, M. (1996), 'The Core Elements of Ethnicity', in J. Hutchinson and A. Smith (eds), *Ethnicity*, Oxford University Press, Oxford.

O'Connor, H. (1997), *The Britain-Russia Center and Former Soviet Women*, Print-out of British East-West Center, personal copy.

Oenen, G. van (1999), 'Roodheet. Hoe restrictief immigratiebeleid de Nederlandse politiek ontregelt', *Migrantenstudies,* No. 2, pp. 113–28.

Ong, A. (2002), 'Disjuncture and Difference in the Global Cultural Economy', in J.X.Inda and R. Rosaldo (eds), *The Anthropology of Globalization*, Blackwell, Malden and Oxford, pp. 172–98.

Ong, A. and Linck, G. (2000), 'Flexible Citizenship', *Anthropos: revue internationale d'ethnologie*, Vol. 95, No. 2, pp. 624–6.

Ortner, S. (1991), 'Reading America: Preliminary Notes on Class and Culture', in R. Fox (ed.), *Recapturing Anthropology: Working in the Present*, School of American Research Press, Santa Fe.

Ostrovskii, A. (1998), 'Russians Are Coming … er, Have Come', *Financial Times*, 24 June.

Panarin, S. (1999), 'Predislovie', in A. Vyatkin, N. Kosmarskaya and S. Panarin (eds), *On the Move: Voluntarily and Involuntarily: Post-Soviet Migrations in Eurasia*, Natalis Press, Moscow.

Petronoti, M. (1995), 'Greek-African Interrelations in Eritrea and Greece, Social Interaction as a Framework for Understanding the Construction of Ethnic Identities', in G. Baumann and T. Sunier (eds), *Post-migration Ethnicity: Cohesion, Commitments, Comparison*, Het Spinhuis Publishers, Amsterdam.

Pickvance, C. (1995), 'Comparative Analysis, Causality and Case Studies in Urban Studies', in A. Rogers and S. Vertovec (eds), *The Urban Context: Ethnicity, Social Networks, and Situational Analysis*, Berg Publishers, Oxford.

Pilkington, H. (1992), 'Going Out in "Style": Girls in Youth Cultural Activity', in M. Buckley (ed.), *Perestroika and Soviet Women*, Cambridge University Press, Cambridge.

Pilkington, H. (1996a) 'Introduction', in H. Pilkington (ed.), *Gender, Generation and Identity in Contemporary Russia*, Routledge, London.

Pilkington, H. (1996b) 'Youth Culture in Contemporary Russia: Gender, Consumption and Identity', in H. Pilkington (ed.), *Gender, Generation and Identity in Contemporary Russia*, Routledge, London.

Pilkington, H. (1996c) 'Farewell to *Tusovka*: Masculinities and Femininities on the Moscow Youth Scene', in H. Pilkington (ed.), *Gender, Generation and Identity in Contemporary Russia*, Routledge, London.

Pilkington, H. (1998), *Migration, Displacement, and Identity in Post-Soviet Russia*, Routledge, London.

Portes, A., Guarnizo, L.E. and Landolt, P. (1999), 'The Study of Transnationalism: Pitfalls and Promises of an Emergent Research Field', *Ethnic and Racial Studies*, Vol. 22, No. 2, pp. 217–37.

Price, C. (1969), 'The Study of Assimilation', in J.A. Jackson (ed.), *Migration*, Cambridge University Press, Cambridge.

Raeff, M. (1990), *Russia Abroad: Cultural History of the Russian Emigration 1919–1939*, Oxford University Press, Oxford.

Raj, D. (1997), 'Shifting Culture and the Global Terrain: Cultural Identity Constructions amongst British Punjabi Hindus', PhD dissertation, University of Cambridge Department of Anthropology and Archaeology.

Ravenstein, E. (1889), 'The Laws of Migration', *Journal of the Statistical Society*, Part XLVIII, June, pp. 167–235.

Rex, J. (2003), 'The Nature of Ethnicity in the Project of Migration', in M.Gibernau and J. Rex (eds), *The Ethnicity: Nationalism, Multiculturalism, and Migration*, Polity Press, Cambridge, pp. 269–83.

Richmond, A.H. (1969), 'Migration in Industrial Societies', in J.A. Jackson (ed.), *Migration*, Cambridge University Press, Cambridge.

Ries, N. (1997), *Russian Talk: Culture and Conversation during Perestroika*, Cornell University Press, Ithaca.

Rogers, A. and Vertovec, S. (1995), 'Introduction', in A. Rogers and S. Vertovec (eds), *The Urban Context: Ethnicity, Social Networks, and Situational Analysis*, Berg Publishers, Oxford.

Rouse, R. (2002), 'Mexican Migration and the Social Space of Postmodernism', in J.X. Inda and R. Rosaldo (eds), *The Anthropology of Globalization*, Blackwell, Malden and Oxford, pp. 157–72.

Salaman, G. (1974), *Community and Occupation: an Exploration of Work/Leisure Relationships*, Cambridge University Press, Cambridge.

Scheepers, P., Schmeets, H. and Felling, A. (1997), 'Fortress Holland? Support for Ethnocentric Policies among the 1994-electorate of The Netherlands', *Ethnic and Racial Studies*, Vol. 20, No. 1, January.

Scheper-Hughes, N. (1992), *Death without Weeping: The Violence of Everyday Life in Brazil*, University of California Press, Berkeley.

Schwartz, T. (1999), 'Migration Configurations and Regimes', in A. Vyatkin, N. Kosmarskaya and S. Panarin (eds), *On the Move: Voluntarily and Involuntarily: Post-Soviet Migrations in Eurasia*, Natalis Press, Moscow.

Shevtsova, L. (1992), 'Post-Soviet Migration Today and Tomorrow (Part I)', *International Migration Review*, Vol. 26, No. 2, pp. 241–59.

Shlapentokh, V., Sendich, M. and Payin, E. (eds) (1994), 'Introduction,' in *The New Russian Diaspora: Russian Minorities in the Former Soviet Republics*, M.E. Sharpe, Armonk, New York.

Shore, C. (1993), 'Ethnicity as Revolutionary Strategy: Communist Identity Construction in Italy', in S. Macdonald (ed.), *Inside European Identities: Ethnography in Western Europe*, Berg, Providence.

Siegel, D. (1998), *The Great Immigration: Russian Jews in Israel*, Berghahn Books, Oxford and New York.

Sik, E. (1994), 'Network Capital in Socialist, Communist, and Post-Communist Societies', *International Contributions to Labor Studies*, Vol. 4, pp. 73–94.

Smith, A.D. (1996), 'Chosen Peoples', in J. Hutchinson and A. Smith (eds), *Ethnicity*, Oxford University Press, Oxford.

Smith, M.P. and Guarnizo, L.E. (eds) (1998), *Transnationalism from Below*, Transaction Publishers, New Brunswick, NJ.

Snel, E., Boom, J. de, Burgers, J. and Engbersen, G. (2000), *Migratie, Integratie en Criminaliteit: migranten uit voormalig Joegoslavië en de Voormalige Sovjet-Unie in Nederland*, RISBO Contractresearch BV, Rotterdam.

Staring, R. (1999), 'Migratiescenario's', in J. Burgers and G. Engbersen (eds), *De ongekende stad 1: overkomst en verblijf van illegale vreemdelingen in Rotterdam*, Boom, Amsterdam.

Staring, R. (2002), 'Reizen Onder Regie: Het migrantieproces van illegale Turken in Nederland', summary of a PhD dissertation for Erasmus University, Rotterdam, Department of Social Anthropology.

Stone-Mediatore, S. (2003) 'Postmodernism, Realism, and the Problem of Identity', *Diaspora: A Journal of Transnational Studies*, Vol. 2, No. 1, Spring, pp. 125–40.

Strathern, M. (1987), 'The Limits of Auto-anthropology', in A. Jackson (ed.), *Anthropology at Home*, Tavistock, London, pp. 16–37.

Strathern, M. (1995), 'Series Editor's Preface', in D. Miller (ed.), *Worlds Apart: Modernity Through the Prism of the Local*, Routledge, London.

Taylor, R.C. (1969), 'Migration and Motivation: A Study of Determinants and Types', in J.A. Jackson (ed.), *Migration*, Cambridge University Press, Cambridge.

Thornton, S. (1995), *Club Cultures: Music, Media and Subcultural Capital*, Polity Press, Cambridge.

Thornton, S. (1997), 'Introduction', in K. Gelder and S. Thornton (eds), *The Subcultural Reader*, Routledge, London.

Tishkov, V.A. (ed.) (1996), *Migratsii I Novye Diaspory*, Institute of Ethnology and Anthropology of the Russian Academy of Sciences, Moscow.

Tonkin, E., Mcdonald, M. and Chapman, M. (1996), 'History and Ethnicity', in J. Hutchinson and A. Smith (eds), *Ethnicity*, Oxford University Press, Oxford.

Tonry, M. (1997), 'Ethnicity, Crime, and Immigration', in M. Tonry (ed.), *Ethnicity, Crime, and Immigration: Comparative and Cross-national Perspectives*, University of Chicago Press, Chicago.

Verkuyten, M. (1997), 'Cultural Discourses in The Netherlands: Talking about Ethnic Minorities in the Inner-City', in N.G. Schiller (ed.), *Identities: Global Studies in Culture and Power*, Vol. 4, No. 1.

Verkuyten, M., Calseijde, S. van de, and Leur, W. de (1999), 'Third-generation South Moluccans in the Netherlands', *Journal of Ethnic and Migration Studies*, Vol. 25, No. 1, January, pp. 66–80.

Vermeulen, H. (1999), 'Immigration, Integration and the Politics of Culture', *The Netherlands Journal of Social Sciences*, Vol. 35, No. 1, pp. 6–21.

Vertovec, S. (1999a), 'Conceiving and Researching Transnationalism', *Ethnic and Racial Studies*, Vol. 22, No. 2, pp. 447–62.

Vertovec, S. (1999b), 'Introduction', in S. Vertovec (ed.), *Migration and Social Cohesion*, Edward Elgar, Cheltenham, pp. xi–xxxvii.

Vertovec, S. (2000), 'Rethinking Remittances', ESRC Transnational Communities Programme Working Paper WPTC-2K-15, Oxford, http://www.transcomm.ox.ac.uk.

Vertovec, S. (2001), 'Transnationalism and Identity', *Journal of Ethnic and Migration Studies*, Vol. 27, No. 4, pp. 573–82.

Vertovec, S. (2002), 'Transnational Networks and Skilled Labour Migration', ESRC Transnational Communities Programme Working Paper WPTC-02-02, Oxford, http://www.transcomm.ox.ac.uk.

Vertovec, S. (2003), 'Migrant Transnationalism and Modes of Transformation', paper for Social Science Research Council, Princeton University, 23–24 May.

Villanueva, M.A. (1998), Book review of *Latinos in New York: Communities in Transition* by G. Haslip-Viera and S.L. Baver, *American Anthropologist*, Vol. 100, No. 1, March.

Vishnevsky, A. and Zayonchakovskaya, Z. (1994), 'Emigration from the Former Soviet Union: The Fourth Wave', in H. Fassmann and R. Munz (eds), *European Migration in the Late Twentieth Century*, Edward Elgar, Aldershot, pp. 239–59.

Vries, M. de (1995), 'The Changing Role of Gossip: Towards a New Identity? Turkish Girls in the Netherlands', in G. Baumann and T. Sunier (eds), *Post-migration Ethnicity: Cohesion, Commitments, Comparison*, Het Spinhuis Publishers, Amsterdam.

Wallman, S. (1979), *Social Anthropology of Work*, Academic Press, London.

Webber, J. (1997), 'Jews and Judaism in Contemporary Europe: Religion or Ethnic Group?', in *Ethnic and Racial Studies*, Vol. 20, No. 2, April.

Weber, M. (1996), 'The Origins of Ethnic Groups', in J. Hutchinson and A. Smith (eds), *Ethnicity*, Oxford University Press, Oxford.

Weiner, A.B. (1992), *Inalienable Possessions: the Paradox of Keeping-while-giving*, University of California Press, Berkeley.

Werbner, P. (1995), 'From Commodities to Gifts', in A. Rogers and S. Vertovec (eds), *The Urban Context: Ethnicity, Social Networks, and Situational Analysis*, Berg Publishers, Oxford.

Willems, F. (1972), 'Manifestations of Discrimination in The Netherlands', in H. van Houte and W. Melgert (ed.), *Foreigners in Our Community, A New European Problem to be Solved*, Keesing Publishers, Amsterdam.

Wolf, E. (1974), *Anthropology*, Norton and Company, New York.

Yasinskaja-Lahti, I. and Liebkind, K. (1999), 'Exploring the Ethnic Identity among Russian-speaking Immigrant Adolescents in Finland', *Journal of Cross-Cultural Psychology*, Vol. 30, No. 4, July, pp. 527–39.

Internet Sites

http://www.salonUSSR.com.
http://www.cultureelcentrum.nl.
http://www.russiancentre.co.uk.
http://www.samsonart.ndirect.co.uk/index1.htm.
http://europa.eu.int/comm/eurostat/Public/datashop/print-catalogue/EN?catalogue =Eurostat.
http://europa.eu.int/abc/governments/index_en.htm#members.
http://www.cbs.nl/.
http://statline.cbs.nl/StatWeb/start.asp?LA=nl&DM=SLNL&lp=Search/Search.
http://www.statistics.gov.uk/.
http://www.statistics.gov.uk/CCI/nscl.asp?ID=7472.

Appendix 1

Legal Migration Statistics

Ways of Entry to Britain and The Netherlands

In both Britain and The Netherlands, the following categories of Russians may officially enter:

1 visitors (tourists, visitors in transit and those seeking to enter for private medical treatment);
2 persons seeking to enter for studies (students, spouses and children of students);
3 persons seeking to enter for training or work experience (working holidaymakers and their children, au pairs, etc.);
4 persons seeking to enter for employment (work permit employees, representatives of overseas press, sole representatives, overseas government employees, etc.);
5 persons seeking to enter as a businessman, self-employed person, investor, writer, composer or artist;
6 family members of British or Dutch citizens (spouses, children, parents, etc.);
7 asylum seekers.

East to West Migration

Table A1a   Number of immigrants in The Netherlands from countries of the former Soviet Union by citizenship and year, 1990–98

	1990	1991	1992	1993	1994	1995	1996	1997	1998
Armenia	*	*	10	118	268	233	83	65	44
Azerbaijan	*	*	0	7	19	70	28	25	27
Belarus	*	*	1	9	18	45	65	75	122
Estonia	*	*	12	29	18	11	29	30	25
Georgia	*	*	9	52	111	232	146	55	91
Kazakhstan	*	*	1	5	1	7	29	40	37
Kyrgyzstan	*	*	1	10	1	1	2	5	6
Latvia	*	*	12	16	21	27	34	40	49
Lithuania	*	*	9	30	26	57	83	95	114
Moldova, Republic of	*	*	0	15	8	11	21	20	35
Russian Federation	*	*	878	821	660	710	797	690	845
Tajikistan	*	*	0	10	6	7	2	0	1
Turkmenistan	*	*	13	13	3	0	0	5	4
Ukraine	*	*	57	149	137	264	292	335	382
Uzbekistan	*	*	0	3	11	10	8	5	16
Total (former) Soviet Union	358	664	1003	1287	1308	1685	1619	1485	1798
Total all countries	117350	120249	116926	119154	92143	96099	108749	109860	122407

* Not available.

Source: Eurostat.

Table A1b Number of immigrants in the United Kingdom from countries of the former Soviet Union by citizenship and year, 1990–98

	1990	1991	1992	1993	1994	1995	1996	1997	1998
Armenia	*	*	*	*	*	*	*	*	694
Azerbaijan	*	*	*	*	*	*	*	*	0
Belarus	*	*	*	*	*	*	*	*	0
Estonia	*	*	*	*	*	*	*	*	0
Georgia	*	*	*	*	*	*	*	*	282
Kazakhstan	*	*	*	*	*	*	*	*	91
Kyrgyzstan	*	*	*	*	*	*	*	*	0
Latvia	*	*	*	*	*	*	*	1000	555
Lithuania	*	*	*	1000	*	*	*	*	140
Moldova, Republic of	*	*	*	*	*	*	*	*	0
Russian Federation	*	*	*	*	*	2000	1000	1000	441
Tajikistan	*	*	*	*	*	*	*	*	0
Turkmenistan	*	*	*	*	*	*	*	*	0
Ukraine	*	*	*	*	*	*	*	*	84
Uzbekistan	*	*	*	*	*	*	*	*	0
Total (former) Soviet Union	*	*	1000	1000	*	2000	1000	2000	2287
Total all countries	267000	267000	216000	210000	253000	245000	258000	285000	332390E

E   Estimated.
*   Not available.

Source: Eurostat.

Table A2a Number of asylum applications in The Netherlands from countries of the former Soviet Union by citizenship and year, 1990–99

	1990	1991	1992	1993	1994	1995	1996	1997	1998	1999
Armenia	*	*	40	352	1082	358	364	432	711	1249
Azerbaijan	*	*	10	23	104	129	185	315	1267	2449
Belarus	*	*	16	0	41	6	7	29	25	40
Estonia	*	*	0	51	82	22	15	0	1	0
Georgia	*	*	25	169	1238	344	188	291	292	321
Kazakhstan	*	*	0	0	18	55	64	105	80	102
Kyrgyzstan	*	*	0	0	0	0	0	0	0	6
Latvia	*	*	14	28	55	11	10	5	3	10
Lithuania	*	*	13	43	67	19	11	15	12	12
Moldova, Republic of	*	*	13	23	95	52	65	34	39	31
Russian Federation	*	*	408	643	1141	621	551	459	517	960
Tajikistan	*	*	0	13	17	10	8	31	40	21
Turkmenistan	*	*	0	0	0	0	0	0	5	0
Ukraine	*	*	78	239	560	249	217	228	227	306
Uzbekistan	*	*	10	11	23	9	10	13	12	13
Total (former) Soviet Union	224	1013	627	1595	4523	1885	1695	1957	3231	5520

* Not available.

Source: Eurostat.

Table A2b Number of asylum applications in the United Kingdom from countries of the former Soviet Union by citizenship and year, 1990–99

	1990	1991	1992	1993	1994	1995	1996	1997	1998	1999
Armenia	*	*	*	*	*	*	5	35	58	93
Azerbaijan	*	*	*	*	*	*	*	15	18	50
Belarus	*	*	*	*	*	*	*	35	111	602
Estonia	*	*	*	*	*	*	5	20	115	456
Georgia	*	*	*	*	*	*	5	30	15	72
Kazakhstan	*	*	*	*	*	*	0	10	6	15
Kyrgyzstan	*	*	*	*	*	*	0	5	2	5
Latvia	*	*	*	*	*	*	5	140	522	517
Lithuania	*	*	*	*	*	*	275	1010	1301	613
Moldova, Republic of	*	*	*	*	*	*	*	20	25	180
Russian Federation	*	*	*	*	*	*	205	180	187	687
Tajikistan	*	*	*	*	*	*	0	0	7	6
Turkmenistan	*	*	*	*	*	*	0	5	3	1
Ukraine	*	*	*	*	*	*	235	490	372	777
Uzbekistan	*	*	*	*	*	*	*	5	21	10
Total (former) Soviet Union	100	245	270	385	595	795	1110	1995	2763	4084

*   Not available.

Source: Eurostat.

Appendix 2

List of Informants*

London

Agniya   F, 29, Russian, arrived 1994 from Murmansk having married a British man, formerly a bookkeeper, presently studying for an English major at the London University.

Aleftina   F, 40, Ukrainian, arrived 1995 from Kiev having married a British man, formerly an accountant, presently a housewife.

Alina   F, 67, Jewish, arrived 1995 from Moscow, joined her husband Michael, formerly a school teacher, presently retired.

Angela   F, 19, Lithuanian, arrived 1998 from Vilnyus having asked for asylum, just divorced from a Lithuanian husband, formerly a trainee hairdresser, presently working odd jobs, having 'British male sponsors'.

Anna   F, 32, Moldovan, arrived 1995 from Kishinev on a business visa (to attend a medical course in Manchester), formerly a surgeon, presently unemployed.

Armen   M, 45, Armenian, arrived 1994 from Erevan as a 'businessman', presently unemployed.

Bulat   M, 39, Georgian, arrived 1996 from Tbilisi invited by friends, formerly a garage owner, presently unemployed.

Daryma   F, 37, Uzbek, arrived 1995 from Tashkent having married a British man, formerly a school teacher, presently a housewife.

Egor   M, 25, Russian, arrived 1997 from Kostroma at the invitation of his friends, formerly and presently an artist.

Galya   F, 30, Russian, arrived 1994 from Ekaterinburg, was married to a British man, used to work as a museum curator, presently working as a teller at a London bank.

Gera   M, 28, Belorussian, arrived 1997 from Gomel, invited by friends, formerly and presently a plumber.

---

*   Only key informants have been included in the Appendix. Others gave random interviews.

Grisha	M, 54, Jewish, arrived 1995 on a temporary contract from Moscow, working for the University College London as a biologist.
Inna	F, 30, Russian, arrived 1997 from Yaroslavl, joined her husband Zhenya, formerly a secretary, presently a housewife.
Konstantin	M, 23, Ukrainian, arrived 1998 as a tourist from Kharkov, doing odd jobs, like street juggling.
Lena	F, 28, Jewish, arrived 1994 from Moscow, first as a tourist, then as an art student, presently working for an architectural firm in Switzerland.
Marina	F, 38, Russian, arrived 1992 from St Petersburg having married a British man, formerly a linguistics lecturer at the university, presently a housewife.
Masha	F, 26, Russian, arrived 1998 from Kazan, invited by friends (possibly tried to arrange a marriage partner through the Internet), working as a masseuse in a Russian-owned health parlour.
Michael	M, 69, Jewish, arrived 1995 from Moscow, was helped to enter UK as an asylum seeker by the Jewish organization, formerly a sociologist and a publisher, presently retired.
Mitya	M, 28, Russian, arrived 1993 (in Ireland) from St Petersburg, on a student visa, presently a research biologist at the Cancer Research Institute outside London.
Nikita	M, 57, Russian, arrived 1990 from Omsk, formerly a 'museum worker', presently an antiques shop owner.
Olga	F, 26, Russian, arrived 1997 from Moscow having married a British man, has worked as a teller for an International Bank in Moscow and in London, entered Slavonic Studies course at the London University.
Petya	M, 65, Russian, arrived 1998 from Estonia to join his family, formerly an accountant, presently retired.
Sasha	M, 30, Kazakh, arrived 1996 from Moscow, continuing his career as an IT consultant, presently working for Anderson's between London and Amsterdam.
Sergei	M, 36, Jewish, arrived 1992 from Moscow, entered at the invitation of a British theatre company, working as a theatre producer and director.
Tolya	M, 40, Russian, arrived 1994 from St Petersburg, formerly and presently employed at a tourist agency.

Valentin   M, 37, Azeri, arrived 1993 from Moscow, formerly a businessman, presently an organizer of Russian cultural events.

Vasya   M, 66, Ukrainian, arrived 1990 on a tourist visa from St Petersburg, formerly a doctor, now retired.

Veronika   F, 40, Jewish, arrived 1997 from Moscow having married a British man, formerly a doctor, presently a housewife.

Zhenya   M, 29, Russian, arrived 1997 from Yaroslavl, an IT specialist on a temporary contract in the UK, presently living in New York with his family.

Zhora   M, 29, Russian, arrived 1994 by the invitation of the Russian artists organization in London from Baku, currently a self-employed artist.

Zora   F, 35, Ukrainian, arrived 1991 from Kiev having married a British man, formerly a textile specialist, presently a housewife.

Zoya   F, 46, Russian, arrived 1997 from Krasnoyarsk, formerly an agriculturalist, presently a volunteer worker for the Russian language Anglican church.

Ellen   F, 34, British, employee at the Russian/British Centre in London.

Jim   M, 37, British, electronics retailer, has Russian customers and friends.

Mr Jones   M, 60, British, owner of a car business, has Russian colleagues and friends.

Lucy   F, 65, British, co-founder and organizer of the Pushkin Club, a lawyer for Russian asylum seekers.

Sam   M, 45, British, car salesman, married to a Russian.

Amsterdam

Alena   F, 32, Jewish, arrived 1992 from Kiev accompanying her Ukrainian husband, formerly a music teacher, presently a bank worker.

Alex   M, 23, Russian, arrived 1998 from Moscow, invited by his friends, formerly an art student, presently a hard rock musician.

Andrei   M, 30, Russian, arrived 1998 from Ekaterinburg, invited by friends, formerly a music technician, presently a construction worker.

Anton	M, 34, Jewish, arrived 1990 from Ekaterinburg having married a Dutch woman, an artist and businessman.
Arina	F, 49, Russian, arrived 1992 from Moscow, invited by friends, formerly an agrarian engineer, presently a retailer at the flower shop.
Asya	F, 25, Russian, arrived 1999 from Moscow with her Dutch partner, formerly a book firm employee, presently a housewife.
Dima	M, 35, Jewish, arrived 1990 from St Petersburg as an 'independent artist', formerly a philosophy student, presently a street artist.
Dina	F, 34, Georgian, arrived 1997 from Tbilisi to visit her aunt, formerly an engineer, now working odd jobs (like baby-sitting and cleaning).
Dusya	F, 31, Russian, arrived 1998 from Ekaterinburg following her husband Andrei, formerly an opera singer, presently a music student at the Dutch Music Academy.
Gennadiy	M, 50, Jewish, arrived from Moscow 1992 as a refugee, formerly a political economist, now a maths teacher.
Igor	M, 31, Russian, arrived 1994 at the invitation of his Dutch partner from Orel, doing odd jobs (like construction and repairs).
Irina	F, 26, Belorussian, arrived 1994 from Germany (left Minsk in 1990 with her mother), an economics student at the Economics School.
Kirill	M, 32, Ukrainian, arrived 1993 from Kiev at the invitation of a Dutch computer firm, formerly and presently a computer specialist.
Lev	M, 26, Uzbek, arrived 1997 from Moscow to attend a medical training course, formerly a doctor, presently unemployed.
Margarita	F, 40, Russian, arrived from St Petersburg in 1992 as an 'independent artist', formerly and presently a poet.
Mariana	F, 47, Russian, arrived 1990 from Moscow having married a Dutch man, formerly working in education sector, presently has her own business selling Russian goods.
Maxim	M, 20, Russian, arrived 1999 from Vologda as a tourist, probably an army deserter, presently a petty thief.
Mitya	M, 55, Russian, arrived 1993 from Moscow, invited by friends, formerly a history teacher, presently giving private Russian lessons.
Nastya	F, 24, Belorussian, arrived 1995 from Grodno having married a Dutch Turk, formerly a textile engineering student, presently

studying computer science at the Free University and working in her husband's restaurant.

Pavel   M, 40, Georgian, arrived 1991 from Moscow, formerly a chef, presently a coffee shop owner.

Raisa   F, 37, Jewish, arrived 1993 from Israel (left Kishinev in 1984 to join her family), working as a criminologist at the Free University.

Shurik   M, 19, Russian, arrived 1999 from Arhangelsk as a tourist, possibly an army deserter, presently a hard rock musician.

Slava   M, 30, Russian, arrived in 1993 from St Petersburg on business, formerly a history student, presently a car salesman.

Sofia   F, 47, Russian, arrived 1993 from Uglich, invited by her family, presently working as an informal barber.

Stepa   M, 70, Jewish, arrived 1990 from Minsk as an asylum seeker, formerly a schoolteacher, presently retired.

Sveta   F, 27, Jewish, arrived 1994 from Ekaterinburg as a tourist, formerly a doctor, presently following a medical studies course to regain her qualifications.

Tanya   F, 28, Russian, arrived 1992 from Odessa with her mother, an actress and a student of literature at the University of Amsterdam.

Vadim   M, 21, Russian, arrived 1991 from Moscow with his mother, a hard rock musician, presently in jail in Russia for drug dealing.

Vika   F, 25, Russian, arrived 1995 from Yaroslavl as a tourist, takes part in her Yugoslavian partner's criminal operations.

Vitya   M, 30, Ukrainian, arrived 1992 from Kiev, invited by friends, a travel agency employer.

Yury   M, 32, Belorussian, arrived 1992 from Vitebsk as a tourist, formerly an electrician, presently homeless and unemployed.

Anneke   F, 28, Dutch, employer at the Russian store Pegasus.

Gerda   F, 34, Dutch, programmer, has Russian friends.

Henk   M, 29, Dutch, fund manager, married to Tanya.

Jan   M, 27, Dutch, used to work in Moscow for a book firm, resides with Asya in Amsterdam.

Richard   M, 33, Dutch, computer systems manager, participates in volunteer projects in Russia and has Russian friends.

Appendix 3

Russian Institutions in London and Amsterdam

Both London and Amsterdam host a number of Russian institutions, ranging from churches to disco clubs. There are more institutions in London than in Amsterdam. Both in London and in Amsterdam, Russian institutions are scattered throughout the city. There is no central point or street, but rather a number of geographic areas with clusters of Russian residents and/or institutions. In Amsterdam, these areas include neighbourhoods like De Pijp, Jordaan, Oud-West, Buitenvelderdt and Indische Buurt. In London, these are Chelsea, Holborn, Knightsbridge, Earls Court and many other areas and neighbourhoods.

Russian institutions that attract the largest numbers of Russians in both London and Amsterdam are Orthodox churches. In Amsterdam there are two Orthodox churches, while in London there are three of them. Both in London and in Amsterdam Moscow Orthodox churches attract a regular congregation of over a hundred members, while on holidays, such as Easter or New Year, there might be up to a thousand visitors in each church. Congregations are not exclusively Russian but include other foreign Orthodoxes, as well as British and Dutch people.

London

Churches and Temples

Hundreds of Russians can be found in the Russian Orthodox Church (Ennismore Gardens) and Russian Church Abroad (Harvard Road). There is selected socialization after the services between members of the established congregation and newcomers.

The Anglican churches, notably St Luke's church in Redcliffe Gardens which has Russian-speaking pastors and services and offers free English courses and Sunday school for Russian children, and Church *Slovo Vechnosti* (The Voice of Eternity), in Granville Rd, which has a Sunday school for children, and Russian audio-videotheque, attract dozens of Russians. There is a relaxed social atmosphere; tea and cookies are usually served after services.

There are groups of Baptists and Jehovah's Witnesses as well as a number of synagogues (notably, Munks synagogue in Golders Green) that welcome Russian congregations (services are not in Russian).

Restaurants, Cafes, Food Shops and Bars

Russians are rarely found visiting Russian restaurants and cafes, although there are about a dozen of them in the London area, including Georgian, Armenian and Azerbaijani restaurants. Most of these places are quite idiosyncratic and cater mostly to the Western public (such as *Borsch and Tears* ar 46 Beauchamp Place, which has live East European music) or an exclusive high brow elite, such as new Russians and supposed 'Mafia', (such as *Nikita's Russian Restaurant* at 65 Ifield Road). *Red* is the supposedly Russian bar that serves different kinds of vodka but has few Russian visitors. Other eateries: *Caviar Kaspia* (18 Bruton Place, Mayfair: restaurant, shop, caviar wholesales), *Tbilisi* (91 Holloway Road), *Trojka-Russian Tea Room and Restaurant* (101 Regents Park Rd; live Russian music).

Russian Publishers and Press

Russian books are sold in international book stores, such as Grant and Cutler (55–57 Great Marlborough Street); Green Skird Books (1 Heron Court). The largest Russian library is housed by the British-Russian Centre, which, aside from books, hosts a sizeable collection of Russian periodicals.

The two main Russian publications in London are London Courier (*Londonskiy Kur'er*) with a readership of about 10,000 and European Herald (*Evropeyskiy Vestnik*) with a readership of about 3,000. *Russian Info*, a humorous newspaper with announcements of Russian cultural events and classifieds, is gaining in popularity.

Russian Bands

Most Russian music is supplied by seasonal musicians or temporarily invited bands from the CIS. Local bands are represented by the *Yuri Stepanov* band and *Loyko*, a gypsy band, both of which regularly play at Russian clubs, restaurants and discos.

Literary Clubs

The Pushkin Club, Pushkin House, 46 Ladbroke Grove, 'welcomes anyone who is interested in Russian culture': mostly literary lectures and poetry readings. Events are free for members, in Russian and in English.[1]

Film Clubs

Kino Kino! Cine Lumiere, Institut Francais, 17 Queensbury Place showing Russian films, advertising through mail and Internet.[2]
The *Lux Centre*, 2–4 Hoxton Square: occasional Russian films.[3]

Anglo-Russian Theatres

The King's Head Theatre, 115 Upper Street: occasional Russian productions by a group of amateur Russian and British actors.[4]

Karmanniy Teatr, Logen Hall, 20 Bedford Way:[5] occasional productions by theatre groups invited from the CIS.

Society for Cooperation in Russian and Soviet Studies

320 Brixton Rd, described as 'library and information resource centre', comprising an extensive Russian-language members' library, information service and archival research. Organizes Russian language courses, publishes the information guide (SCR 1998–99 Russian Information Guide). Its associated educational charity, British-Soviet Educational Trust, offers small grants for British cultural or educational initiatives in the CIS.[6]

Society Balls, Charitable Events, Art Fairs and Auctions

Organized by members of the 'aristocratic wave', variable venues, events attract mostly wealthy Western public and occasionally 'new Russians'.[7]

Russian Commercial and Cultural Services

IVS (International Venue Service) organizes Russian parties in night clubs like Stringfellows as well as services for Russian tourists, like tours and accommodation.

BCI Centre, which has seven employees of which only one is British, organizes conferences and seminars for Russians in London, mostly courses aimed at professional improvement of statisticians and managers.[8]

Russian Night Clubs and Discotheques

Stringfellows, a large night club, welcomes Russians every last Friday of the month.[9]

International Sportsmen Club hosts Russian parties and concerts every other month.[10]

Astoria: monthly Russian concerts and disco nights since January 1999.[11]

Russian Club Night Aquarium: bi-monthly discotheque with Russian music.[12]

Russian Art

Association of Russian Artists in Great Britain, 16 Dartmouth Row, Greenwich. Most recent exhibition took place in November 1998 at the Alchemy Gallery in Farringdon Road, London.[13]

Amsterdam

Churches

Russisch-Orthodoxe Kerk H Nicolaas Kerkstraat 342/344. Every Saturday and Sunday service attracts about 50 people, more than half of whom are Dutch Orthodoxes or members of the post-Revolutionary and post-Second World War Russian migration. The church shop sells regular worship objects (candles, paper icons, etc.) as well as Tatiana, the priest's wife's, booklet about religious life in Russia.[14]

Russisch Orthodoxe Buitenlandse Kerk, Muiderstraat 10. The Foreign Orthodox church which does not recognize the Moscow Metropolitan and has traditionally rejected the 'Soviet' church and is thus at odds with the other Amsterdam church. The Foreign Orthodox church has irregular services. It is housed in a small building and poorly maintained. It attracts a regular congregation of around two dozen Russians, mostly earlier wave migrants.[15]

Restaurants, Cafes, Food Shops, and Bars

Oblomov. Throughout the 1990s, a few Russian clubs and cafes attempted to establish themselves in Amsterdam on a permanent basis. Existing between 1997 and 1999, Café *Oblomov* was the only true Russian cafe and club in Amsterdam. Not only did it serve Russian food and drinks and exhibit Russian paraphernalia, like samovars and balalaikas, but it also advertised and sold tickets for most Russian events in Amsterdam. Some of these events were held in *Oblomov* itself, while others took place elsewhere. These events included invited Russian singers and writers, both from the CIS and from the local Russian population; Russian evenings and Russian games. Most *Oblomov* habitués were Russians, although there were a few Dutch, Afghans and Yugoslavians. *Oblomov* attracted quite a few 'mixed background' Russians, such as Israeli, American or Australian citizens; a few Russia-based businessmen; long-time Amsterdam residents and recent arrivals. The atmosphere was rather friendly, and those who frequented the place developed strong social ties with each other and with the owners.

Kalinka, opened after the demise of *Oblomov* in November 1999, is not popular with the former *Oblomov* habitués. It was christened 'Erevanka' because of the predominance of Armenian visitors and owners.

Russisch/Pools Restaurant Polonia, Derde Oosterparkstraat 72. Not popular with Russians.

Russian Food Shop (Oosdorpplein)

Sells mostly canned goods, also sausages and *pelmeni*. Has Kazakh owners. Not very popular with Russians, mostly used by Dutch customers from the neighbourhood.

Book Stores

The Russian and East European book store, *Pegasus*, caters to the popular tastes of Russians, distributing mostly Russian pulp and translated detective stories. The owner of *Pegasus* also sends books to Russian prisoners in The Netherlands.

There is also an Internet site listed under http://www.russkyclub.com (a family-run Russian translation agency based in Hilversum) called *Lira* where Russian books, audio and video tapes can be ordered.

Russian Commercial and Cultural Services

Stichting CIRC Atelier, Oostelijke Handelskade 29A: Russian travel and information agency, occasionally organizes Russian events.

Het Rusland Centrum (Inclusive of Stichting Rusland Centrum, CIRC Rusland Reizen, and Russia Experts), Peperstraat 11–13. Travel, information, events, also distributes books and other publications about Russia, has a small Russian library.[16]

Schools

There is a Russian school where the children of Russian parents are taught Russian literature and culture. There are between 15 to 30 students each year, aged 4–15, although membership fluctuates.

Another Russian school is affiliated with the Orthodox Church and generally invites the children of congregation members.

Films and Plays

Dutch cinemas and theatres occasionally offer Russian films and performances which draw some Russian people. Most Russian plays (mostly by Chekhov or Gogol) are performed in Dutch and attract mostly Dutch people.[17]

In March 1999 The Filmmuseum showed a sequence of 1930s Russian films, including *Volga Volga, Dama na Kachelyah, Traktoristy, Komissary* and *Vesyelye Rebyata*. The *Rialto* cinema on Centuurlaan occasionally shows Russian and East European films, such as *V toy strane* about village life in Russia (shown in June 1999) or *Kolia*, about political events in Czechoslovakia and Russia.

Internet Groups

'Russen in Nederland' (http://www.rusland.net) features cultural announcements and advertisements. The latter includes those searching for Russian car business partners, Russian women in Russia's advertisements looking for partners, and Dutch men's advertisements searching for Russian women. Other sections include odd bits and pieces such as a Russian sculptor's gallery in Amsterdam, Cold War advertisements like 'Better a rocket in the garden than a Russian in the kitchen' and Russian recipes.

There are a couple of smaller sites in other cities like Rotterdam (advertising a Russian restaurant at http://www.xs4all.nl/~janvw).

Art and Music

Most of the Russian artists and musicians are self-employed and hold temporary visas. Some of the street artists and musicians are 'seasonal' or 'visiting' on short-term contracts. They can be found performing in parks or on major squares (Liedseplein and Rembrandtplein) and bridges. Established artists and musicians are sometimes invited from the CIS by private Dutch galleries or music halls.

Notes

1   Sample presentation: January 1999: *Odna Lyubov' Dushi Moei, The One Love of My Soul*, a play about Pushkin and Maria Volkonskaya, written and performed by Mlada Kalashnikova. Of the 40 people present, most were older and middle aged. 'Older wave' and a few British people speaking Russian. Also, a criminal-looking Russian businessman, presently an asylum seeker, was present (Lucy Daniels, one of the founding members and organizers of the club events, is his lawyer); a couple of middle-aged recently arrived wives of Russian bankers and British citizens. Mlada Kalashnikova (professional actress, lives between Oxford and Russia): rather old-fashioned inspiring performance, good acting and memory, documentary content. Lively atmosphere, tea and cookies.

2   *Declaration of Love* by Averbach (1978), 19 January 1999. A film about intellectuals' ideals and idealism spanning almost 60 years of Communist history. About 100 people, almost half of them Russian-speaking, some French and British. Introduction by Vitalii and Lyudmila: brief history and review of Kino!'s activities.

3   *Hands* by Aristakisyan, 24 January 1999. A film about materially and physically deprived people in Kishinev, a call for dissemination of the system by non-cooperation, anarchistic peaceful utopia. Small viewing hall housing 40 viewers, mostly non-Russian.

4   Sample show: *A Chekhov Circus* (5 January 1999). Housed in a small room adjacent to the theatre bar. Only six people in the audience, including the actor's mother and actress's friend. Four actors: two British males of whom one has a degree in Russian and has worked as a presenter on Russian television, and two Russian women. Tatiana, trained at the GITIS Theatre Institute, worked in Moscow and Tbilisi. Natasha trained at City Lit Actor's Studio, related to me ART-VICs plans for expansion and acquisition of a permanent building.

5   Sample: *Lencom,* a play by J. Cocto, attracted about 20 mostly older Russian spectators.

6   Visit: housed in a dilapidated building in a seedy part of Brixton, little space inside. Greeted by Jane Rosen and her assistant, both English-speaking. Urged to pay membership fee of £10, offered a tour of the premises: library, office, book shop, all filled with paper materials, untidy and outdated. Large collection, friendly and helpful personnel, conspicuously poor.

7   Sample: *War and Peace* Ball, 9 February 1999, in the ballroom of Dorchester Hotel. Dress Code: Costume of 1812, admission £175. Under the patronage of Her Highness Russian Princess Maria.

8   From an interview with an employee: 'We use telemarketing to find clients. In five years about a thousand professionals requested our services. We acted as a tour agency, helping them with obtaining visas, organizing accommodation, etc. These days there is less demand for these services and training courses as people are able to arrange their own visits and there are too many competitors, people opening their own companies, our prices have to drop. So we concentrate more on entertainment business now, organizing about 8–9 parties each year at the International Sportsmen Club. Other cultural organizers are ISC and IVS (International Venue Service) which organizes Russian parties at Stringfellows. There are also companies which use the proceeds from the tickets for their events for charities, like orphans in Murmansk. We wish to start an all-Russian club and look for a suitable building' (Galina).

9   Sample party: August 1998. Admission: £20. About 400 people, mostly Russians. The programme consisted of disco and karaoke. Guests, mostly habitués invited through 'people they knew' conversed in groups at separate tables, but very loud music and a festive atmosphere soon drove many to the dance floor. Although there were a couple of people over 40, the majority of guests were professionals between 18 and 35.

10   Sample party: September 1998. Admission: £10 with a free shot of vodka. About 300 people. Yuri Stepanov band. Animated atmosphere, people talking, small disco room with Russian pop and dance music. Visitors: mostly professionals in their 30s, quite a few young girls, a few British accompanying Russian friends or Russian language students.

11   Concert of *Chizh and Co*, a rock group from Russia, attracted about 200 mostly young Russian professionals.

12   Sample: 21 January 1999. Main room: Russian pop and dance; Red room: house and speed garage; swimming pool with jacuzzi. Admission free for women before 10 p.m., 7 p.m. for men. Two spacious, festively decorated rooms. Mostly visitors under 30, asylum seekers. A number of older professionals. Many ethnic Lithuanians.

13   Profile of one of the artists, from *British East-West Journal*, December 1998, No. 111: Peter Belyi, born 1971, Leningrad, based in UK since 1995. 'He has taken part in more than 20 exhibitions in Russia and UK since 1995. His work is held in permanent collections of the *Victoria and Albert Museum* and in the *State Russian Museum*'.

14   Sample service on the eve of *Preobrazhenie*, the Transfiguration, 1998. At the entrance, we were offered the chance to buy candles and a pamphlet written by the priest's wife about her recent trip and impressions of Moscow. The building offered an intimate atmosphere exhibiting reproductions of Rublev's icons and a centrally placed diptych of the Holy Family. Low ceiling at the ground floor and high vault at the back, above the chorus, kept the conversations below to their acoustical minimum while amplifying the voices above. There were about 15 people present in the church, mostly young. Many were non-Russian: a few Serbs and Dutch, one American. The service took place in two languages, Russian and Dutch, while the female chorus positioned on the balcony facing the altar

sang predominantly in Russian. First, the Russian country and government were blessed in Russian, then the Low Country and Queen Beatrice in Dutch. The Dutch translation did not always follow the Russian text, but served as its continuation, and sometimes a new theme was introduced in Dutch first, rather than in Russian. The priest, himself a Dutch convert to the Russian Orthodox faith, easily alternated the two languages, although, due to his advanced years, confused a few ritual steps, such as stepping down from the centre and not from the left side of the altar.

15 Sample service: 7 March 1999. The Orthodox priest has arrived from Paris. Service in a small room of a regular house, altar made of thin wood or carton, faded curtain used to close the altar off. Hosted about 30 people, including the choir, mostly Dutch or representatives of the old Russian migration (Society *Otchisna*, etc.) and a couple of Russian teenage hard-rockers. Service was very intimate (perhaps because of the limited space), pleas for more donations were made by the old priest. Paris priest gets paid 200 guilders per service, rent costs 300 guilders per month, donations are just over 100 guilders at each service. Services are held no more than once a month, next one being 17 April 1999. After service: tea and coffee in another small room, reminiscent of the old dacha kitchens.

16 Sample event housed by the *Centrum*: The opening of the *Buratino* exhibit on 5 March 1999 attracted mostly friends of the artists and families of the Dutch personnel (about 50 people), including children. A Russian school representative and a couple of Russian wives of the personnel were present. The opening signified the beginning of a cultural programme which includes lectures and painting exhibits which evolve around the supposedly popular Russian folklore character Pinocchio Buratino. The reception included drinks, Russian folk singing and a few toasts and was rather low-key, although sociable. The Russian Centre organizes some Russian events, such as exhibitions of Russian artists or boat trips (like the one to Zaandam in June 1999 in commemoration of Pushkin's birthday), but such events attract only very limited Russian attention; they are mostly targeted towards the Russia-oriented Dutch. However, a Russian language play about the life of Pushkin, organized by Amsterdamse Poesjkin-comite in September, attracted a few dozen Russians.

17 In the course of my fieldwork, two plays were organized by the local Russian residents, employing local Russian actors, namely *Pushkin: Youth and Childhood* (performance at Crea Teatre, 14–15 September 1999); and *De Emigranten* (performance at Stadsschouwburg (Leidseplein 26), 23–28 November). Both performances attracted about 50 people, half of whom were Russian.

Printed in Great Britain
by Amazon

68712648R00145